The Wholly Book of Exodus

The Wholly Book of Exodus

By
Jay Dubya

http://www.eBookstand.com
http://www.CyberRead.com

Published by
eBookstand
Division of CyberRead, Inc
1929_4

Copyright © 2005 by Jay Dubya
All rights reserved. No part of this publication may be reproduced
or transmitted in any form or by any means, electronic or
mechanical, including photocopy, recording, or any information
storage and retrieval system, without permission in writing from the
copyright owner.

ISBN 1-58909-258-9

Printed in the United States of America

Other Books by Jay Dubya
Adult Fiction

Black Leather and Blue Denim, A '50s Novel
The Great Teen Fruit War, A 1960' Novel
Frat' Brats, A '60s Novel
Ron Coyote, Man of La Mangia
So Ya' Wanna' Be A Teacher
Pieces of Eight
Pieces of Eight, Part II
Pieces of Eight, Part III
Pieces of Eight, Part IV
The Wholly Book of Genesis
Nine New Novellas
Nine New Novellas, Part II
Nine New Novellas, Part III
Nine New Novellas, Part IV
Fractured Frazzled Folk Fables & Fairy Farces
FFFF&FF, Part II
Mauled Maimed Mangled Mutilated Mythology
Thirteen Sick Tasteless Classics
Thirteen Sick tasteless Classics, Part II
Thirteen Sick Tasteless Classics, Part III
Thirteen Sick Tasteless Classics, Part IV

Young Adult Fantasy Novels and Stories
Pot of Gold
Enchanta
Space Bugs, Earth Invasion
The Eighteen Story Gingerbread House

Contents

Chapter 1	"Jacob's Descendents in Egypt"	1
Chapter 2	"Birth and Adoption of Moses"	7
Chapter 3	"The Call of Moses"	13
Chapter 4	"Confirmation of Moses' Mission"	19
Chapter 5	"Pharaoh's Obduracy"	25
Chapter 6	"Renewal of God's Promise"	33
Chapter 7	"The Plagues"	39
Chapter 8	"The Gnats and the Flies"	45
Chapter 9	"The Pestilence"	51
Chapter 10	"The Locusts"	59
Chapter 11	"The Death of the First-born"	67
Chapter 12	"The Passover Ritual Prescribed"	71
Chapter 13	"Consecration of First-born"	79
Chapter 14	"The Red Sea"	85
Chapter 15	"At Mirah and Elim"	91
Chapter 16	"The Quail and Manna"	97
Chapter 17	"Water from the Rock"	103
Chapter 18	"Meeting with Jethro"	107
Chapter 19	"Arrival at Sinai"	115
Chapter 20	"The Ten Commandments"	121
Chapter 21	"Laws Regarding Slaves"	127
Chapter 22	"Social Laws"	135
Chapter 23	"Religious Laws"	141
Chapter 24	"Ratification of the Covenant"	149
Chapter 25	"The Table"	153
Chapter 26	"Tent Cloth, Walls and Veils"	159
Chapter 27	"The Altar of Holocausts"	165
Chapter 28	"The Priestly Vestments"	171
Chapter 29	"Consecration of the Priests"	179
Chapter 30	"Altar of Incense and Oil"	189
Chapter 31	"Choice of Artisans"	197

Contents (continued)

Chapter 32	"The Golden Calf"	201
Chapter 33	"Moses and God"	207
Chapter 34	"Renewal of the Tablets"	213
Chapter 35	"Sabbath Regulations"	221
Chapter 36	"Tent Cloth and Coverings"	227
Chapter 37	"The Ark"	233
Chapter 38	"The Altar of Holocausts"	237
Chapter 39	"The Vestments"	241
Chapter 40	"Erection of the Dwelling"	247

Background

On April 1, 2002 Mohammed Kareem Jihad, a fourteen-year-old April Fool Palestinian revolutionary, was ascending a rocky ledge along rugged cliffs that bordered the western banks of the *Dead Sea*. Exhausted from his climbing enterprise, young Jihad stopped to rest his weary body. The vernal radical lit a *Camel* cigarette and surveyed the landscape below. Much to his frustration everything seemed calm and serene.

When Mohammed Kareem Jihad leaned backwards his gaunt frame slipped through a narrow crevice between two limestone crags. The disoriented youth rose to his knees, inspected his shadowy surroundings and soon realized that he had fallen into a cave (containing a remarkable ancient artifact). In the center of the small hollow was an urn, a well' preserved remnant from Hebrew antiquity.

Instead of sticking his hand into the urn to feel for any contents Mohammed followed his dreadful terroristic instincts by pulling the pin of a hand grenade and tossing the explosive device into what was surely a great archeological discovery. When the bomb exploded prematurely Mohammed Kareem Jihad had not yet fully exited the cave. Besides shrapnel, two leather objects bound with straps (strapnel) blasted out of the ancient urn and collided with the back of the Palestinian lad's skull, knocking him unconscious.

When Mohammed Kareem Jihad finally regained his faculties *(his rich uncle owned two radical Arab universities)*, he perceptively noticed and then grabbed the leather pouches and fled the scene of destruction. After descending the perilous cliffs the young militant thought, 'I'll bet whatever is inside these two leather packages is worth at least a carton of cigarettes,' so the youth mounted his stolen desert "quad" and motored to the city of Jericho, where his economically struggling father owned a popular café.

Inside the café Professor Phillip Collins of the Semitic Semantic Institute was seated at a table with Dr. Allen Qaeda from the Arab Aramaic Academy. Mohammed Kareem Jihad rushed into the dismal café and approached the cozy table where the two distinguished scholars were conversing.

"How much will you give me for these two leather pouches?" the boy anxiously asked Professor Al Qaeda. "I need to buy some weapons right away!"

"Let's unravel them and see what ya' got!" the suddenly curious researcher replied. The good academic doctor gently unwound the dusty cords that bound the leather wrappings. Inside both packages Dr. Allen Qaeda discovered dozens of remarkably well' preserved papyrus sheets with ancient writings carelessly scribbled on the archaic scrolls.

"Why it's the first two books of the Old Testament!" Professor Al Qaeda exclaimed in astonishment. "*The Book of Genesis* and the *Book of Exodus*!"

Professor Phil Collins, who knew plenty about Genesis, rendered his authoritative impressions. "This translation has much more detail than the presently read first two books of the Old Testament!" he enthusiastically observed and shared. "This type of papyrus dates back to at least 900 BC, which makes it a lot older than the Dead Sea Scrolls that had been re-written by the Essenes during an ancient creative writing class."

"If this historical account is accurate," interrupted Professor Al Qaeda, "then this great discovery will present a *wholly* new perspective to religious history, which is presently very controversial to begin with."

Young Mohammed Kareem Jihad was growing very impatient with the scholarly adults' intellectual evaluation and speculation concerning his fabulous find. "How much are they worth?" he insisted on knowing.

"Two cartons of American cigarettes, definitely!" Professor Phil Collins promised.

"And we'll even throw in an AK-47 and two slightly used hand grenades," Dr. Al Qaeda added.

"Sold!" an elated Mohammed Kareem Jihad gleefully shouted. "Now I can blow up my' younger sister's doll collection and her Jewish friends too!"

And so, Dr. Al Qaeda and my uncle Professor Phil Collins (on my mother's side of the family) became the legitimate owners of the only authentic "First Two Books of the Wholly Bible." The remainder of the "unabridged" Old Testament had been thoroughly obliterated inside the urn when Mohammed Kareem Jihad's hand grenade had quite effectively exploded.

Fortunately Uncle Phil Collins had made a computer file in English of his meticulous translation of the great archeological treasure. Uncle Phil very thoughtfully and confidentially had electronically sent "Wholly Genesis" and "Wholly Exodus" to me as e-mail attachments. The careful deciphering represented my relative's fantastic interpretation of the ancient Hebrew writing, which I had electronically received on April 10, 2002. Regrettably, on April 11th, Uncle Phil and Dr. Al Qaeda were blown to smithereens by an errant Palestinian rocket while refining their study of the ancient scrolls in Professor Collins' Jerusalem home. The papyrus sheets and the original computer file had also been destroyed in the malicious terrorist attack.

My treasured e-mail translations are the only remaining evidence of *The Wholly Book of Genesis and The Wholly Book of Exodus*. Uncle Phil sincerely believed that the versions presently in my possession are the original and most reliable documentation of the "Word of Moses," who was believed to be the organizer of the popular *Genesis* and *Exodus* interpretations that appear in the standard *Bible*. Uncle Phil Collins and Professor Al Qaeda strongly believed that Moses had fabricated the Biblical Genesis and Exodus stories around 1400 BC. But since writing (and bona fide alphabets) did not appear until the time after Homer and King David, around 1,000 BC, the Biblical stories had been handed-down and distorted because of the practice of oral tradition with storytellers adding and subtracting important details.

Uncle Phil Collins and Dr. Al Qaeda professed that young Mohammed Kareem Jihad's accidental discovery represented the true unabridged stories of *Genesis* and of *Exodus*. They maintained that the new versions are much more valid in scope and content since the accounts had been written hundreds of years earlier than the stories that now appear in the first two books of the *Bible*. Thus, Mohammed's find is closer to Moses' language and intent than later popularly read interpretations of *Genesis* and *Exodus*. "Careless Hebrew historians and ancient priests recklessly modified the *Wholly Genesis* and *Wholly Exodus* versions into more pious, moral and self-righteous texts," Uncle Phil academically stated in his final e-mail letter. "They did it to satisfy their own selfish purposes and agendas."

Uncle Phil' also indicated in his e-mail, "Moses, who lived approximately 1450 BC around the time of Pharaoh Thutmose III of Egypt, didn't know how to write, even though he had put the stories of *Genesis* and *Exodus* together much like Homer had done with the *Iliad* and the *Odyssey*. In fact nobody knew how to write with any rhetorical expression skills until half a millennium later." According to Uncle Phil, "Moses barely knew the numerals one to ten signifying the *Ten Commandments* etched on the twin stone tablets," my mother's older brother attested.

Now that the essential background of *The Wholly Book of Genesis and The Wholly Book of Exodus* is fully known, only the astute readers can be the best judges of the merits of Mohammed Kareem Jihad's discovery and Uncle Phil Collins' exceptional claims. I have placed in *italics* the language that ancient scholars had shrewdly edited out of the *Wholly Book of Genesis* and I have plainly and clearly left the standard and generally accepted script in *Times New Roman* type.

Jay Dubya

Chapter One
"Jacob's Descendents in Egypt"

The second book of the Pentateuch is called *The Wholly Book of Exodus*, meaning *"Let's get the hell out of here before we are savagely butchered to death by these mercurial-tempered mighty pissed-off Egyptians!"*

Exodus describes the rapid departure of the Israelites *(Jacob's people and clan)* from Egypt, continuing the nightmare adventures of the *Lord's* ill' starred' "chosen people" *(cursed and punished Hebrews)* and the text begins where the *Wholly Book of Genesis* leaves off. *Exodus* recounts the oppression by the Egyptians of Jacob's descendents and their miraculous deliverance by God through Moses,'*(how they all filtered through Moses remains a mystery to this day),* who then *guilefully guided the Israelites out of Egypt without even the aid of a compass, a fortune teller or a crudely-drawn map.*

Moses led the Israelites through the Red Sea *(which was really blue)* to *famous* Mount Sinai *where nasty sinus infections were often cured by sneezing into a wicked gusty wind with real gusto from atop the desolate mountain's peak.* There', Moses entered into a special covenant with the Lord where God 'laid down the law' for all *the doltish Hebrews* to *faithfully* obey His Ten Commandments *(Demandments).* Hence, the saying originated *"to lay down the law,"* which when translated into colloquial English means *'to read the riot act."*

These are the *everyday* names of the sons of Israel *(Jacob)* that were accompanied by their households. *(Their' households weren't really households at all. They were crude tents that held many wives, children, concubines, prostitutes, whores, hookers and harlots).* These were the people that migrated with Jacob into Egypt and later *trekked* back to the "Promised Land *of Unfulfilled Promises the Almighty Lord had made to Abraham and to his sons Isaac and Jacob."*

The sons of Jacob were the following *devious and unscrupulous* men: Reuben, *the undisputed sandwich king,* Simeon, Judah and *next was* Levi, *who had invented a strong blue denim-material used for work apparel.* Some other sons' of Jacob were Issachar, *who looked like a burned-out ember,* Zebulan, *who formed a bizarre bazaar four piece singing group called Led Zebulan* and then there was *Dandy* Dan, Naphtali, Gad, *Egad* and Asher', *who was in charge of performing Hebrew cremations.* The total number of the direct descendents of Jacob was seventy *individuals.* Joseph *(Jacob's eleventh of twelve sons)* was already *well situated in a position of power* in Egypt, *being smart enough to stay a good distance away from his crazy family and all of his demented relatives. In Joseph's case, absence made his heart grow more forgetful of his warped and shameful heritage.*

Now Joseph and all his *obnoxious and malicious* brothers and that whole generation died, *but not all at the same time, in the same place or on the exact same day.* The Israelites were prolific and fruitful *because they liked to screw-around all the damned time instead of working and producing like loyal slaves should work and produce.* They became so numerous and so strong that the land was filled with them *like a colossal locust invasion or like swarming bees inside an overcrowded hive. The ancient prehistoric New Stone Age Hebrews were notorious avid pumpers and humpers, no doubt about it.*

Then a new king, who knew nothing of Joseph, came to power in Egypt. *The king's name is unimportant because he knew nothing of Jacob and of Joseph, nor did he ever care to know about them. But somehow, this unknown personage managed to become king of the most potent civilization of that era.* He *(the new Egyptian anonymous king)* said to his *inattentive* subjects *and predicates,* "Look how numerous and powerful the Israelite people are growing, more so than we ourselves," the new Pharaoh declared *to his apathetic listeners. "It is all because the Hebrew men have been circumcised and can squirt their prolific seeds further into vaginas than we uncircumcised but lesser endowed Egyptian men can shoot our juices."*

"The fact that the Hebrew men can have all these children proves that they all aren't stupid jerk offs like you think they are!" a cynical court adviser retorted while interrupting Pharaoh's lackluster speech. "Your statements do not circumvent circumcision!"

"Come, let us deal shrewdly with them *(the Israelites)* to stop their increase *in population*; otherwise, in times of war they too may 'join' our *myriad* enemies, *who for some reason always become torn apart and disconnected at their bellybuttons during brutal 'naval' battles.* The *not-too-brilliant* Israelites might *defy their history and surprisingly* fight *extensively* against us, and so leave the country *after whipping our asses good,"* the anonymous Pharaoh verbally concluded.

Accordingly, *the Egyptian* taskmasters were set over the *enslaved* Israelites to *vilely* oppress them with forced 'labor', *especially the women that were giving birth.* Thus 'they' *(the Israelites, here comes the recurrent pronoun-antecedent problem again)* had to *obediently* build for Pharaoh the supply cities of Pithom and Raamses *without any blueprints or available usable materials.*

Yet the more they *(the Israelites)* were *mercilessly* oppressed, the more they *(the libido-oriented Israelites)* multiplied and spread *like fertile rabbits since they always screwed around a lot and seldom worked for their industrious Egyptian masters and taskmasters.*

The *dominating* Egyptians then dreaded the *circumcised* Hebrew men and reduced them and their families to cruel slavery, making life, *vinegar and lemons'* even bitterer for them *during those un-enlightening barbarous times.* The Israelites performed hard work in mortar and brick *many millennia before brick and mortar stores and shops became popular.* They *(the Israelites)* had to do all kinds of field work-*and they were cruelly demoted to field representatives that never had field days, even though some were the best in their fields.* Thus is the whole cruel fate of slaves. *The Israelites had been reduced to mere beasts of burden and were even challenged in court by the strong "National Egyptian Donkey Union."*

The anonymous powerful king of Egypt *(who wasn't important enough to have a name even though he had the authority to repeatedly bust the Israelites' balls and to deflate their women's flabby tits)* told something *in the form of a command* to the Hebrew midwives, one of whom was called Shiphrah and the other *named* Puah. "*Listen to me.* When you act as midwives for the Hebrew women' and see them giving birth, *try pushing the little sucker back into its mother's snatcheroo.* If it is a boy, kill him, but if it is a girl, she may live," *the anonymous* Pharaoh commanded. "*And quite frankly it's seldom that I'm this goddamned sentimental. You're both just lucky you two bitches caught me in one of my better fuckin' moods today."*

The midwives, however, feared God more than *they feared* Pharaoh *because they had heard all about the deluge of Noah's time and all about Sodom and Gomorrah where fire and brimstone had penetrated up people's delicate ass holes. And if a person had a hairy ass hole, then the flames from the fire and brimstone were fiercer than ever and raged completely out of control, cauterizing sensitive ass hole after sensitive ass hole.* The *now three* midwives *(Shiphrah, Shipwreck and Puah)* did not do what the king of Egypt had ordered them, but let the boys live. *Of course, there were tens of thousands of pregnant Israelites (and remarkably all of them women) and only three overworked midwives to accommodate the needs of all of them randomly spread out over the vast desert country's entire length and breadth. The beleaguered midwives really needed shorter hours and better working conditions but the only unions that the horny Hebrew women knew were post-pubescent Israelites continuously having intercourse and then putting up with the whining babies that resulted from their indiscriminate copulations.*

So the *(anonymous) Egyptian* King summoned the *defiant* midwives and *candidly* asked them, "Why have you acted thus *by failing to act?* You have allowed the boys to live. *Don't you know the damned difference between subtraction and addition? Haven't you learned anything from your female ancestor Basemath?" (The mother of arithmetic mentioned extensively in the Wholly Book of Genesis).*

The midwives answered Pharaoh *all together, which was a bad habit all the Israelites had,* "The Hebrew women are not like the Egyptian women," they all chanted in unison, *simultaneously having the exact same thoughts and words.* "They are robust *and busty* and certainly give birth *before afterbirth* and *all that happy nonsense happens even* before the *overtaxed and overworked* midwife arrives *from a remote part of the country. It ain't easy for just the three of us to work this whole friggin' land all by ourselves, ya' know anonymous Kingy, and that's no friggin' bull shit either!"*

Therefore God 'dealt' well with the midwives, *even giving each of them a free deck of playing cards.* The people *(the Israelites)* too, increased and grew strong *because most of them finally went through puberty at age five and were adequately breast-fed until age twenty-one.*

And because the *three overwhelmed Hebrew* midwives feared God, He built up more families for them, *making the poor midwives hustle and scurry all over the damned place, arriving too late to deliver any Hebrew babies into poverty and slavery. The overburdened midwives became frustrated, not even having sufficient time to play solitaire with the decks of cards the Lord had generously given them.*

Pharaoh, *feeling rather petulant,* then commanded all his subjects, *predicates, direct objects and predicate nominatives,*

"Throw into the river *(the Nile)* every boy that is born to the 'Hebrews', *except for the children of Reuben, for 'he brews' some damned good coffee and beer to go with his succulent sandwiches. However,"* the anonymous king proclaimed and pontificated, "you may let all the girls live *so that I may increase my harem at my majestic palace. But I want you to 'a-'nile'-alate' all of those fertile little Hebrew pecker heads as soon as possible in order to accommodate my arbitrary and capricious will."*

Chapter Two
"Birth and Adoption of Moses"

Now a certain man *(we don't know who he is)* of the house of Levi married a Levite' woman *in the first ever all blue denim incestual wedding.* The unidentified woman conceived and bore a son, *who right now is also unidentified, his name lost in history's abyss.* Seeing that he was a goodly *(not godly)* child, she *(the mother)* hid him *(the infant who was not yet ready for the infantry)* for three *months in a clothes hamper in order to hamper Pharaoh's soldiers from finding him. This particular infant abandonment method' was often employed by many psychopathic Hebrew women many years before child abuse laws had been officially instituted.*

When she *(the unidentified mother)* could hide him *(the Levite child by incest)* no longer, she took *(stole at her convenience)* a papyrus basket, daubed it with bitumen, *sulfur, arsenic* and pitch, and putting the child in it, placed it *(the basket)* on the river 'bank' *next to the teller's window.* His sister *(the discarded kid's)* stationed herself at a distance to find out what would happen to him. *Would he drown? Would he swim like a fish? Would he magically turn into an amphibian or a reptile? Would he be just another little shrimp in a basket?*

Pharaoh's *(the anonymous king's)* daughter *(the unknown offspring of the anonymous king)* came down to the *filthy, dirty, slimy* river to bathe. Her maids walked 'along' the riverbank, *a long riverbank at that. They were looking for little discarded Hebrew infants drifting by in baskets in the turbulent river rapids. "Whatever floats your boat?" you might say. The boy was a basket case even before he had been discovered.*

Noticing the basket among the reeds, she *(the anonymous Pharaoh's unknown daughter)* sent her handmaid to fetch it. On opening it *(the basket)*, she lowered, and lo *and behold*, there was a baby boy, crying *inside! (It had been crying for an hour, but the basket was a soundproof one when its lid was shut).*

She *(the unknown daughter of the anonymous Pharaoh)* was moved with pity for him and said *(to anyone that cared to listen)*, "It is one of the Hebrews' children. *He looks like he's really having a bawl in there!"*

Then his *(the shrimp in the basket's)* sister asked Pharaoh's unknown daughter *(who had been cleverly set up to have her sympathy exploited)*, "Shall I go and call one of the Hebrew women' *who are always pregnant* to nurse the *refugee* child for you? *This little ornery wiener could end up being a real pain-in-the-ass weaner if ya' know what I mean!"*

"Yes, *please* do so," she *(the unknown daughter of the anonymous Pharaoh)* answered. So the maiden went and called the child's own mother, *whom she just happened to know out of the thousands of pregnant Hebrew ladies and concubines walking around the city's palatial government district.*

Pharaoh's daughter said *to the big-breasted mother*, "Take this child, *this little sucker* and nurse it for me *because my tits are embarrassingly small and contain not a drop of milk even though I'm now eight and a half months pregnant. Shit! Why couldn't I have big knockers just like the Hebrew women do?"*

The woman' *who wore a breastplate over her knockers* therefore took the *hungry little muncher'* child and nursed it *all the way through nursery school.* When the child grew *(it was already a teenager in three months),* she *(the Hebrew breast-feeder with the big boobs)* brought him *(the little wiener that was a bona fide weaner)* to Pharaoh's daughter, *who had forgotten all about the tiny tot's rather mediocre existence.*

She *(anonymous Pharaoh's unknown daughter)* adopted him *(the child, not the Pharaoh)* as her son and called him Moses; for she said, "I drew him out of the water, and Moses means to draw a child *on papyrus while he and I are both underwater. The name Moses is the closest I could come to accurately depicting the true strange chain of events."*

On one occasion *(there were thousands of occasions, perhaps millions),* after Moses had grown up *(as you can already tell, the boy's certainly extraordinary becoming an adult in one mere paragraph),* he visited his *enslaved* kinsmen. Moses witnessed their forced labor and he saw an Egyptian striking a Hebrew *that was on strike and that refused to work.* "Strike one," *Moses said as he lifted his right thumb into the air.* "Three strikes and you're out of this messed-up ass-backwards world!" *he yelled at the heartless Egyptian doing the lashing.*

Looking about and seeing no one *that would report him*, he *(Moses)* immediately slew the Egyptian *(With what? His 'bear' hands?)* Then he hid him in the sand *without even having the courtesy of dragging his homicide victim anywhere to conduct a decent civilized burial.*

The next day he *(Moses, the criminal and killer)* went out again, *getting permission from his nurse that was still nursing him through nursery school.* Now two' *erratic* Hebrews are fighting (*even though this story is taking place thousands of years ago*). So he *(Moses, the man of the hour)* asked the culprit *(there were two culprits fighting),* "Why are you striking your fellow Hebrew *when you should be beating the shit out of a fuckin' Egyptian? Where's your friggin' loyalty to your race?"*

But he *(one of the two culprits, probably the more aggressive bully)* replied, "Who has appointed you ruler and judge over us, *you stupid power hungry ass hole!" the tough brawler yelled at Moses.* "Are you thinking of killing me as you killed the Egyptian *by some unknown secret means?"*

Then Moses became afraid and said, "The affair between you two *homosexuals* must certainly be known. *Which one of you creeps was dating the dead Egyptian' taskmaster? Tell me the truth or I'll castrate you both!"*

"Both of us' were!" the smaller weakling that had previously been taking a severe pummeling answered Moses. "We're now fighting over who's most qualified to date you! You should feel honored by our altercation!"

Pharaoh *(the nameless anonymous king)*, too, heard of the 'affair' *and became jealous that a male love triangle was going on without his involvement in a nifty foursome arrangement.* He sought to put Moses to death *for conspiring in a love triangle with two other Hebrews without giving the king a chance to hop into the sack with the three principal players.*

Moses, however, fled from him *(the jealous, greedy, gay anonymous Pharaoh)* and walked *in a sandy strip dividing two dirt roads* until he reached the land of 'Midian'. As he *(Moses)* was seated there by a well', seven daughters *that were well-wishers* came to draw water, *which is pretty damned hard to draw with any coal, crayon, stencil or pencil.* The girls were daughters of a priest' of Midian *who obviously did not practice celibacy or abstinence.* They *(the daughters)* had visited the well to get water and fill the trough for their father's *thirsty* flocks. *Moses had erroneously thought that the lengthy trough was a public urinal and the itinerant had just taken a massive leak into it.*

But some *(no number given; too indefinite)* belligerent hooligan shepherds came and 'drove' them *(the seven daughters)* away *without even using a chariot for transportation.* Then Moses got up and defended them *(the seven daughters)* and *he mercifully* watered their flock, *just to bust the chops and the lamb chops of the rude, rowdy hick redneck shepherds.*

When *they (the seven daughters; another serious pronoun-noun antecedent problem evident here)* returned to their father Reuel', *who was a priest and was also often called Father Reuel,* he said to them, *"What the fuck's going on here?* How is it that you have returned home so soon today? *You horny girls almost caught me masturbating!"*

They *(the girls)* answered *all together as a group of seven'*, "An Egyptian saved us from the interference of the *rowdy* shepherds *so Daddy, can we all lose our virginity to this noble wonderful man?* He even drew water for us and *dutifully* watered the flock. *He's our hero!"*

"Where is the man?" he *(Father Reuel, the father of the seven sexy broads)* asked *his curvaceous horny daughters*. "Why did you leave him there *without showing him a little cleavage to entice him to me?" the bisexual priest complained.* "Invite him to have something to eat *and then we could have a real orgy because he valiantly stood up to those mean ninety-year-old sex-starved shepherds!"*

Moses agreed to live with him *(Father Reuel, who as already established did not believe in abstinence and who was reputed to be the first priest child molester/pedophile on record)*. The man then gave his daughter Zipporah in marriage, *and poor Moses didn't have any say in the matter. He only knew that Zipporah was the most ugly hag this side of Hades.*

She *(Zipporah)* bore him *(Moses)* a son, *although Moses claims that he only had oral sex (and no other kind) with Zipporah only once, but then she had farted loudly in his face, completely ruining his orgasm and his sweet afterglow.* He *(Moses)* named the infant Gershom, *which roughly means "big fart."* Moses said, "I am a stranger in a foreign land *where the gaseous woman eat too many damned green vegetables."*

A long time passed, *but no one knows exactly how long, so why even mention it if we can't be accurate and specific?* The *nearly blind* king of Egypt died *while mistaking a cactus for a Hebrew woman's big breast and then choking to death on the plant's sharp thorny needles.*

Still the Israelites cried 'out' *after graduating from the Empire Umpire School,* because they wanted 'out' of slavery. As their cry for release *and liberation* went up to God, He' heard their groaning *and thought they were having raunchy sex with the notorious pedophile Father Reuel and his seven hot-to-trot voluptuous teasing daughters.*

The Lord was *very* mindful of His' covenant with Abraham, Isaac and Jacob. He saw the Israelites and knew *that the promise of "the Promised Land" had not yet been fulfilled in Biblical history. Why promise something if the Promiser cannot or does not deliver it?*

Chapter Three
"The Call of Moses"

Meanwhile Moses was tending the flock of his father-in-law Jethro, the *high and low* priest of Midian', *who was also known in that remote sector of the ancient world as Father Reuel. Although he was no Homer Jethro was both the high and low priest of Midian not only because he was the lone priest living there but also because the emotionally volatile religious personage was a certifiable manic-depressant.*

"I am the boss of this house," Moses once told his wife Zipporah.

"You might think so," Zipporah replied with amusement, "but Father Reuel's (rules)."

One day Moses *was* leading the flock *of sheep* across the desert, *trying to starve the animals to death or kill them by virtue of heat exhaustion and dehydration.* He came to Horeb *because obviously Horeb would not come to him.* Horeb was the mountain of God, *for each mountain, river, desert, tree and blade of grass had some special god that had dominion over it. So Moses went to the mountain, and the mountain did not come to him as taught in other religions with certain suspect prophets of God.*

There *(at Horeb)* an angel of the Lord *(we don't know which one, but that's not important here)* appeared to him *(Moses)* in fire *that was* flaming out of a bush.

"I must really be bushed," the fatigued shepherd said to no one in particular. "I just wish Zipporah's bush would be as hot and as on fire as this one is! Wow! I'm getting a super hard-on just thinking about it!"

As 'he' looked on, 'he' *(Moses, here we go with those dumb pronoun difficulties again)* was surprised to see that the bush, though on fire, was not consumed. 'Why would I want to consume a thorny bush?' Moses thought. 'I'm not that damned hungry! I could choke to death on a thorn or on one of Zipporah's wet farts for that matter!'

So Moses *judiciously* decided, 'I must go over to this remarkable sight and see why the *strange magical* bush is not burned to incineration. Maybe I can piss the damned fire out. I have really healthy kidneys.'

When the Lord saw him *(Moses)* coming over to look at it *(the bush)* more closely, *for Moses was a bona fide bush inspector*, God called out to him from the bush *country*, "Moses! Moses! *I hope you are not a bushwhacker!"*

He (Moses) answered, "Here I am Lord. *I really like your splendid talking bush. How long have You' been practicing ventriloquism? It's actually a dying art form, ya' know!"*

God said, "Come no nearer *unless you have fire insurance and have made all of your scheduled payments*! Remove the sandals from your feet *because naturally shoes haven't been invented yet.* The place where you 'stand' is holy ground, *and sinners just can't stand being here. They always fall down because they just can't stand for it!"*

"Who are You really?" Moses inquisitively asked. "Where are the smoke and mirrors? This is a pretty neat trick You got going for You! Fire without any observable holy smokes!"

"I am the God of your father Abraham," *the formerly enigmatic Voice said.*

"Jacob was reputed to be my father's distant ancestor, Isaac was rumored to be my great-grandfather's father, and Abraham was possibly my great-great-grandfather who in the final analysis wasn't so great after all!" Moses clarified and exclaimed. *"Let's keep our definition of terms and our basic facts straight here!"*

"I am the God of Abraham," the Voice *reiterated and* continued, "the God of Isaac, the God of Jacob."

Moses 'hid' his face *and stuck it in his knapsack*, for he was afraid to look at God *and maybe have fire and brimstone shoot up his butt hole just like once had happened to targeted victims living in Sodom and Gomorrah. God's severe methods of punishment were even worse than those employed by the bellicose and widely barbaric Ass-searians.*

But the Lord said, "I have witnessed the affliction of My' people in Egypt, *but now Moses you have to do something significant about it!* I have heard their cry of complaint against their *oppressive* slave drivers, *but you Moses have to do something significant about it!* I know *very* well what they are suffering, *but you Moses have to do something significant about it!"*

"This is the last time I'm ever going to take a flock of sheep up on this mountain for the very demanding Father Jethro Reuel!" Moses vehemently protested. "He's a damned priest, not me! Why don't You' simply appear to Father Jethro instead of to little old me and make one of Your' religious people do the damned dirty work for You'?"

"Therefore," *the Lord deliberately continued*, "I have come down to *Earth* to rescue them from the hands of the Egyptians and lead them out of that land into a good and spacious land *worthy of migration and invasion.*"

"*I believe that Your' timing and Your' landing coordinates are a little off target,*" Moses cynically stated. "*If You' Lord are going to do those specified things, You' should have descended in Egypt instead of alighting down on this barren forsaken mountain ridge. Get Your' damned Divine Intervention routine correct next time, will You' please!*"

"The new land will be flowing with milk and honey," the Lord *emphatically* said, "and the country *is now occupied by and is* of the *crazy* Canaanites, *the horrific* Hittites, *the amorous* Amorites, *the terrible Troglodytes, the petulant* Perizzites, *the horrendous* Hivites and *the unpredictable Jeb-Bushites.*"

"*Do you mean to say that the Hebrews are going to have to have battles and conflicts with all of those people just so Your' unfulfilled promise to my forefathers can be completed?*" Moses objected. "*No way!*"

The Lord ignored Moses' *dramatic* entreaty. "So indeed the cry of the Israelites has reached Me' *way up here on this remote and desolate mountain peak since the heinous Hebrews have really loud voices and can scream exceptionally well, even here in bush country,*" the Lord indicated to Moses. "I have truly noted that the Egyptians are oppressing them *but I have done nothing about it. That's where you come in,*" God expressly emphasized. "Come now *Moses*! I will send you to Pharaoh, but I forget his real name, to lead My' *chosen* people, the *irascible* Israelites out of Egypt. *I'm sure Pharaoh will cooperate with you without any complications to My' marvelous plan. Otherwise I'll have to become quite vindictive!*"

But *the intrepid* Moses said to God, "Who am I that I should go to *the anonymous* Pharaoh *with the unknown daughters* and *then audaciously* lead the Israelites out of Egypt? *I think I'd rather be castrated and have my dick and balls cut off and then chopped into small pieces of tender loins to boot!*"

He *(God)* answered, "I will be with you, *which is just like saying Moses that you're on your own.* This shall be your proof that it is I Who' have sent you *to Pharaoh,*" the Lord *precisely* declared. "When you bring My' people out of Egypt, *remember that they got there because I had caused severe famine all over the world, especially in Canaan.* Then you will worship God on this very mountain *because I desperately need some home-style adoration and some damned genuine grass-root homage and basic respect around here!"*

"But *Lord*," said Moses to God, "when I go to the *insolent* Israelites and say to them, 'The God of your fathers has sent me to you, *they'll all think that I'm full of shit!"* Moses strenuously argued. "If they ask me, 'What is His' name? *What is His' I.D. number? Why doesn't He'* do something relevant about this slavery bull shit?' What am I to tell them?"

God *authoritatively* replied, "I am Who' am. *That is the most esoteric thing I can say to you My' dear Moses, right now. Are you erudite enough to comprehend it*? *I am Who' am,"* the Lord very deliberately reiterated. Then He' added, "This is what you shall tell the Israelites: "I am sent to you. *That is the coded message that those dimwits, My' chosen people, will finally understand, for indeed, they are trivial numskulls of the lowest caliber."*

God spoke further to Moses, "Thus shall you say to the *imbecile* Israelites: *'The Lord, the God of your fathers has not reneged on you despite His' extensive promises to Abraham, Isaac, and Jacob, and despite the all-essential famine and slavery issues.* The Lord, the God of your fathers, the God of Abraham, the God of Isaac, the God of Jacob, has sent me to you'," *the Lord repeated to Moses in a strong effort to drive home His main idea through monotonous repetition.*

"How many times must I tell You' Lord," Moses balked. "Jacob probably was not my father, Isaac was not my grandfather, and Abraham was not my great-grandfather. Everyone believes and gossips that I'm an illegitimate offspring. Listen up for a change, will You' please? Communications is a two-way street. Abraham, Isaac and Jacob were undeniably retards but now I think and actually believe that 'I thoroughly suck' just like Isaac sucked."

God overlooked Moses' mild protest and proceeded with verbal alacrity. "This is My' name forever, *even though My' name is not 'Forever'*. This is My' *given* title for all generations *dear Moses, although you currently have no title or deeds to the lands I had promised you in Canaan."*

Then God elaborated, "Go *Moses,* and assemble the elders, *who are too weak and feeble to do anything of merit or importance, let alone stand up in erect postures with impressive erections. Those arthritic fools!* Tell them *dear Moses*: 'The Lord, the God of your fathers, the God of Abraham, *of* Isaac and *of* Jacob, has appeared to me and said: *'You primitive people don't have forefathers. You only have three fathers, Abraham, Isaac and Jacob'."*

"And You' expect the Hebrews to believe any of this happy horse crap?" Moses asked. "Horse shit is one full level below basic bull shit!"

"Tell them," the Lord commanded with conviction, "I am concerned about you and about the way you are being treated in Egypt."

"Wouldn't 'mistreated' be a better word to use?" Moses defiantly questioned. "I mean Lord the Hebrews have little credibility in the civilized world because we have these severe communications' handicaps, many of which incidentally originate with You', our Lord! If we became more educated and suddenly out-of-character abandoned our pastoral way of life, then we could get along with other cultures better and wouldn't consequently be reduced to subservient slaves," Moses yelled to the amazing burning, talking bush. "We gotta' evolve and get out of the damned Stone Age and into the bitchin' Bronze Age. The damned Bronze Age is where it's at!"

God persisted in His' eloquent discourse. "Tell them Moses that I have decided to lead you out of the misery of Egypt *into even more greater misery and conflict in Canaan*, the land of the Canaanites, Hittites, *Troglodytes*, Amorites, Perizzites, Hivites and Jeb-Bushites. It is a *marvelous* land flowing with milk and honey, *and if you believe that, I have two under-priced Mediterranean Seas to sell you for a mere ten thousand shekels.*"

"If You' are going to lead them out of Egypt," Moses insisted, "then why do I have to lead the dependent and inferior Israelites out of Egypt?"

The determined Lord continued with his inflexible rhetoric. "Thus they *(the Hebrews)* will heed your message Moses. Then you and the *worthless, geriatric* elders of Israel shall go to the *anonymous* king of Egypt and *bluntly* say to him: 'The Lord, the God of the *cursed disconsolate* Hebrews, has sent us 'word,' *a new type of prescribed programming of a moral nature*. Permit us, then, to go a three-day journey *to nowhere* in the desert, that we may offer sacrifice *on a barren mountain with a unique burning bush* to the Lord, our *traditional* God'."

"Who's gonna' believe such an incredibly ridiculous story?" Moses boldly challenged. "Do You' think I'm an idiot? Do You' think the Hebrews are absolute morons? Do You' think the anonymous Pharaoh is a total imbecile? Do You' think at all?"

The Lord was adamant about His' focused instructions. "Yet I know that the *anonymous* king of Egypt will not allow you to go unless he is forced. I *therefore* will stretch out My' hand *so that all can see My' fantastic fingers and My' lithe ligaments,"* the Lord predicted. "I will smite Egypt by doing all kinds of wondrous *destructive* deeds there."

"Your wondrous deeds are usually nothing more than mindless tragedy calamity, catastrophe and terrible devastation combined," Moses intelligently pointed out. *"Why must You' always have to punish humans and be vengeful? Can't we just do something constructive and contributory for a change?"*

God was determined to exercise His' Almighty will by imposing it on Moses. "After that, he *(the anonymous Pharaoh that didn't even know Moses' name or care to know him)* will send you away and attempt to slaughter the Hebrews later on with advancing soldiers, armies and chariots."

"Wouldn't it be a lot easier just for the accursed Israelites to simply remain as slaves in Egypt?" Moses shrewdly advanced. *"A lot of trouble could be avoided in the future if the Hebrews just stayed put there!"*

Moses' noble but unconvincing objections did not thwart God. "I will even make the Egyptians so well-disposed toward this people that, when you leave, you will not go empty-handed," *the Lord exactly explained.* "Every woman shall ask her neighbor and her house guest for silver and gold articles and for clothing *to extort in order* to put on your sons and daughters. Thus you will dispoil (*Is this really a word? Oh sorry! Our mistake! We' meant to state the word "despoil"*) the *untrustworthy* Egyptians."

"Oh, I get it now," Moses derived and acknowledged. *"The Hebrews are not strong enough to be authentic marauders and plunderers. We can't use force to claim the wealth of Egypt and bring it to tiny Canaan with us,"* Moses argued and stated. *"We must persuade, coerce and extort the Egyptians to give us their heirlooms, and what they don't donate to our cause and agenda,"* Moses maintained, *"we will brazenly steal before we depart and finally exit the scene. Your supreme strategy all makes absolute sense now Lord."*

Chapter Four
"Confirmation of Moses' Mission"

"But," objected Moses *to the Lord's supreme Voice*, "suppose they *(the Hebrews)* will not believe me, nor listen to my plea? *Those jerks don't believe that it is raining if there's a major hurricane blowing around their tents that have already blown away! Do You' have any secret weapons and threats readily available such as earthquakes or volcanic eruptions? I know You' Lord are indeed a mover and a shaker,"* Moses asserted. "If You do visit Egypt with a huge earthquake, make sure everyone knows it wasn't my 'fault'! For they *(those apostate nefarious retarded Israelites)* may say, 'The Lord did not appear to you Moses. *Stop drinking so much lousy potent wine so start thinking in a more acceptable sober manner that doesn't stress everyone out'!"*

The Lord therefore asked him *(Moses)*, "What is that in your hand?"

"*Can't You' recognize simple everyday' objects?*" Moses testily replied. "*It's* a staff!"

"*You must have a very large hand if you can fit your entire 'staff' in it,*" the Lord jested. "*How many secretaries* do you have in your *staff?*"

"*Enough to give me a very serious 'staph' infection!*" Moses rankled.

The Lord then said *to His principal servant*, "Throw it *(the staff)* on the ground."

When he *(Moses)* threw it *(the staff)* on the ground, it was *instantaneously* changed into a serpent *laden with loco staphylococcus infection all over its slimy scaly skin. The Lord's transformation demonstration was quite impressive.*

Being very bashful upon first introductions, Moses 'shied' away from it *(the grotesque infected serpent)*. '*I despise snakes more than I loathe chronic constipation!*' he considered.

"Now put out your hand," the Lord said to *the astonished* Moses, "*so that I may read your palms.* Then take hold of its tail *and tie the poisonous viper into a magnificent figure-eight-knot. Can you count that high Moses?"*

So he *(Moses)* 'put out his hand' *which had accidentally caught fire from the burning bush,* and laid hold of it *(the slimy, bacteria-infected serpent)* and it *(the voodoo snake)* remarkably became a staff *without any infection* in his hand.

19

"This will take place so that they *(the Israelites)* may believe," He' continued *(to Moses)*, "that the Lord God, the God of their fathers, *Who' practices supernatural miracles and not mere mundane magic tricks,* did appear to you. *I am* the God of Abraham, the God of Isaac, and the God of Jacob', *who are all dead now and their souls lost somewhere in the vast universe out there that I have created out of boredom. Moses, I've always said that those three deceased Hebrew guys were really 'out there'!"*

Again the Lord said to him *(Moses) because he was a slow learner just like his mentally challenged ancestors and his ignoramus peers,* "Put your hand in your bosom *without penetrating you chest, diaphragm or stomach.*"

He *(Moses)* put it *(his hand, we know not which one)* in his bosom, and when he withdrew it, to his surprise his hand was as leprous as snow *just like the leprous staph infection of the viper's scaly skin had been.*

The Lord, *who was on a roll and not on a biscuit* then said *to his main worshiper,* "Now, put your hand back in your bosom *without penetrating your chest cavity.*" Moses put his hand *(let's say his right hand)* back in his bosom, and when he *again* withdrew it, to his *utter* surprise, it was again like the rest of his body, *hairy, wrinkled, scummy and oily. Moses was very glad that his hands were once again 'bosom' buddies'.*

"If they *(the Hebrews)* will not believe you, nor heed the message of the first sign," *the Lord said and emphasized,* "then they' should believe the message of the second sign. *If the stubborn fools don't obey you, then they all will immediately contract staph infection on and in their reproductive organs. I guarantee you' Moses that punishment will be far worse than any ten venereal diseases imaginable!"*

"Can't we just have the vicious viper simply bite all of the skeptical disbelievers?" Moses suggested. "That (instant death) would alleviate a lot of needless suffering among my cynical people."

The Lord was so intent on His' next comment that He' completely ignored Moses' rather sage remark. "And if they *(the doubting mentally retarded Israelites)* will not believe even those two signs, nor heed your plea, take some *polluted* water from the river and pour it on the dry land. The water you will take from the river will become blood on the dry land," *the Lord attested.* "*That change will be My' blood transfusion to my anemic people and My' final proof! Moses, I want My' often errant Israelites to symbolically* understand that they are stupid red-blooded Hebrew rednecks to the core."

Moses, however, said to the Lord, "If You' please, Lord, I have never been eloquent *and have never taken any speech courses* in the past *nor have I taken them recently.* Now that You' have spoken to Your' *humble* servant," *Moses nervously said, "I can't understand why You' just don't appear to the Israelites and do this crazy stuff Yourself'!* I am slow of speech and of tongue *but I have a nice 'stutter' step when playing certain games," Moses related.* "But why do You' have to dump all this heavy messenger responsibility stuff on little old me?"

The Lord *cryptically* said to him *(Moses):* "Who gives one man speech and makes another deaf and dumb? Or who gives sight to one and makes another blind? *I tend to really severely handicap those that get on My' Almighty nerves! Now Moses, I would even handicap a horserace if I felt I had to!"*

"Can't You' just take a psychology course and become a little more benign and reasonable?" Moses *courageously inquired.* "In my opinion violence and punishment are a little too drastic for the fearful Israelites to live with!"

"Go then *with dispatch!*" *the Lord prompted.* "It is I Who' will assist you in speaking and will teach you what *persuasive rhetoric* you are to say. *Moses,* I will make you as scholarly and as wise as any Egyptian *presently residing in any of the anonymous Pharaoh's insane asylums."*

Yet he *(Moses)* insisted *and persisted,* "If You' please, Lord, send someone else *to do Your' malicious dirty work! Get one of Your' more garrulous non-union slaves to be my worthy substitute."*

Then the Lord *lost His' Almighty patience and temper and* became very angry with Moses and said, "Have you not your brother, Aaron the Levite? I know that he is an eloquent speaker *when no one is around to hear him talking to himself'.* Besides, he *(Aaron)* is now on his way to meet you," *the omniscient and ubiquitous Lord revealed.* "When he sees you, his heart will be glad, *but you should shun his homosexual tendencies and his deliberate advances.* You are to speak to him then, and put the *appropriate* words in his mouth."

"Now just wait an olive pickin' minute," Moses *boldly countered.* "How can I put words in his mouth? Should I make him swallow the Wholly Book of Genesis? And if Aaron is such a gifted orator, why do I have to awkwardly tell him the necessary words to speak?" *Moses Adam-antly protested.* "Did You' mean I should put *ideas into his mind so that he could communicate them into the right words? Please be more specific Lord!"*

The Lord was not convinced of anything by Moses' shallow thoughts and by his hollow ineffectual arguments. "I will assist both of you *dumbbells* in speaking and will teach the two of you *nitwits* what you are to do. He (Aaron) shall speak to the people for you *until you satisfactorily polish-up your rusty lecturing and oratorical skills,"* the Lord sternly directed. "He (Aaron) shall be your 'spokesman', *even though he has never made a wheel and has never been a big wheel around these remote parts.* You shall be as God to him, *but don't let the prestige go to your head or I shall make you' start having babies through the tiny hole at the end of your male genitalia.* Take this staff in your hand *Moses, and watch out for nasty splinters.* With it *(the staff)* you are to perform the signs *I have already described, but please, no cosines or other forms of advanced trigonometry are to be exhibited.*"

After this *non-enlightening discussion* Moses returned to his *cantankerous* father-in-law Jethro *Reuel, the first documented priest or man in the Old Testament to have valid first and last names.* "*Father Jethro*, let me go back, please, to my kinsmen in Egypt to see whether they are still living *low on the hog. I need more adventure and conflict in my life and to tell you the truth I am homesick and tired of being a fugitive from cruel Egyptian justice,"* Moses declared to normally phlegmatic Father Reuel.

Jethro *Reuel aptly* replied, "Go in peace, *but come back in one piece."*

In Midian *(in the center of the roadway)* the Lord said to *an already confused* Moses, "Go back to Egypt, for all the men who sought your life are dead, *intentionally killed by contagious and vile staph infection."*

So Moses took his wife (*Who cares about her name*?) and his sons (*Who cares about their names either*?) and started back to the land of Egypt with them riding his *(the)* ass *all the way.* The staff of God he carried with him, *and Moses threatened to use its awesome magical powers to frighten on purpose his wife and children as long as they kept riding his ass all the way to Egypt.*

The Lord said to him *(Moses during his arduous trip),* "On your return to Egypt (*which is happening now in real time*), see that you perform *in a fantastic circus act before the anonymous* Pharaoh all the wonders I have put in your power."

"*Can't You' just teach my unfaithful wife how to use the idiotic staff?"* Moses recommended and pleaded. "*Zipporah's so macho that she could club everybody that disobeys her to death without ever needing the silly aid of any awesome infected staff that can convert into a viper!"*

"I will make him *(the anonymous Pharaoh)* obstinate, however, so that he will not let the people go," *the Lord confidentially divulged to Moses. "I don't want to make it too easy a mission for you, you know! Suffering and struggle must be your hallmarks on this Earth!"*

"Thanks but no thanks," Moses mumbled and protested. "Why couldn't I have been born a happy pagan or a blithe Canaanite? Then I wouldn't be subjected to such asinine brutal long-term frustrating assignments."

"So you shall say to *the anonymous* Pharaoh," *the Lord stated with true authority,* "thus says the Lord. 'Israel is My' son, my first-born, *and I am still trying to figure out how he became a people and how those people soon will become a country'. Anyway My' dear Moses,* hence I tell you *with conviction,* 'Let My' son go so that he may serve you *in restaurants without using tennis rackets.'* If you refuse to let him go,' the Lord warned, 'I will kill your son, your' first-born *and hang his naked body in the center of your city's most popular bizarre bazaar.'* Tell that particular threat to the hard-headed Pharaoh!"

On a journey at a place *(how specific can you get?)* where they *(Moses and his wonderful family)* spent the night, the *relentless* Lord *again* came upon Moses and would have killed him *out of intense animosity and from sheer frustration.*

But Zipporah *(who refused to commit a second circumcision on Moses with a zipper)* took a piece of flint' *stone* and cut off her son's foreskin *so that he could be 'in like Flint'.* "This damned foreskin must come off, *but one skin should have been enough. Why four?"* she shouted *like a bona-fide maniac.*

"Ow!" her son screamed. *"Can't you just break my balls instead of shaving tender skin off my dick? I could get a serious staff-infection if I unintentionally get an erection with all the dirt you have corroded on that grimy flint stone you're using."*

"Give me some skin!" Zipporah yelled at her apprehensive son *without even the courtesy of extending her right hand.*

Touching 'his' person *(Moses' anonymous son's: whose name was Gershom in chapter two),* she *(Zipporah) illogically* said, "You are a spouse of blood to me." Then God let Moses go after holding him down during the entire agonizing *(dual?)* circumcision. At that she (Zipporah) said *like a practitioner of incest,* "A spouse of blood.

This bloody foreskin mess is far worse than any damned period I ever had since I lost my lousy maidenhead!" She was speaking in regard to the ongoing circumcision *(but was it Moses' or Gershom's, or both of their peckers that had been blatantly butchered by Zipporah?).*

The Lord *felt loquacious at that moment and* said to Aaron, "Go into the desert to meet Moses', *who is a little skinnier in his tenderloin area than he was just yesterday."*

So he *(Aaron)* went *into the desert,* and when they met at the mountain of God, Aaron kissed him, *but Moses howled with pain because his sensitive penis had been savagely banged into during Aaron's strong physical embrace.*

Moses informed him *(Aaron)* of all the Lord had said in sending him, and of the various *frightening* signs that had enjoined upon him. *Aaron withdrew from his anguished brother's embrace, wishing the hell that he had stayed in Egypt being pissed on by the nefarious Egyptians and being whipped by his belligerent taskmasters.*

Then Moses and Aaron went and assembled all the senile elders of the Israelites, *which was a hard task to accomplish because the feeble old gents would aimlessly wander off again after being retrieved and reassembled. The elders preferred dissembling to assembling.*

Aaron told them *(the demented elders)* everything the Lord had said to Moses *but the mentally deficient hoary old men were too forgetful to remember all that Aaron had told them.* Moses *then dramatically* performed the signs *with the staff turning into the serpent, but the decrepit aged gents could not comprehend or recollect what they had just witnessed ten seconds before.*

However, the *people (especially the senile elders)* believed *what they failed to remember,* and when they heard that the Lord was concerned about them and had seen their *mental* affliction, *they were still smart enough and had the wherewithal to do the proper thing.* They *(all the obedient elders and other Israelites)* bowed down in worship *out of fear of sudden and instant retribution and certain violent death.*

Chapter Five
"Pharaoh's Obduracy"

In case you are wondering, obduracy means hardening of feelings, which usually is a telltale symptom of the last stages of hardening of the arteries. The anonymous Pharaoh's attitude toward the enslaved Israelites gradually changes from apathy to stubborn contempt as this monotonous chapter progresses from beginning to end.

After that, *(Excuse me? After what?)* Moses and Aaron, *the unambitious 'Ma' boys* went to *the anonymous* Pharaoh, *who always eagerly entertained slaves coming to his palace because the King simply enjoyed randomly bull shitting with various sub-commoners. The Egyptian King had nothing better to do with his leisure time especially when he wasn't sexually screwing prostitutes or when he wasn't economically screwing all his overtaxed and undersexed resident citizens.*

"Thus said the Lord, the God of Israel," *Moses and Aaron both stated in unison without ever having graduated from or attended parroting school. The King was not influenced by the men's utterance.*

"Your foreign God has no jurisdiction here in Egypt," Pharaoh *angrily stated, "so don't give me any Ra-Ra pep talk about His notorious temper and wrath! Go tell it on a mountain out in the middle of nowhere."*

"The Lord then said," the two persistent slave/guests recited in unperturbed dual voices, "Let My' people go, that they may celebrate a feast to Me' in the desert. *Let them play a 'home game' for a change instead of being the 'visiting team' all the damned time in Egypt."*

The anonymous Pharaoh *that liked to listen to the testimonies of grieving slaves all day long* answered *his visitors,* "Who is the Lord that I should lead His' plea to let Israel go *and secede from Egypt? Give me His' address so that my accountants can place Him' on our tax rolls!" Pharaoh imaginatively joked.* "I do not know the Lord *to whom you allude,* and I have never been introduced to Him by an acquaintance. Even if I had been *formally introduced to the Lord,"* the *anonymous* Pharaoh emphasized *with a grim expression on his countenance,* "I would not let Israel go *because it is hard to remove a slave country and its people from within the host country and its contented people. Is this Israel a country, a person, a people or all three possibilities, that's what the fuck I want to know? What the hell* is going on here anyway?" A momentary pause resulted as the two Israelites gathered their wits.

They *(the Ma boys)* replied, "The God of the Hebrews has sent us word *that threat of plague, famine, earthquake or death to Egypt by fire and brimstone works much better than national internal chaos within Egypt resulting from slave rebellion and insurrection does,"* Aaron finished as Moses merely lip-synced towards the end of the response. *"What say you Pharaoh?"*

"Tell your avaricious Lord to get or import some genuine good-spirited worshipers from Babylonia or cretins from Crete and to stop busting my regal chops," the anonymous Pharaoh ordered. "And tell Him' to get some elite worshipers of a higher caliber than those rather base and lazy Hebrew slaves that you two clowns are attempting to illegally unionize and represent. I have an innate repugnance toward insurrection and toward those who inspire it!"

"God told us," Moses and Aaron simultaneously said, "Let us go on a three days' journey in the desert *to conduct an orchestrated rebellion rally and a series of non-violent peaceful demonstrations against Pharaoh* so that we may *freely* sacrifice to the Lord our God."

"You and your people are nothing more than meager slaves and therefore must 'sacrifice' and toil for me, or otherwise be sacrificed yourself'," the anonymous Pharaoh retorted. "Be wise! Know and learn to accept your place and station in the damned pecking order!"

"*If you do not comply with our unreasonable demands,"* Moses and Aaron both said together, "otherwise God will punish 'us' with pestilence or *with* the sword. *He has little patience with non-compliance!*"

"As long as He' just punishes the Hebrews and not the Egyptians," Pharaoh merrily laughed, "who really gives a flying shit about His antics and ranting?"

The *anonymous* king of Egypt' *who liked to hear slaves bitch and moan about their myriad ordeals and travails then* answered them *(Moses and Aaron)*, "What do you mean, Moses and Aaron *(the King now suddenly knows them on a first name basis)*, by taking the people away from their work?" Pharaoh challenged their confrontational point of view. "How can my slaves be working in Egypt when they are on some holiday vacation in the eastern desert worshiping your totally vindictive Lord? This entire fiasco and your idiotic request are both preposterous to say the least!" the *anonymous Pharaoh'* who now knew Moses and Aaron on a first name basis replied.

"You'll be sorry!" Moses and Aaron both mercilessly threatened and predicted. "You will soon feel the intense wrath of the Lord and we guarantee that you and your subjects will not relish it one iota!" both florid-faced visiting Israelites remarkably chanted in unison.

"First you came here to bust my chops and now you're busting my balls!" the anonymous Pharaoh screamed. "Off to your labor! Look how numerous the people of the land are already," continued the paranoid anonymous Pharaoh, who was good enough to have his name recorded in history book chronicles but not good enough to be named in the Old Testament of the Bible. "Yet you *(Moses and Aaron)* would give them *(the Israelites)* rest from their *common* labor! Your people are so numerous because they screw around all day long with each other rather than indulge in the pursuit of work!" Pharaoh accurately accused. "Your Lord has threatened Egypt with a pestilence! I already have a damned pestilence in my land, and it's called you lazy Israelites! Listen to me you simple-minded Dickheads! I call the shots in my kingdom! Not your anonymous voodoo Lord!" the anonymous Pharaoh vehemently hollered.

That same day *(Tuesday? Month? Year?)* the very pissed-off anonymous Pharaoh gave the taskmasters *(loyal Egyptian accountants, officials and pimps)* and the foremen *(bully-type Israelites)* of the people this order: *"That's the last straw!* You shall no longer supply the people *(Hebrew slaves)* with straw for their' brick-making *(straw was laboriously mixed with clay to give the sun-dried bricks greater consistency)* as you have previously done. Let them go and gather straw themselves *so that they (the enslaved Israelites) can make hay while the sun still shines!"*

"But your Excellency," said an astute adviser, "wouldn't such an activity as gathering straw slow down the vital construction of buildings and monuments in our great land? What if the insolent and indolent Hebrews all contract hay fever? Those ornery slaves are too snot-nosed already without the additional problem of having nasty hay fever!"

"You shall levy upon them *all the way from here to the levee* the same quota of bricks as they have previously made," *the* anonymous Pharaoh directed his subordinates. "Do not reduce it. They *(the Hebrews)* are lazy *and screw around all day long. That's why there are so many of them around to bust our nuggets!" the furious king pointed out.* "That is why they are crying: 'Let us go to offer sacrifice to our God.' *The imbeciles say that because the ungrateful fools don't like sacrificing their time and effort to build marvelous edifices for me, their anonymous Pharaoh',"* the livid King responded.

"This dumb work assignment you have prescribed could really backfire on the entire nation," interrupted an anonymous scribe' who never had the authority to prescribe anything including medicine. *"Your punishment might ultimately lead to revolution and turmoil throughout your great kingdom!"*

"Regardless," yelled the crimson faced anonymous Pharaoh to his half-concerned counselors. "Increase the *assigned* work for the men, so that they keep their mind *(minds)* on it and pay no attention to lying words *and to screwing their women all day long anywhere they could park their carcasses. I hereby proclaim that straw is the law and that their ass is grass! That is it in a peanut shell gentlemen!"*

So the *fearful* taskmasters and foremen of the people went out *of the palace* and told them *(the Israelite slaves),* "Get your fat lard asses in gear. I *(we)* will not provide you with straw. Go and gather the *cheap* straw yourselves, wherever you can find it," *all of the taskmasters and foreman simultaneously commanded all of the apathetic but horny slaves in the country.* "Yet there must not be the slightest reduction in your work," *they continued all together,* "even *if you roll around with your hot promiscuous hussies in the straw that you gather and then proceed to pump the bitches like there's no fuckin' tomorrow! The Pharaoh wants to have 'No Porking Zones' all over the damned country!"*

The *horny* people *(Israelite slaves),* then, scattered throughout the land of Egypt and meanwhile built nothing *but amorous relationships.* They gathered their straw *and screwed their women in straw mangers and in haystacks all the way from the Nile to the extremities of the vast surrounding deserts. This all transpired while the dedicated taskmasters kept driving them on, imperatively saying, "Hop off your loose woman and get out of the freakin' haystack so that I may mount and then incessantly ride your bitch like a stud stallion would skillfully perform his instinctive duties in heat,"* they all said in unison to non-attentive Hebrew slaves standing still as statues all over Egypt. "Finish your work *while I ambitiously pump your sex partner for you,* and make sure it's the same daily amount *of work* as when your straw was supplied *in the past before Pharaoh had declared his stupid edict. Pharaoh's stupid edict doesn't seem so stupid now after all! Oohhhh! Ahhhhh! Oohhhhh! Ahhhh!"*

The foremen of the Israelites *(who were actually non-union Israelites)* whom the taskmasters of the *anonymous* Pharaoh had placed over them', were beaten. The *victimized* foremen were *interrogated by the Pharaoh's taskmasters and* asked *under threat of death,* "Why have you not completed your prescribed amount of bricks *as prescribed by the King and recorded by the scribes?"* The grieving foremen then protested the taskmasters' unjustified criticism.

"There is less yesterday and today as there was before! *You're all screwing around just like the lustful slave women 'under you' are! Hey, I want some of that action!"* exclaimed all the sex-starved foremen all over Egypt as they immediately forgot their arguments and their grievances with their demanding taskmasters that had just recently brutally and maliciously whipped and beaten the crap out of them.

Then the *abused* Israelite foremen came and made an appeal to *the anonymous* Pharaoh: "Why do you treat *(mistreat and abuse)* your servants *(slaves)* in this *uncivilized* manner? No straw is supplied to your servants *(slaves),* and still we are told to make bricks *for your bricks and mortar stores in your bizarre bazaars all over the damned country,"* the disgruntled Israelite foremen all said in unison. *"Just* look at how your *loyal* servants *(slaves)* are beaten *like hanging rugs*! It is you' King who are at fault *for this unnecessary travesty!"*

The anonymous but eminent Pharaoh answered, "It is just because you are lazy *and so horny that you always want to get laid in straw mangers and in haystacks* that you keep saying, 'Let us go and offer sacrifice to the Lord,' *the King aptly admonished the hurting foremen.* "Off to work *you lazy lethargic lackadaisical oafs!* Straw shall not be provided for you, *although you have at your convenience all of the Hebrew' women you wish to screw,"* the incensed King acknowledged. *"However, you must still deliver your quota of bricks even if your dicks are warm inside hot greasy Hebrew' women's ovens and even though you have to find and gather your own damned straw!"*

The Israelite foremen knew they were in a sorry plight, *but they really didn't care that much since they were getting laid in straw mangers and in haystacks all over Egypt with much greater frequency than normal.* They had been told not to reduce the daily amount of bricks *but as everybody knows, it is hard to reduce bricks from their normal size anyway even without experiencing adversity. So it really didn't matter to the sex-starved foremen as long as they were getting their rocks off more often (than before) in straw mangers and in haystacks all throughout Egypt. In that sense bricks were very much like vaginas: one size fitted all.*

When therefore they *(the Israelite fore-playing foremen)* left *the anonymous but very important* Pharaoh, they came upon Moses and Aaron *taking dual craps in a popular and often frequented downtown public hopper.* Moses and Aaron had been waiting to meet them *(the foremen),* so they (the foremen) said to them (Moses and Aaron), "The Lord look *(looks)* upon you and judge," *(judges; let's get third person singular right, here! Okay!)* the aggravated foremen all said together. "You have brought us into bad odor with Pharaoh and his servants *(the king and his court had terrible cases of halitosis and were experiencing chronic gastritis conditions).* You two *unimpressive jerk offs* have put a sword *(swords)* in their hands to slay us. *Finish taking your smelly dumps so that we can beat the future shit out of both of you simple-minded fuck heads!"* the indignant foremen all said together *without any designated rehearsal or script to read.*

Moses again had recourse to the Lord and said *(no setting here; where was he at the time?),* "My sweet Lord, why do You' treat *(mistreat)* this, *Your'* chosen people so badly? And why did You' send me *on such an unscrupulous and foolhardy mission?"* Moses demanded to know. "*I'm liable to get decapitated following Your' inflexible instructions!*"

"Are you Moses' questioning My' supreme integrity?" the Lord countered. "Do you want the fire and brimstone treatment *(mistreatment)* up the old wazoo now or later? You'd better choose your words wisely!"

"Ever since I went to Pharaoh to speak in Your' *Almighty* name he has mistreated this *accursed* people of Yours'," Moses sobbed. "Why didn't You' go and speak with Pharaoh Yourself' instead of assigning an incompetent flunky like me to do Your' unattainable bidding?" Moses requested of the Lord. "Please give me an adequate explanation!"

"Because I'm the Boss in this operation and you're just a mortal who' is in the wrong place at the wrong time," the Lord observed and communicated. "You Moses are merely a poor weak actor cavorting around on My' grand illustrious stage. The world is My' theater, and you'd just better remember that you sniveling *pipsqueak! You are at best a silly puppet in My' ever-evolving magnificent variety show."*

"You have done nothing to rescue Your' people from the drudgery of slavery," *Moses pathetically cried. "Why do You' torment me thus?"*

"Because Moses," *the Lord's distinct Voice thundered from Heaven, "sometimes you just piss Me' off!"*

Chapter Six
"Renewal of God's Promise"

Then the *Almighty* Lord answered Moses *(remember, Moses hasn't even asked a question yet in this chapter)*, "You shall see what I shall do *as much-deserved punishment* to *the anonymous* Pharaoh. *He will wish that he was chopped liver or basic minced' meat when I finally get through with him."*

"What will You' do to the dirty bastard?" Moses curiously asked. "Give him a lifetime supply of jock itch or canker sores all over his personals? What devious methods has Your' omnipotent mind schemed up?"

"Forced by My' mighty hand," *the Lord said,* "he *(the anonymous Pharaoh)* will send them *(the Israelites)* away, *away, away down south in Canaan.* Compelled by My' outstretched arm, he *(the anonymous important Pharaoh)* will drive them *(the Hebrew slaves)* from his land, *but will not drive them away in expensive chariots."*

God also said to Moses, "I am the Lord. *You oughta' know that by down, you lackluster slow learner.* As God the Almighty I appeared to Abraham, Isaac and Jacob, *but I couldn't appear to all three of them at the same time because they all lived during different times,"* the Lord clarified for the benefit of Moses. *"I'm still trying to figure out exactly how to do such a fantastic feat!"*

"At least something You' have said seems almost logical," Moses considerately admitted. "Is Heaven a big mental institution or what?"

"I did not make My' *sacred* name known to them," *the Lord continued,* "since I felt your father and forefathers were too doltish to remember It'. At any rate Moses,* I also established My' covenant with them *(Abraham, Isaac and Jacob),* to give them the *wonderful* land of Canaan."

"But Canaan belongs to the Canaanites," Moses interrupted with strong principles, "and You' had no deed or title to that land. You were giving away territory that You' do did not own. You merely promised my father and forefathers that land. Why do You' have this compulsive fixation about Canaan?"

"*You are learning to think and speak too well for your own good,"* the Lord admonished. "Don't you know that I had created the whole Earth that incidentally includes Canaan? Your ancestors were living in the land of Canaan as *illegal* aliens, *not to mention immoral* aliens. And now *that* I have heard the *continuous* groaning of the Israelites, *I must tell you that their noises do not sound too pleasant to My' super-sensitive ears."*

"Can't You' just get lost in eternal space or infinite time somewhere?" Moses insisted. "Go bother Your' enemies instead of annoying and pestering Your' faithful worshipers."

"The Egyptians are treating *(mistreating)* My' people as slaves, and I am *still* mindful of the covenant. *I plan to kick Pharaoh's butt really good this time,"* the Lord forecasted. "Therefore, say to the Israelites: I am the Lord. I will free you from the forced labor of the Egyptians and will deliver you from their slavery. *You know Moses, I am pretty awesome when I get my dander up!"*

"Why must there always be conflict in substitution of misery?" Moses challenged. "The people are now content living in their despicable misery. The Israelites will hate a change to conflict more than they have despised their unhappiness associated with Egyptian slavery."

"*Moses,* I will rescue you by my outstretched arm and with mighty acts of judgment," *the Lord predicted.*

"Why do You' say You' will rescue me?" Moses audaciously challenged. "I'm not drowning in a river or dying in a fire! I am perfectly satisfied wallowing like a content swine in absolute mediocrity."

"Moses," the Lord strongly stated, "I shall take you from My' own people and you shall have me as Your' God."

"Oh great!" Moses yelled at the Voice without form. "I will be Your' only worshiper while everyone else is getting laid and drunk and having terrific slave orgies in straw mangers and in soft haystacks."

"Moses," the Lord interrupted, "you will know that I, the Lord, am your God when I free you from the labor of the Egyptians and bring you up in the land which I swore to give to Abraham, to Isaac and to Jacob. I will give it to you as your own possession-I, the Lord!"

"Yeah, yeah! Promises, promises!" Moses exclaimed. "Hollow, empty promises!" Moses muttered, shaking his head from shoulder to shoulder. "I must be hallucinating all of this crazy bull shit. Why couldn't I just have been able to stay in my mother's womb for my entire life or have luckily drowned in the Nile when my basket finally sank to the bottom of the river'. What a bummer this is! A real royal pain-in-the-ass bummer!"

But when Moses told this *(the Lord's promises)* to the Israelites, they would not listen to him because of their dejection, hard slavery *and their ability to get laid in hard straw mangers and on soft haystacks all over Egypt whenever they wanted.*

Then the determined Lord said to Moses (where were they? No setting), "Go and tell Pharaoh, the *nameless* King of Egypt *(No daaaaa!),* to let the Israelites leave the land."

But Moses protested to the Lord, *"Please make more reasonable demands of me,"* he *futilely* argued. "If the Israelites would not listen to me, how could it be that Pharaoh will listen to me *and my unfeasible bull crap that is really Your' profound rhetoric,* poor *public* speaker that I am!"

Still, the Lord, to *satisfactorily* bring the Israelites out of Egypt, spoke to Moses and Aaron and gave them the *explicit* orders regarding both' the Israelites and Pharaoh, King of Egypt *and that specific part of the civilized world.*

"I don't like this scenario one bit," Moses told Aaron after the Lord's formless Voice departed the scene.

"You're right," Aaron agreed. *"I regret to acknowledge that there aren't any hard straw mangers and soft haystacks out in the hot, arid, sultry eastern desert."*

These are the 'heads' of the ancestral 'houses', even though way back in prehistoric times the Hebrews lived mostly in tents instead of in houses and that the houses didn't have any toilets (heads) in them. So, there weren't really any 'heads' in the ancestral houses. In fact, there weren't even outhouses back then for people to take private dumps in. The sons of Reuben, the first-born of Jacob *and also known as the Hebrew kosher rye sandwich king:* Hanoch, *Hammock,* Pallu, Hezron, *Doo-ron-ron,* Carmi and *Karma. These are the sons of Reuben, and all had wry senses of humor to go along with their hybrid rye bread sandwiches.*

The sons of Simeon were Jemuel, Ohad, Jachin, *Jachinoff,* Zohar, and Shaul, *whose mother always had cold shoulders and gave them to every stranger that she ever met.* Shaul was the son of a Canaanite woman' *who was the first to stitch together a garment to cover her cold shoulders.* These are the clans of Simeon.

The names of the sons of Levi in their genealogical *and gynecological order (notice that wives, daughters, sisters, aunts and nieces are unimportant and immaterial to ancient male Biblical chauvinism'):* Gershon, *Gershwin,* Kohath, *Strauss, Denim* and Merari. Levi lived for one hundred and thirty-seven years *and seldom came out of his tent made of a durable blue canvass material.*

The sons of Gershon, as 'heads' of clans', *meaning that they' all looked like primitive outhouses.* They were Libni, *Lip-knee* and Shimei.

The sons of Kohath *(have you readers dozed off and gone to sleep yet?)* were Amran, Izhar, *Iz-hardyhar-har,* Hebron and Uzziel. Kohath lived one hundred and thirty-three years *and didn't do a blessed thing in his lackluster lifetime except screw around and manufacture a whole lot of babies with his big circumcised dick.*

The sons of Merari were Mahli, Mushi and *Mushy', who was soft in disciplining his many children.* These are the clans of Levi in their genealogical, *general logical and gynecological* 'orders *from headquarters'.*

Amran married his aunt Jochebed *in bed because he was worried that there wasn't enough incest in his inbred family. Joch*ebed *was athletic in the sack* and bore him *(Amran)* Aaron, *Errand, Errant,* Moses, *Molasses, Mosaic* and Miriam. Amran lived one hundred and thirty-seven years, *and who gives a shit about that except maybe Amran', who was very happy to die anyway and get the fuck outa' here!*

The sons of Izhar were Korah, *Coral, Corral,* Negpheg and Zichri.

The sons of Uzziel were Mishael, *Guided-mishael,* Elzaphan and Sithri.

Aaron married Amminadab's daughter, Elisheba. *Aaron' then appointed himself a high priest on marijuana', officiated at his' own wedding ceremony and even went against family tradition and screwed hi*s *own wife that night.* Elisheba was the sister of Nahshon *and the brother of U-nighted-nah-shons.* Elisheba bore him *(Aaron)* Nadab, *Nabob,* Abihu, *Hoo-gives-a-crap,* Eleazar, *Elsinore* and Ithamar, *all in one amazing pregnancy.*

The sons of Kora were all *son-of-a-bitches.* They were Assir, *Wise-asser,* Elkanah, Abiasaph *and I'll-be-a-sap.* These are the clans of the Korahites', *who lived in isolation somewhere in the Kora Heights.*

Aaron's son, Eleazar, married one of Putiel's daughters *(which "one" is not important here because she was merely a girl),* and the unknown woman bore him *(Eleazer)* Phinehas. These are the heads of the ancestral clans of the Levites.

This is the Aaron and the Moses to whom the Lord said, "Lead the Israelites from the land of Egypt, *but make sure you go east.* Lead them company by company, *firm by firm, and corporation by corporation."*

These are the ones' who spoke *to the anonymous* Pharaoh, King of Egypt *(how dumb could we be?)*. *They were assigned* to bring the Israelites out of Egypt *after the Lord had caused a severe famine that had brought many of the Hebrews to Egypt in the first place.* These were the same Moses and Aaron, *since there' were thousands of Israelites named Moses and Aaron around way back then along with hundreds of sets of brothers (many of them identical twins) named Moses and Aaron.*

On the day the Lord spoke to Moses *(date documentation is not given here because there were no calendars or almanacs back in those abject primitive times)* in Egypt He' said, "*Listen up guys! I'm speaking to you two knuckleheads!* I am the Lord. Repeat to *that slow-learner described to all as the anonymous* Pharaoh, King of Egypt, all that I *presently remind and* tell you."

But Moses objected to the Lord, "Since I am a poor speaker, how can it be that Pharaoh will listen to me?"

"*Look Birdbrain!*" thundered the Lord's Voice *(without form) from Heaven*. "*Just do what I tell you to do and cease your inane protesting. Protestants are not supposed to be around down there on earth until thousands of years in the future!*"

Chapter Seven
"The Plagues"

The Lord answered him' *(Moses),* "See! I have made you as God to Pharaoh. And Aaron your brother *(we already know this redundant fact)* shall act as your *special* prophet," *the Lord firmly stated.* "But if you give Me' a hard time, you Moses will be demoted and I will make Aaron as God to you. The name of the game is My' way or no way! Either please Me' or learn to suffer more than you have to!"

"Oh well!" sighed Moses with a trace of sorrow, "a hero today and a goat or a scapegoat tomorrow. You have all the damned trump cards Lord!"

"*Moses*, you shall tell him *(the anonymous Pharaoh)* all that I command you," the Lord forcefully declared, *"because the ridiculous King has nothing better to do with his valuable time than to sit down and commiserate with an incompetent Hebrew slave like you.* In turn, your brother Aaron *(does everybody by now know who Aaron is in this story?)* shall tell Pharaoh to let the Israelites leave his *already wealthy* land."

"Pharaoh might like the idea of getting rid of us," Moses agreed. "He could then send his armies and his charioteers to slaughter us all out on the open plains. He's a brilliant military strategist, that's for damned sure!"

"Yet," *the Lord abruptly interrupted Moses,* "I shall make Pharaoh so obstinate that, despite the many *punitive* signs and wonders that I will work in the land of Egypt, he will not listen to you," the Lord claimed. *"But dear Moses, I do believe that you are equal to the task I may assign, no matter how formidable it might be for an old hoary coot like you."*

"Couldn't You' just resurrect Abraham from the dead to do this impossible mission for You'?" Moses politely suggested. "This sounds more like his type of work that is better suited to his raunchy personality than to mine."

"Therefore Moses," the Lord proceeded, "I will lay My' *giant* hand on Egypt. By great acts of judgment I will bring the 'hosts' *of comedy clubs and nightclubs* of my people together, the Israelites, out of Egypt. The Egyptians will learn that I am the Lord," *the Voice proceeded,* "as I stretch out My' *giant* hand against Egypt *and crush the anonymous Pharaoh and his supreme armies as if they were colonies of ants.* I will then lead the Israelites out of their' midst, *but that in itself really won't mean anything to the world audience* learning about My' play because the punished Pharaoh and his armies will have already been dead from being crushed by My' giant hand."

Moses and Aaron *didn't want to get on the Lord's "shit list" so they* did *exactly* as He' had commanded them. Moses was eighty years old and Aaron was eighty-three when they spoke to Pharaoh *for the umpteenth time, for the anonymous king liked bullshitting with rank slaves and criminals for much-needed diversion from contact with phony egotistical educated scholars, priests, charlatans and a shekel-a-dozen magicians. The ever alert King especially enjoyed talking to enslaved senior non-citizens like Moses and Aaron to comprehend precisely how pissed-off they were regarding their' people's forced captivity in Egypt.*

The Lord told Moses and Aaron, "If *the anonymous* Pharaoh demands that you work a sign or wonder, you *(Moses)* shall say to Aaron: Take your staff and throw it down before Pharaoh. It will change into a snake *that ought to scare the feces right out of the shocked King's buttocks.*"

Then Moses and Aaron went to Pharaoh *(who had all of the time in the world to listen to them about their mediocre plight)* and did as the Lord *had* commanded. Aaron threw the staff down before *the relaxed* Pharaoh and his *equally disinterested* servants, and it was *instantly* changed into a *wriggling venomous* snake. *Pharaoh had seen that exact same trick many times before, so he' and his court were not al all impressed by the Lord's mundane hackneyed demonstration.*

Pharaoh, in turn, summoned wise men and *flying* sorcerers, and also the *opinionated* magicians of Egypt, *who all just happened to be on call in the vicinity of the palace.* They did likewise by their magic art, *duplicating the trite illusion with the staff turning into the vicious poisonous snake. Moses and Aaron were quite startled that the Lord's reptilian magic had been so easily duplicated.*

The anonymous Pharaoh was also a magician of sorts because every evening he would 'turn' his royal chariot (along with its four horses) into his driveway, and then he would show off some more by turning them into his palace.

But then Aaron's staff *was hungry and* swallowed their *(the magicians')* staffs, *so Pharaoh was seriously considering adding Aaron to his bureaucratic staff.*

Pharaoh, however, was obstinate and would not listen to them *(Aaron and Moses), since he had once seen the hungry staff' magic sleight-of-hand trick performed in a crowded downtown city supper club.* This was just as the Lord had foretold, *but why He' had made Moses and Aaron suffer through the humiliating ordeal and all the associated embarrassment at Pharaoh's court that already had been His' knowledge remains a Biblical mystery to this very day. Such is the way of the Almighty.*

Then the Lord said to Moses *(after Moses and Aaron had left Pharaoh's palace),* "Pharaoh is obdurate in refusing to let the people go."

"Why not just kill all the Egyptians in the world and then we could forget all about Canaan and take over Egypt?" Moses intelligently questioned the Almighty Lord. *"If we could have Egypt and its many riches and crops all to ourselves, who on earth would need or want the worthless Promised Land that still belongs to the stubborn Canaanites?"*

The Lord had other things on His' omniscient mind. "That would be too easy Moses," He' suavely and nonchalantly maintained. "Tomorrow morning, when he *(the anonymous Pharaoh)* sets out for the river 'bank' *to deposit his monies in the Bank of the Nile,* go and present yourself by the riverbank *even though you have no shekels to deposit anywhere.* Hold in your hand the staff that had *just before* turned into a serpent *but is now a splintery staff again.*"

"Do you think that someone as busy and as important as the anonymous Pharaoh has time to give common illiterate Hebrew slaves a private audience or an exclusive interview by the riverbank while he is making a deposit in the Bank of the Nile?" Moses curiously asked the awesome supernatural Voice. *He might ignore me because I don't even know lower-glyphics let alone hieroglyphics!"*

"Say to him *(Pharaoh),"* the all-too-focused Lord instructed, "The Hebrew God sent me to you with this *specific* message: 'Let My' people go to worship the Lord in the desert *so that we can imaginatively plan and conduct raucous protest demonstrations and wild political insurrection against your imperial authority.* But as yet you *(the anonymous Pharaoh)* have not listened *one iota to my pertinent appeal. You might desperately need an emergency ear' operation, or you Kingy might have too much damned wax build-up'.*"

"Exactly what is phase two of Your' grandiose scheme?" Moses requested to know. *"It's getting very close to my bedtime and I have to potty and wipe my rear end with cactus bristles."*

"The *insistent* Lord now says *for Moses to say*, 'This' is how you *(the King)* shall know that I am the Lord. I will strike the water of the river *(the Nile)* with the staff I hold, and it shall be changed into blood, *type O positive, I believe'*," *the Lord revealed to His human messenger.* "The fish in the river shall die *and rot. It is such a pleasure killing innocent fish.* The river itself will become so polluted that the Egyptians will be unable to drink its water *or even bathe in it. However Moses, there is an upside to this fabulous catastrophe. All bona-fide, red-blooded card-carrying hemophiliacs can jump into the bloody Nile and be cured of their life-threatening affliction.*"

The Lord next said to *the flabbergasted* Moses, "Say to Aaron, *for this will be his cue according to My' script:* 'Take your staff and stretch-out your hand over the waters of Egypt, and *don't worry. I will make your hand grow hundreds of miles long and hundreds of miles wide so that it can cover all of Egypt's waters'*," *the Lord promised His' obedient servant.* "As you can see Moses, I like to use heavy-handed tactics against sinners and also against My' mortal enemies.*"

"Wow!" Aaron jubilantly shouted. "I will have a 'big hand' in this incredible Exodus project!"

"Egypt's streams and canals and pool *and cesspools*, all of its water supplies will become blood *for thankful hemophiliacs,*" *the Lord indicated to his cognizant and fascinated listeners.* "Throughout the land of Egypt there shall be blood, even in the wooden pails and in the stone jars *that all the native drunks drink from and get 'stoned' from. I think I've covered the whole game-board with My' foolproof plan to be efficiently executed by you two stupid fools.*"

Moses and Aaron did as the Lord had commanded *because they did not desire to be the objects of His' famous violent temper and vindictive wrath.* Aaron raised his staff and struck the waters of the river in full view of Pharaoh and his servants. *The assembled Egyptians were wondering what the hell the crazy slaves were doing next to the riverbank and why they were not busy working on national construction projects or rolling around with loose women in straw mangers or on soft haystacks.* "Those miserable jerks have no money to deposit in the Bank of the Nile," Pharaoh said to his illustrious loyal royal counselors and to his personal cash management account executives.

All of the water of the river was *immediately* changed into *type O positive* blood. The fish in the river died *from over-consumption and from protein gluttony,* and the river itself became so polluted that the Egyptians could not drink its waters *or swim, shit or take pisses in it like they normally and routinely had done for centuries.* There was type' O Positive blood throughout the *semi-tropical* land of Egypt, *and the authors of Exodus know this extraordinary knowledge of type O Positive blood from the distant future solely by Divine Revelation. But the important concept to remember here is that the river's banks had suddenly been transformed into blood banks.*

But the *unperturbed* Egyptian magicians did the same *exhibition* by *employing* their *secret black* magic arts. So Pharaoh remained obstinate and would not listen to Moses and Aaron, *even though the Nile River was now twice as polluted as it had just been from the Lord's supernatural act. Pharaoh should have made his dumb 'flying sorcerers' eliminate the Lord's river' blood instead of doubling the pollution content by duplicating Aaron's marvelous staff' feat.* All of this *incredible bloody bullshit* was just as the Lord had foretold.

He (Pharaoh) turned away and went into his house *(actually, a luxurious palace)* with no concern even for this, *for the anonymous Pharaoh never gave a small shit about anyone except himself and his royal fat ass.*

Seven days passed *(that's one full week, folks)* after the Lord had struck the river *(actually it had been Aaron that had struck the Nile with his wooden staff).* Then the Lord' *(Who never got laryngitis or even a sore throat)* said to Moses, "Go to Pharaoh and tell him: 'Thus says the Lord: Let My' people go to worship Me' *so that they can permanently escape slavery in Egypt, causing your country great economic disaster and financial ruin.* If you refuse to let them go," the Lord *imperatively* threatened, "I warn you, I will send a plague of *hyperactive prolific* frogs *and toads* all over your territory'."

"*Holy Moses!*" *yelled Aaron to his younger brother. "Instead of wooden staffs, we can now pester the anonymous Pharaoh with billions and billions of tad-'poles'."*

"Remember the crucial frog plague part," the Lord reminded *the two rather dense brothers.* "The river will teem *with teams of* frogs. They will come up into Pharaoh's palace *and make him croak (here, die).* They will come up into the King's palace and into his bedroom and onto his bed," the Lord predicted *to His two favorite actors.* "They *(the frogs)* will invade the houses of the King's servants, too. And the King's subjects, and also his *direct and indirect* objects *will suffer from the overwhelming devastation,"* the Lord said in a wild rage. "Even objects like ovens and kneading bowls, *and also the homes of those ' needing kneading bowls will consequently suffer. I really like seeing sinners and My enemies agonize and anguish,"* the Lord admitted. "Tell Pharaoh this," the Lord commanded. "The frogs will swarm *like bees* all over you and your land and all over your subjects, *all over* your' *direct and indirect* objects and *also* all over your *innocent* servants."

"Anything else Boss?" the totally astounded Aaron and Moses asked in unison.

"Yes," the Lord thundered. "Give the Pharaoh the two-minute warning about the frogs. And please remember to remind Pharaoh, it's also leap year! So hop to it, men!"

Chapter Eight
"The Gnats and the Flies"

The Lord told Moses, "Say to Aaron, 'Stretch your *giant* hand and your *magnified* staff over the streams and canals, the pools and *cesspools* to make frogs *and toads* overrun the land of Egypt. *You can do it. I have confidence in you two dolts. If you don't believe in yourself, then at least you should believe in Me'* and in My' *incomparable power."*

Aaron stretched out his hand *and amazingly it enlarged to the entire size of all Egypt.* The hand stretched over the waters of Egypt, and the *horny bullfrogs* came up *during the well-timed mating season* and covered the land of Egypt *with their horny, green, sticky slimy bodies.*

But the *anonymous Pharaoh's anonymous* magicians did the same with their *black* art *saying the Egyptian magic word repeatedly, "Ribbit, ribbit, ribbit!"* They too made frogs overrun the land of Egypt, *and if Pharaoh had half a brain, he would have had the 'flying sorcerers' undo the Lord's curse rather than doubling it with twice as many horny, green, sticky, slimy frogs during the height of mating season. The entire country was a major amphibian mess that even compelled the Hebrews to temporarily forget about having sex.*

Then Pharaoh summoned Moses and Aaron (*To his palace?*) and said, *"I want you two stooges to* pray the Lord to remove the frogs from me, from my subjects, *predicates and from my direct and indirect objects.* Then I will let your people go to offer sacrifice to the Lord. *And if you believe that, I have Mesopotamia and Canaan to sell you for two lousy shekels each."*

Moses *boldly* answered *the anonymous* Pharaoh, "Do me the favor of appointing the time when I am to pray for you, and for your subjects *and for your' direct and indirect objects. At that time,"* Moses said and specified, "the frogs may be taken away from you and your houses and be left only in the river *to mate and mate some more. I suggest that you 'appoint' the appropriate time so that you are not disappointed."*

"Tomorrow," said *the perplexed anonymous* Pharaoh.

"Then," Moses replied, "it shall be as you have said, so that you may learn that there is none like the Lord, our God. The frogs shall leave you and your house *to go and get laid in the beds of the riverbank.* Only in the *wet and wild* river *beds* shall they be left *to live and then to croak."*

"And if you (Pharaoh) don't do as Moses demands," Aaron interrupted and added, "then you will turn into a horny, green, sticky, slimy frog and have to mate with the other horny, green, sticky, slimy bastards all assembled down at the infested riverbank."

After Moses and Aaron left Pharaoh's presence, Moses implored the Lord to fulfill the promise he *(Moses)* had made to the Pharaoh *(how about using the word 'King' as a much needed synonym here)* about *the horny, sex-starved green, sticky slimy* frogs. The Lord did as Moses had asked *just to see what was going to happen, even though He' knew exactly what was going to happen when He' had planned the whole sequence of events on His' lonely throne in Heaven.*

The *sex-driven* frogs in the houses, in the courtyards, *in the courthouses, in the courtiers' houses* and in the fields *all spontaneously* died off. Heaps and heaps of them were gathered up *for the new Egyptian culinary delicacy, frogs' legs. There' was plenty of noxious stench' resulting from rotting* in the land *not only from the dead decaying frogs but also from all of the Egyptians' farting and also from their' uncontrollable smelly wet farting from consuming too many horny, sticky, green, slimy frogs' legs.*

But when *the abominable* Pharaoh saw that there was respite, he *again* became obdurate and would not listen to them *(Moses and Aaron), just as the skeptical and cynical Israelites also had never listened to them either. This phenomenon all happened* just as the Lord had foretold *and had known all along from the outset of the infant Moses' exciting Nile River white water adventure in the picnic basket.*

Thereupon the Lord said to Moses, "Tell Aaron to stretch out his staff and strike the dust of the earth, that it may be turned into *hungry* gnats *unnaturally throughout the land of Egypt and its many populated suburbs. I want to really 'bug' the Pharaoh and his people with those bothersome gnats."*

They *(Aaron and Moses)* did so *(even though only Aaron was supposed to implement the very destructive staff-to-gnat infestation ploy).* Aaron stretched out his hand', *which had been recently getting mighty good exercise,* and with his staff *the crazed fellow* struck the dust of the earth, and gnats came up upon man and beast *to cause even more turmoil and even more havoc than that which had existed with the nuisance frogs.* The dust of the earth was turned into gnats throughout the *entire* land of Egypt *and soon there was no more* dust, 'dirt' or gossip left to be seen or heard anywhere within hundreds of miles.

Though exercising stupid mimicking, the imperial anonymous magicians tried to bring forth gnats by their' *black* magic arts, *but* they could not do so. *They were too dumb and too shallow to realize that their second-rate magic had to eliminate the gnats created by Aaron's staff and not to insanely double the magnitude of the devastating plague that haunted the anonymous Pharaoh's formerly tranquil kingdom.*

As the *persistent* gnats infested *and infected both* man and beast, the *dimwitted anonymous* magicians said to *the anonymous* Pharaoh *all at the same time,* "This is the finger of God. *If you want to feel the impact of God's total body,"* the self-centered magicians all said in unison, "then just continue being obdurate, you simple-minded dumb ass, you!"

Yet Pharaoh remained obstinate *in addition to being obdurate* and would not listen to them *(the flying sorcerers),* just as the Lord had foretold *and knew all along according to the script He' had written for His' giant theater He' had established down on what is known as the earth.*

Pharaoh went to his quarters and pouted and sulked but his general frustration was to no avail. The Lord would not give any merit to his theatrical 'sob story'.

Again the Lord told Moses, "Early tomorrow morning present yourself to Pharaoh when he goes forth to the water, and say *to the stubborn bumbling idiot:* 'This' says the *omnipotent* Lord: Let My' people go to worship Me' *in the desert so that they can conspire rebellion and revolution against your questionable authority.* If you will not let My' people go, I warn you, *you bungling fool,* I will loose swarms of flies *and maggots* upon you and your *innocent* servants, your subjects, *your indirect and direct objects* and on your houses. *I will then pulverize your testicles, grinding them into road kill for the hungry swarming insects to consume!"* the Lord *vociferously dictated to Moses.*

"Lord, the Israelites are perfectly happy here in Egypt having intercourse and oral sex in straw mangers and in soft haystacks that are infested with trillions and trillions of gnats," Moses maintained and argued. "This business of leaving Egypt to go to Canaan does not set too well with Your' many treasonous worshipers. They'd rather stay here in Egypt despite the plagues and screw each other to death!"

The Lord was just as stubborn and just as obdurate as the Pharaoh was in 'their' personal power struggle. "The houses of the Egyptians and the very ground on which they stand shall be filled with swarms of flies," *the Lord explained to Moses, who immediately checked to see if he had a fly or a makeshift zipper sewn on his crude-looking tunic.*

"Will anyone be safe from this horrendous torment?" Moses inquired. "I mean, shouldn't Aaron and I have some refuge from all of this devastation since we are supposed to be Your' loyal main men. Are there no privileges connected with our vital roles in Your' divine plan?"

"On the day of the devastation I shall make an exception," *the Lord reluctantly compromised.* "The exception will be the land of Goshen, *far from the ocean.* There shall be no flies in the land where My' people dwell. *Goshen will be officially proclaimed a 'No Fly Zone'.* In that way that you may know that I am the Lord within the earth."

"*Goshen far from the ocean* is also a long way from the Nile close to the crocodile'," *Moses observed and related.* "Not many of the Hebrews are athletic enough to run cross' country let alone trek across the hot arid desert or swim the river with a carnivorous croc' latched onto his or her ass."

"Tell Pharaoh I will make this distinction between my people and your *(the King's)* people," the Lord informed. "This sign shall take place tomorrow *when I get into My' nasty mood again, which will happen very soon."*

This *prediction* the Lord did *enact*. Thick swarms of *voracious* flies entered the houses of Pharaoh and the houses of his servants, *which incidentally were also the houses of Pharaoh.* Throughout Egypt the land was infested with flies, *and there weren't any "No Fly Zones" to offer the population sanctuary from the extreme devastation.*

Then *obstinate, obdurate* Pharaoh again summoned Moses and Aaron *to his palace* and said to them, "Go and offer sacrifice to your God in this land, *for He' needs lots of love, adoration and the fear of His' chosen people to sustain Himself'. Your dictatorial Lord has emotional needs too, you know!"* the anonymous Pharaoh succinctly *lectured.*

But Moses *sullenly* replied *to Pharaoh,* "It is not right to do so, for the sacrifices we offer to the Lord our God are *regarded as* an abomination to the Egyptians. *Can't You' wait until the Hebrews get* to Goshen far from the ocean to worship our God far away from the pagan Egyptians?"

"Ah, so that's where you Israelites are heading," Pharaoh laughed. "To Goshen far from the ocean. I should have known your intentions. How gullible you idiots are to divulge your deepest secret to the King of your avowed enemy!"

Moses was so engrossed in his own thought processes that he had completely ignored Pharaoh's clever discovery about Goshen far from the ocean. "If before their very eyes we *(the Israelites)* offer sacrifices which are an abomination to them *(the Egyptian population, soldiers and army)*, will not the Egyptians *egregiously* 'stone' us *at one of their boisterous rock festivals?"*

"What are you suggesting?" asked the savvy King. "Give me a viable solution to your quandary, even though I don't give a lethal tsetse fly about any aspect of it."

Moses courteously replied, "We *(the Israelites)* must go on a three days' journey in the desert to offer sacrifice to the Lord our God as He' commands, *or else He' will surely bust our balls more than He's currently busting your testicles with this sadistically cruel fly invasion."*

"Well then," said Pharaoh *before clearing his throat,* "I will let you *and your people* go and offer sacrifice to the Lord, your *vengeful* God, in the *hot sultry* desert *as He' has stipulated.* However, you must not go too far away, must pray for me *and then you must immediately return to Egypt like the good and obedient slaves I know you all are."*

Moses answered, "As soon as I leave your presence, I will pray to the Lord that the flies may depart from Pharaoh and his servants, his subjects, *predicates and his direct and indirect objects. And Pharaoh,"* Moses candidly added, *"the insects will leave tomorrow during the daytime because the Lord my God does not run a fly-by-night operation."*

"Are there any other things I need to know about your mass evacuation, er, I meant to say your planned worshiping excursion out in the eastern desert?" asked the anonymous King of Egypt. "I'm getting very weary listening to your ludicrous drivel."

"I warn you," Moses told the King, "Pharaoh must not play false again by refusing to let the people go to offer sacrifice with the Lord. *If you fail to cooperate,"* Moses yelled and qualified, *"your ass will be where your mouth is and your penis will be your brain attached to your shoulders, you arrogant dickhead!"*

When Moses left Pharaoh's presence, he prayed to the Lord, *Who' unfortunately was away traveling in Ethiopia on an important international business trip. But the Lord had advanced remote control communications, so* He' *heard the Hebrew's prayer and did precisely* as Moses had asked.

Meanwhile the anonymous Pharaoh was wishing that he had a frog in his throat to catch the pesky pestering flies that were swarming around his face and head.

He *(the Lord, masculine by preference)* removed the flies from Pharaoh and from his servants, and from his subjects, *predicates and also from all' of the King's direct and indirect objects and predicate nominatives, too.* Not one *single or married* fly remained. But once more *the anonymous* Pharaoh became obdurate and would not let the *Israelite* people go *out into the hot arid eastern desert to defiantly escape his tyranny by fleeing to Canaan.*

Chapter Nine
"The Pestilence"

Then the Lord said to Moses *(at an unknown setting)*, "Go to the *anonymous Pharaoh* and tell him: 'Thus says the Lord the God of the Hebrews: Let My' people '*desert' you and* go *to* worship Me' *in the desert*. If you refuse to let them go and persist in holding them *against their will*, I warn you, the Lord will afflict all your livestock in the field." *(Actually, there were many 'fields' in Egypt that contained livestock).*

"But Lord," Moses said, "can't You' think of anything original or perhaps more benign like maybe being kind to the anonymous Pharaoh instead of giving him a multitude of threats of plagues, misery and devastation? You can get more results from humans by giving them sugar to eat rather than by making them taste and drink bitter vinegar."

The Lord terminated Moses' objection by saying, "All of Pharaoh's livestock will be afflicted *and soon become dead'* stock. Tell him: 'All the livestock in your field *(fields)*, all your horses, camels, herds and flocks, *and especially all o*f your asses will *soon* be dead'."

"That last part where You' said all of 'your asses' will be dead might be the clincher that convinces Pharaoh," Moses interrupted. "You should have been more specific Lord by saying to the Monarch that all your dumb asses and all your smart asses in Egypt will be dead. That blanket statement would have included all of the asshole Egyptians too as well as the animals."

"It will be a very severe pestilence that will kill all of the *anonymous* Pharaoh's livestock," *the Lord confidentially divulged to Moses*. "But the Lord will distinguish between the livestock of Israel and the livestock *of the smart asses and the livestock of the dumb asses of Egypt*. None of the livestock belonging to the Israelites will die."

And setting a definite time *schedule,* the Lord *willfully* added, "Tomorrow the Lord will do this in the land *since I have nothing better to do tomorrow although time itself is meaningless to good old eternal and infinite Me'."*

"You're going to kick their asses good!" Moses proudly exclaimed. "There might even be plenty of disease haunting the Egyptians when the dead carcasses of all the smart asses and all the dumb asses start rotting in the field (fields)!"

And on the next day the Lord did so *as He' had predicted*. All of the *anonymous Pharaoh's* livestock *belonging to the Egyptian smart asses and to the Egyptian dumb asses* died *in the field (fields)*. However, not one beast belonging to the Israelites died *because the Hebrews had God on their side and a hundred squads of experienced field veterinarians patiently roaming around out in the 'field'*.

But though Pharaoh's messengers informed him that not even one beast of the Israelites had died, he *(the King)* still remained obdurate. He would not let the people *(Israelite slaves)* go *and have their political demonstration (disguised as a worship ceremony) and then enact their mass Exodus to Canaan, which was all propagandized as praying to their Lord in the unbearable hot sultry eastern desert.*

"But my wife is still alive," Pharaoh complained to his remaining attentive aides. "When according to Moses all animals are supposed to be dead she's been a real beastly 'beast' ever since I've married the nasty bitch!"

Then the Lord said to Moses and Aaron *(who were trying to hide in an empty cistern to avoid the Lord's Voice)*, "Take a double handful of soot from a furnace, and in the presence of Pharaoh let Moses scatter it toward the sky."

"*Lord, do you mean two double handfuls of soot, one for Aaron and one for me, or just two scoops to share between the two of us?" Moses perceptively and intelligently asked.*

The Lord's inimitable Mind was focused on what He' wanted to say next, so He' overlooked Moses' very smart question. "The soot will then turn into fine dust, *but the dust will not be so fine for the perplexed Egyptians to appreciate*. It will spread over the whole land of Egypt and cause festering boils on man and beast throughout the *entire condemned* land."

"Boy, I'd hate to be working in an Egyptian 'boiler-room' near a furnace when that holy crap happens," Moses said as he wiped some thick sweat from his brow. "All of the Egyptians will suddenly become 'welterweights' with all of those boils and welts all over their skinny black bodies."

So they *(Moses and Aaron, the mentally dull God fulfillment boys)* took soot from a *dirty* furnace *that hadn't been cleaned in several centuries,* and the two *obedient Hebrews* stood in the presence of the *now-disgruntled* Pharaoh, *who should have learned by that eventful time to avoid any and all contact with Moses and Aaron.*

Moses *discreetly* scattered it *(the soot)* toward the sky, and it caused festering boils on man and beast *that made them itch all over and not just in their genital areas either.*

The *anonymous* magicians could not stand in Moses' presence *because most of them had already scratched their balls off and were itching to get the hell away from "the crazy bastard!"* There were boils on the *anonymous* magicians no less than on the rest of the *anonymous* Egyptians *and even the shrunken and withered magic wands between the wizards' legs weren't so magical right then and there.*

But the *indomitable* Lord made Pharaoh obstinate, *so you see Pharaoh really never had control of his own obduracy.* He' (Pharaoh) would not listen to them *(the testicle-less' anonymous magicians, who never had brass balls in the first place)* just as the Lord had *marvelously* foretold.

Then the Lord told Moses, "Early tomorrow morning present yourself to Pharaoh and say to him: 'Thus' says the Lord of the Hebrews. Let My' people go *into the desert and conspire their escape from your jurisdiction and also plan rebellion against your authority under the clever guise of worshipping Me'.*"

"Lord, admit it," Moses articulated, "*isn't this pattern of events and those exact same words You' keep repeating becoming a little redundant just like the rest of this unliterary Wholly Book of Exodus?*"

"Tell the anonymous Pharaoh," the Lord loquaciously stated, "This time I will hurl all my blows upon you, your servants, and your subjects,' *predicates and your direct and indirect objects. Not even your predicate nominatives will be spared from My' all-encompassing wrath. You will receive left jabs, uppercuts, right' crosses, left hooks and a totally savage flurry of punches to the abdomen.*"

"Isn't that hitting below the belt?" Moses asked in a concerned voice. "Can't you use some wrestling moves to complement all this boxing brutality stuff?"

"The Pharaoh will know that there is none like Me' on the whole earth *that can beat the living feces out of him and his people like the Lord can execute,*" the supernatural authoritarian Voice told Moses.

"Are you really going to hit the Egyptians with your Almighty fists?" Moses inquired. "Please don't hit the Egyptian women. I've been keeping my eyes on them and most of the dolls are already knockouts."

"For by now, tell Pharaoh," the Lord proceeded in his garrulous dissertation, "I would have stretched out my hand and struck you and your servants with such pestilence as would wipe you from the earth *so that then I wouldn't even have to waste My' invaluable time knocking you all out with My' fantastic array of blows. It's hard to knock out dead people, you know Moses. Although I must confess, I do enjoy administering right crosses and left hooks,*" the Lord confided to His' chief adherent.

"Why haven't You' pummeled the Egyptians and given them a real beating before?" Moses boldly challenged. "You might not have had to visit them with all these plagues and pestilences if first You' would just have given them a serious boxing demonstration to teach them a vital lesson."

"Tell Pharaoh that this is why I have spared him up to this time," the Lord instructed Moses. "I want to show *the anonymous Pharaoh* My' *great undeniable* power and to make My' name resound around the world."

"*Isn't that a tad egotistical?*" Moses aptly criticized. "*Why must You' always hurt people instead of helping them? Why must there always be trauma to this nauseating ongoing drama?*"

"Ask Pharaoh," the Lord said *while ignoring Moses' entreaty*, "will you still block the way for My' people by refusing to let them go *and have an Exodus from Egypt via the eastern desert?* I warn you, then, tomorrow at this hour *(let's be more accurate here)* I will rain down such fierce hail' as there has never been in Egypt from the day the nation was founded up to the present. *I mean, who really keeps track of such time or meteorology*?"

"Oh, I get it now!" Moses yelled gleefully in the direction of the Heavenly' Voice. "The Egyptians and the Israelites alike will holler out, 'Hail' the Lord'! But truthfully, I like the boxing idea better than the hailstorm idea. Then the Egyptians wouldn't be so hale and hearty after that awesome display of pugilism!"

"Therefore tell Pharaoh," the Lord further directed Moses, "order all your livestock and whatever else you have in your open fields to be brought to a place of safety. *(It would have to be a pretty small place to accommodate all of Egypt's livestock since all of the country's livestock was already dead from severe pestilence, and those animals that had survived the plague had aggressively scratched themselves to death from the itchy boils the Lord had sent).*

"I wish You' wouldn't change Your' omniscient omnipotent mind so often," Moses complained. "First You' kill the livestock *with a pestilence. Then You' kill all of the Egyptians with knockout punches. Next You' afflict the livestock and the Egyptians with boils when they're already supposed to be dead,"* Moses argued. *"And now You' are going to hit the country with a savage hailstorm when nobody's around to appreciate it except maybe the spared Israelites! What a fantastic show-off You' are!"*

"Tell Pharaoh," the Lord commanded, "whatever man or beast remains in the field and is not brought to shelter shall die when the hail comes upon them. *Of course, the roofs of the shelters may collapse from the weight of the colossal hailstones and then crush the remaining animals and people anyway."*

Some of Pharaoh's servants finally *wised-up* and feared the warning of the Lord and hurried their servants *(even the anonymous Pharaoh's anonymous servants had their own anonymous servants)* and livestock off to shelter *(there was only one damned shelter in the whole gigantic kingdom)*. Other Egyptians, however, did not take the Lord's warning to heart. *This was because the predicted pestilence, the spectacular boxing knockout exhibition and the annoying boil harassment had never fully materialized.* They *(the pissed off Egyptian farmers) foolishly* left their livestock *and 'wood' stock'* in the fields.

The Lord then said to Moses, "Stretch out your 'hand' toward the sky *to see how much rheumatism and arthritis you have*. Hail will fall upon the entire land of Egypt, on man, on beast and on every living growing thing in Egypt *because I like to see the Egyptians suffer when I am not making the Israelites suffer under the Egyptians,"* the Lord admitted. *"I really enjoy being the producer and the director of this tremendous epic mortal play!"*

When Moses stretched out his staff *(somehow his hand became a wooden staff)* toward the sky, the Lord *mercilessly (when He' could have been merciful)* sent forth peals of thunder. Lightning flashed toward the earth, and the Lord rained down hail upon the land of Egypt. *The bolts of lightning made the Egyptians bolt toward their shelters and then swiftly bolt their doors.*

It *(the devastating hailstorm)* struck down every 'man' and beast that was in the open throughout the land of Egypt, *but since women were not struck down with the men, it must have been a discriminating gender-biased hailstorm that the Lord had sent down to earth.* It *(the hailstorm)* beat down every growing thing, *so no men could get erections during the fierce typhoon.* It *(the hailstorm)* splintered every tree in the fields *since no crops grew in the fields', only forests of trees, so as you can plainly see, they weren't fields at all but only forests and woods.*

Only in the land of Goshen *far from the ocean*, where the Israelites dwelt, was there no hail. *They just had a normal-type hurricane instead. This is because the invincible Lord liked to 'precipitate' things.*

Then *the anonymous* Pharaoh 'summoned' Moses, *who was coming to visit the King's palace anyway to appeal a parking ticket he had gotten for his oxcart being parked in a "Chariot Only" parking zone.*

Aaron was with Moses, and Pharaoh said *to the all-too-frequent slave visitors to his magnificent palace,* "I *obviously* have sinned again! The Lord is just, *and besides that, He's a real ball-buster with some imaginatively cruel weapons of nature at His' Almighty' disposal.* It is I and my subjects, *predicates and my direct and indirect objects* that are at fault."

"Don't worry royal Kingy," Moses and Aaron said in unison, "the Israelites had a bad hurricane in Goshen, too, but it was not nearly as severe as the wicked hailstorm typhoon that hit here in central Egypt."

"Pray to the Lord, for we have had enough of God's thunder and hail," *the anonymous Pharaoh implored Moses and Aaron.* "*I have no more balls to be broken!* I have decided to let you *(the Israelites)* go *and have your political demonstration and then your planned eastern Exodus from Egypt to Canaan.* You need stay no longer."

Moses replied, "As soon as I leave the city, *of course with traffic and weather permitting,* I will extend my hands to the Lord. *Ever since I was a little kid I had this amazing ability to make my hands much bigger and longer than normal and then retract them back into my wrists.*"

"What will you say when you extend your hands to the Lord?" Pharaoh cynically asked. "Are you going to ask Him' for an extended leave from Egypt?"

"The thunder will cease and there will be no more hail *to thwart you,*" Moses predicted to the King. "Thus Pharaoh, you shall learn that the earth is the Lord's *and not yours*. But you and your servants *and your anonymous servants' anonymous servants*, I know, do not yet *sufficiently* fear the Lord."

"Moses, how do I know that this is not all some form of religious quackery being employed here?" *the anonymous but articulate Pharaoh disagreed.* "It all seems like a kind of primitive *extortion to coerce me to either allow the Israelites to return from slavery to Canaan, which they do not own, or to coerce me into giving you all my wealth and property if the recalcitrant Hebrew slaves stay here in Egypt,"* the embittered Pharaoh hypothesized and verbalized. *"Then the noble Egyptians will become the slaves of the lowlife, uneducated shepherding Israelites. Is that your sinister clandestine plan? Do you want your Israelites to go from barns to noble?"*

Now the flax and the barley were ruined *by the turbulent hailstorm,* because the barley was *barely* in ear and the flax in bud *and the kingdom in complete turmoil.* But the wheat and the spelt were not ruined by the *incredibly fiercest hailstorm in Biblical history, much of which as we all know is ludicrous glorified mythology.* The wheat and the spelt grow much later *in the season, as we all don't know or care to know.*

When Moses *finally* had left Pharaoh's presence and had gone out of the city *limits in the midst of the ferocious hailstorm,* he extended his *magical* hand to the Lord *way up in Heaven.* Then the thunder and the *furious* hail ceased and the rain no longer poured down upon the earth, *and this is precisely what usually happens when storms leave an area.*

But *the 'stubborn'* Pharaoh *had been born with a stubbed head. He* saw that the 'rain', hail and thunder had ceased, so he sinned again *to protect his own 'reign'.* He and his *anonymous* servants and his *anonymous servants' anonymous servants again* became obdurate. In his *(the anonymous King's)* obstinacy he would not let the *disruptive* Israelites go to the *eastern* desert, *which had been obliterated and flooded by the terrible hailstorm.* This *truth* the Lord had foretold to Moses.

Chapter Ten
"The Locusts"

Then the Lord said to Moses, "Go to Pharaoh *and bother him some more since he is disgusted and tired of seeing you.* I have *deliberately* made him and his servants obdurate *against their free wills just because I enjoy playing hardball and busting on them every time I have the splendid opportunity to do so,"* the Lord shared with Moses. "I have made the anonymous Pharaoh and his servants obstinate so that *I may show-off and* perform these many horrible *and astonishing* signs of Mine' among them. *Then* you may *proudly brag as you* recount to your son and grandson (*daughters and granddaughters are not even worth a pittance*) how ruthlessly I *have* dealt with the Egyptians and what signs I had *cruelly and callously* wrought among them, so that you may know that I am the *judgmental* Lord *and do just about everything arbitrarily*."

So Moses and Aaron *obediently* went to *the disgusted anonymous* Pharaoh', *who was thoroughly repulsed to see them and wished he could remain anonymous to his two slave visitors that inexplicably had access to him and his royal palace any time the vagabonds so desired.*

Moses and Aaron *together* told him, "Thus say the Lord, the *omnipotent* God of the Hebrews *that discriminates against the Egyptians and doesn't want any of them worshiping Him:* 'How long will you refuse to submit *your manuscripts* to Me' *to be incorporated into My' main script? For the too manyeth time,* let My' people go worship Me' in the desert *so that they can foment rebellion and revolution and then ultimately make a quick exit stage right to Canaan.*"

"Oh Yeah you retarded dingle-heads!" Pharaoh vociferously shouted at his two haughty indigent visitors. "What will be the consequence this time if I do not comply with your War Lord's insistence? This next threat or next warning should be a real doozy!"

"The Lord said," Moses and Aaron mutually recited, "If you *(the anonymous Pharaoh)* refuse to let My' people go, I warn you, tomorrow I will bring locusts *from every locust tree in the world* into your *already accursed* country. They shall cover the ground so that the ground itself will not be visible, *although it will not be invisible either. You just won't be able to see it because of the tremendous locust invasion!*"

"Gee guys," the cunning Pharaoh told his chief anonymous counselors and councilors, *"we'll have to cordon off Locust Street in the downtown district. Then what?"* the King curiously asked Moses and Aaron.

"They (the voracious locusts) shall thoroughly cover the ground and you and your afflicted people will feel as if you are all knee high to a grasshopper," the two visiting slaves recited together. "They will eat up the remnant you *have* saved unhurt from the *nasty* hailstorm, as well as all of the foliage that has sprouted in your *affected* fields. They shall fill the houses of your servants, *and your servants' servants, and your anonymous servants' anonymous servants' anonymous servants.* Such a *horrific* sight your fathers or grandfathers have not seen from the day they first settled on the soil up to the present day."

"What shall I have to do to prevent this wicked plague of the grasshoppers from occurring?" the distraught King asked Moses and Aaron.

"Let the Israelites 'desert' Egypt and go out into the remote 'desert' to eat 'dessert' and then worship the Lord," Moses and Aaron intoned in unison. *"If you don't do that, then your ass will be grass and the grasshoppers will eat your royal butt up, anus, hemorrhoids, colon and all. Then you won't have a grass pot to piss' in or a 'grass hopper' to take a shit in!"* the zany brothers recited together.

With that *being addressed*, he *(Moses)* turned and left Pharaoh. *(Aaron was with him, but apparently the author of Exodus didn't think it was important to mention the older brother in this particular passage).*

But Pharaoh's servants said to him *all together,* "What the fuck's the matter with you, you obdurate asshole! How long must He' *(the Lord and Moses)* be a menace to us *and to our civilization*? Let the men go to worship the Lord, their' God," *the anonymous counselors and councilors advised their superior.* "Do you not yet realize that Egypt is being destroyed, *you dumb stupid obdurate bastard!"*

So Moses and Aaron were brought back *by the local constable* to Pharaoh, who *imperially* said to them, *"What the fuck's going on here?* Yes, you may go and worship the Lord your God. But how many of you will go *out into the eastern hot sultry desert to burn your sensitive tootsies and fat asses on the ember-like sand? Give me a damned head count!"*

"Young and old must go with us," Moses answered *while Aaron was having an intense sneezing fit, shooting quantities of snot all over the regal throne room in all directions.* "Our sons and our daughters as well as our flocks and herds must accompany us so that it will be a total evacuation *that will then evolve into a total Hebrew Exodus to Canaan.* That is what a feast of the Lord means to us. *It means conspiracy, abandonment of the King, treason, defiance, insolence, dissimulation, duplicity, escape from harsh reality and mass Exodus under the pretense of worship. Pretty nifty scheme, wouldn't you agree anonymous Pharaoh?"*

"Your Lord should please help you annihilate and exterminate yourselves," Pharaoh ranted like a peeved maniac, "if I ever let your little *tykes (ones)* go with you *I will be exhausting my future supply of cheap slave labor. I might be a colossal asshole, but I am not a dunce-type asshole like you two dipsticks are!* Clearly," Pharaoh *said with conviction*, "you *two dimwits* have some *sinister* evil *plot* in mind. No, no! Just your men can go *into the eastern desert and risk your worthless lives* to worship the Lord. After all," Pharaoh *concluded with an austere expression on his visage*, "that is what you *really* want."

"Everyone must follow me into the desert," Moses *confidently demanded, thinking that the Lord's temper and power were his indispensable trump cards.* "All of the Israelites, men, women, children, concubines, prostitutes and harlots. Everybody! Is that perfectly clear?"

"Moses, do you eat donkey shit for breakfast along with stupid asses?" *belittled the sometimes sarcastic Pharaoh.* "Everybody knows that little kids don't know what the hell they're doing and that they don't know a damned thing about worshiping the Lord or anyone else! And teenagers only know about juvenile delinquency and about rebellion against authority! That's a royal crock of bullshit you're trying to sell me!" *Pharaoh screamed like a delirious mental patient.*

With that *being stated* they *(Moses and the still sneezing Aaron)* were driven *by charioteers in their' previously confiscated primitive Hebrew oxcart* from the *nameless* Pharaoh's presence *and taken to their humble tent near Goshen, far from the ocean.*

The Lord then said to Moses, "Stretch out your *blessed magic* hand over the land of Egypt, that locusts may swarm over it *(the land and not Moses' hand)* and eat up all the vegetation and whatever the hail has left. *I shall grant you the power and the glory to enact this miracle for accurately following My' capricious directions!"*

So Moses stretched out his *plain wooden* staff', which *enlarged and* cast *its shadow* over the land of Egypt, and the Lord 'sent' an east wind *special delivery* that blew over the land all day and all that night.

At dawn the east wind brought the locusts, *and Pharaoh evaluated that the Lord's tactics weren't exactly 'cricket'*. They swarmed over the whole land of Egypt and settled down on every part of it *to munch, especially landing upon the Pharaoh's newly acquired grass ass.*

Never before had there been such a fierce swarm of locusts, nor will there ever be *again*. They covered the whole surface of the ground, buzzing around *and having loud sex in the midst of their wild frenetic activity*. The earth was black with them, *for the black locusts had covered the entire planet.*

They *(the ravenous black locusts that looked nothing like ravens) ravenously* ate up all of the vegetation in the land and all of the fruit of whatever trees the hail had spared. Nothing green was left on any tree or plant in Egypt, *so tomatoes and apples had to ripen-up in a hurry to avoid being eaten by the voracious and despicable insect attack. The jinxed Pharaoh had to cover his ass for the blame he was receiving from his subjects for the latest pestilence, so the King sat his sensitive grass ass on a grass hopper to protect it from the ravaging hordes of flying and hopping grass-ass eating insects. In fact (counting the King's green toilet) there were grasshoppers all over the damned place!*

Hastily Pharaoh summoned Moses and Aaron *to his grasshopper throne and said,* "You idiots were right! My ass is grass! I hope your next threat is not a half-assed one or I won't be able to wipe my smelly butt-hole after taking a royal crap!"

Moses and Aaron simply gazed in astonishment with their' mouths agape at the anonymous Pharaoh protecting his grassy ass on the grass' hopper' throne.

Pharaoh said *to his frequent slave guests,* "I have sinned against the Lord, your God, and *also* against you' *two disingenuous imbeciles.* But now Butt' holes," *Pharaoh continued in a diminished tone of voice,* "please do forgive my *grievous* sin once more, and pray the Lord, your God to take at least this deadly pest from me *so that I can at least shit in peace upon the hole in my real throne. If you don't, I promise and swear that I will use your tongues for toilet paper for as long as I may live!"*

When Moses left the presence of Pharaoh *(perhaps Aaron got lost during another sneezing fit somewhere in the King's massive toilet/throne room),* he prayed to the Lord. The Lord changed the wind to a very strong west wind, *which stunk like a sick cumulus fart that had a terrible odor' which lasted for over three hours in the atmosphere above Egypt. Everyone including Moses and the Pharaoh wished they were long dead.*

The west wind took up the swarming locusts and hurled them into the Red Sea *(which turned from blue to black in a hurry).* But though not a single *or virgin* locust remained within the confines of Egypt, the Lord made Pharaoh obstinate, *and the adamant King even lost control of his bladder and bowels.* But the *anonymous puppet* Pharaoh *of the Lord* would not let the *subservient* Israelites go *to the rebellious religious rally scheduled for out in the hot sultry eastern desert.*

Then the Lord said to Moses *from the clouds,* "Stretch out your *magic* hand toward the sky, that over much of Egypt there may be such 'intense' darkness '*in tents'* everywhere. The darkness will be so intense *in tents* that 'one' can feel it, *but the number two definitely won't be able to feel anything! So Moses, if you're taking a leak, watch out for number one, but you'll be absolutely safe with number two!"*

So Moses stretched out his magical hand toward the sky, and there was dense darkness throughout the land of Egypt for three days, *which meant that there had to be dense darkness all over the world because the earth had to have stopped rotating on its axis. So let's not be so damned provincial here with all of this malice toward Egypt crap!*

Men could not see one another, *and everyone was better off because of that.* Men could not move from where they were for three days, *and this meant that nobody aggravated anyone else for seventy-two wonderfully serene hours.* But all of the *not-too-brilliant* Israelites had light where they dwelt *because the Lord planned that the Hebrews should not experience the 'Dark Ages' until the sand grains of several millennia would pass through time's expansive hourglass.*

Pharaoh then summoned Moses and Aaron *(who both needed new sandals from walking back and forth to the distant palace so often)* and said, *"How did you find your way here in the dark? In fact, how did my messengers ever find you so that you could find your way here?"*

"That's one of our dark secrets," Moses jested, *"how to survive blackouts and brownouts from Heaven. This phenomenon could actually lead to the beginning of Hebrew science!"*

"Haven't you ever heard of torches and lanterns?" Aaron remarked to his royal host. "You're living in the damned Bronze Age, aren't you?"

Pharaoh then said, "Go and worship the Lord *in the hot sultry eastern desert.* Your little ones *(monsters)* too, may go *and die* with you too *so that they will not some day grow up to be fools like you two numbskulls are.* But your flocks and herds," Pharaoh pointed out, "must remain *as collateral to guarantee your safe return to slavery in my country.*"

Moses *honestly* replied, "You must also grant us sacrifices and 'holocausts' *that are safe from the militant Aryans over in Mesopotamia.*"

Then Aaron *adroitly chimed in*. "The sacrifices we will offer up to the Lord, our God."

"Don't you have any reasonable demands to make to me?" the anonymous Pharaoh asked from atop his royal grass' hopper throne. "I'm scared shitless and am entirely constipated because of you two jerk offs and your very vindictive Lord."

"Our livestock must also go with us, and not an animal must be left behind, *not even one goat's 'behind' shall be left behind,*" Moses insisted and persevered. "Some of them we must sacrifice to the Lord, our God, but we ourselves shall not know which ones we must sacrifice to Him' until we arrive at the place itself. *That's why we must take all of our animals!*"

"Do you take me for a fool!" exclaimed Pharaoh in the dark from his royal grass' hopper' throne. "You don't have to sacrifice all of your bleating sheep and stubborn goats!" the incensed King bellowed. "Choose the twelve best ones you have and leave the rest behind for my starving people to eat. Show some compassion towards your former benign masters!"

But the Lord made Pharaoh obstinate, *which meant that the King had to be stubborn and obdurate too. Pharaoh's obstinacy was intensified by his severe abominable abdominal constipation,* so he *again* would not let the Hebrews go into *the hot sultry* desert *to pretend to worship while they were enacting a traitorous Exodus from Egypt into Canaan to steal land that their crazy Lord had promised their daft forefathers.*

"Leave my presence, and see to it that you do not appear *in the dark* before me again! The day you appear before me *in the dark* again you will die!" Pharaoh said to him *(Moses) in the dark from his high grass' hopper' throne.* "I badly need a powerful laxative," *the King said to his chief anonymous attendant that wasn't there during Moses and Aaron's nonsensical audience with the anonymous Pharaoh.*

Moses *arrogantly* replied *on his way out of the dark grasshopper' throne' room,* "Well said *anonymous constipated Pharaoh*! I will never appear *or disappear* before you *in the dark* again!"

Chapter Eleven
"The Death of the First-born"

Then the Lord said to Moses *because the Lord enjoyed speaking to only one human being on the entire earth,* "One more plague I will bring upon Pharaoh and upon Egypt, *for I am running out of insects and small destructive animals to plague the haughty Pharaoh and his countrymen with. What else can I now use to victimize the dastardly Egyptians?"*

"You still have a terrific arsenal of natural disasters at your disposal that You' haven't yet utilized against the anonymous Pharaoh," *Forget implementing insects! Moses injected into the grandiose conspiracy conversation.* "What about a nice violent earthquake or a giant meteor shower crashing directly into the center of Pharaoh's plush palace? That ought to really get his attention if he ever gets off of his grass' hopper' throne to investigate the damage!"

"Well Moses," *the Lord's booming Voice interrupted,* "after that he *(the Pharaoh)* will let you depart his *unfortunate* country *for the eastern desert heading toward Canaan. In fact My'* favorite *follower*, he will not merely let you *and My' people* go; he will drive you away *and be happy to see you and the dregs of society Israelites depart."*

"What should I tell the ever dissatisfied Israelite people?" *Moses asked the frightful Voice.* "How much luggage and personal possessions should each person take on this five hundred mile trek east through the hot sultry desert? Our sandals don't offer our feet much protection."

"Instruct your people *(actually, My' people)* that every man is to ask his neighbor," the Lord *austerely* said, "and every woman her neighbor for silver and gold articles and for clothing. *It is possible that the men and the women might have different neighbors that are not Israelites', who obviously have little gold, silver or clothing to contribute to our noble cause. Moses, I suggest that the resident neighbors would be more than happy to make the necessary contributions.*"

"If the neighbors do not provide or donate the gold, silver and clothing," *Moses speculated and stated,* "are we then to steal those items from our unfortunate victimized Egyptian friends and neighbors?"

The Lord did not respond to Moses' question because He' was too busy contemplating something important in the near future called the Ten Commandments that might involve a moral code of behavior concerning the art of stealing. *Such was Heaven's mysterious Mindset.*

The Lord indeed made the *dastardly bastardly* Egyptians well' disposed toward the people *(the now rebellious Hebrew slaves).* Moses himself was very highly regarded by Pharaoh's *anonymous* servants *and the other various anonymous people of the land'*, who knew little psychology or sociology and were not very good judges of character. Stubborn Pharaoh and his myriad counselors and councilors, however, had a keener perception of Moses' surreptitious motives and intentions than did the average Egyptian citizen.

Moses then said *practicing his memorized lines*, "Thus says the Lord: 'At precisely midnight My' angel will go forth *on an expedition* through Egypt. Every first-born in the land shall die, from the first-born of Pharaoh *on the grass' hopper'* throne to the first-born of the slave girl at the hand-mill, as well as the first-born of the animals *that have no souls or consciences at stake with which to be arbitrarily punished'.*"

The Lord attentively listened to Moses' rendition of His' murderous plot to liberate His' people from slavery and to plunder the country. It all sounded very barbaric and uncivilized for any justification of a moral crusade. All of the Egyptian first born were to be eliminated.

"Then there shall be loud wailing throughout the *anonymous* people *synonymous* with the land of Egypt," *Moses continued like a talented actor on a stage with an audience' of One', the Almighty Author of the tragic macabre script.* "Wailing *such* as this has never been heard and will it ever be heard again, *not even in the impoverished worldwide whaling industry,"* the ambitious junior thespian brilliantly added. "But among the Israelites and their animals not even a dog shall growl, so that you shall know how the Lord distinguishes between the *wicked* Egyptians and the *innocent* Israelites," *Moses projected his stellar voice in a very masculine baritone.*

"Excellent rendition Moses! Most excellent indeed!" *the exuberant Lord congratulated His' chief 'spokesman' (who also manufactured oxcart wheels in his spare time).* "Praiseworthy indeed My' special prophet! Splendid! Fantastic! Bravo! Now go directly to Pharaoh and enact the entire speech just as you have recently rehearsed it!"

"All of these *pusillanimous* servants of your *anonymous* people *synonymous with Egypt* shall then come down to me," *Moses acted his lines in the continuation of his memorized message to Pharaoh,* "and prostrate *your prostates* before Me, they shall beg Me, 'Leave us, You and Your' dim-witty slave followers! *Leave us now!'* Only then will I depart." With that *speech finally delivered at the palace after much rehearsal* he *(Moses)* left Pharaoh's presence *on the grass' hopper' throne.*

The Lord *next* said to Moses, "*The disenchanted* Pharaoh refuses to listen to you that My' wonders may be multiplied in the land of Egypt." *Moses was puzzled at his Divine Master's very evident animosity.*

"*Forgive my aggressiveness Lord,*" *Moses said with a degree of guilt,* "but the Egyptians interpret Your' wonders as detrimental curses, abominations, plagues, and as natural and unnatural disasters. They think that You' have sadistic tendencies and that Your' obdurate behavior and misbehavior reflects severe psychological problems.*"

Thus, although Moses *and his sidekick* Aaron performed these various wonders *(actually, acting out ugly threats)* in Pharaoh's presence *on his green grass' hopper' throne,* the Lord made the King *even more* obstinate, and he would not let the Israelites leave the land.

"*Pharaoh is but a manipulated hand' puppet in the Lord's spectacular theater show,*" *Moses melodramatically told Aaron.* "He wants to be as powerful as the Lord but that far-fetched aspiration is but wishful thinking. The King is merely the Lord's pawn just as you and I are!*"

"*Indeed Moses, the Lord is making it all look as if the Pharaoh is the antagonist in this drama causing all the bizarre problems,*" *Aaron recognized and shared,* "but it is the Lord' Who is definitely busting everybody's chops, yours, mine, and the suffering Egyptians,*" *Aaron concluded to his younger brother.* "And when He's not focusing His' mercurial temper and attention on busting on you, me and the Pharaoh,*" *Aaron eloquently summarized,* "then He' goes back to the theme of deluging the Hebrews with false promises about Canaan and the travails and ordeals associated with our horrible slavery. And when He's through trying to play the protagonist's role,*" *Aaron deducted and stated,* "then the Lord persists in scaring the shit out of us by reminding the Hebrews all about the great flood of Noah and all about the nasty fire and *brimstone shooting out of everybody's ass' holes in Sodom and Gomorrah."*

"What an ongoing nightmare!" Moses concurred. "Aaron, why couldn't we have been born in Heaven instead of here on earth? All of this inexplicable supernatural stuff might have made more sense to us then!"

Chapter Twelve
"The Passover Ritual Prescribed"

The Lord said to Moses and Aaron *because no one else would listen to Him'*, "In the land of Egypt this month *(er sorry, we don't know which month)* shall stand at the head of your calendar of *unnamed* months. You shall reckon it the first month of the year, which I'll name some time in the future at My' convenience and at My' discretion."

"Oh good," answered the now effervescent Moses, "once the months are finally identified I can draw pictures of my twelve favorite gorgeous women and put one well-endowed lady in the calendar with each month of thirty days."

The Lord had other things on His' very abstract Mind besides entertaining Moses' silly prattle. "Tell the whole community of Israel, *even the sinning gay and lesbian community*," the Lord said, "tell them this: 'On' the tenth day of the *unknown* month every one of your families must procure for itself *a cured* lamb *without disease*. There will be one lamb apiece for each *favored Israelite* household'."

"What about the poorest families that cannot afford to procure a sick or a cured lamb?" Moses sincerely inquired. "Should they steal one from a well-to-do Egyptian?"

"If a family is too small for a whole *rack of* lamb," *the Lord responded without valuing Moses' exact inquiry*, "it shall join the nearest household in procuring one and then sharing the lamb in proportion to the number of persons that partake of it. *Arithmetically that exact sum will be put over the base times the hypotenuse divided by three.*"

"Could the lamb be a speckled female specimen?" Moses requested to know.

"Quit 'lambasting' Me' with your disturbing mortal moral interrogations!" the Lord warned his neurotic advocate. "You can be as stubborn as a mule and a royal pain in the 'ass'. *Of course Moses, I'm referring to animals there*," the Lord clarified. "But if you insist on knowing, the lamb must be a year-old male without blemish. You may take it from either the sheep or the 'goats' *as long as the latter has no goatee.*"

"When should the lamb be prepared for slaughter, er, sorry there My' Lord, sacrifice?" Moses apologetically asked. "Sometimes I have trouble distinguishing what terminology I should use!"

"You shall keep it until the fourteenth *unknown* day of this *unknown* month, and then with the whole 'assembly' of Israel present *and snuggly squeezed into the local school auditorium,*" *the Lord further explained,* "it shall be slaughtered during the evening twilight."

"Wow, whoever gets to break the lamb's chops gets the first lamb chops!" Moses gleefully marveled. "Then we can get ready to leave Egypt and be on the lam to Canaan. What a terrific story this is building into!"

"They *(the lamb butchers)* shall take some of its blood and apply it to the two doorposts and *to* the lintel of every house in which they partake of the lamb," *the Lord further elaborated.* "That same night they shall eat its roasted flesh with unleavened bread and bitter herbs, but the lamb should not be eaten raw or boiled, but roasted whole *like dry roasted peanuts. Moses, we're going to have us a barbecue, Dude! Tell all the Israelite Dudettes too!"*

"Gee, I sure hope I'm selected to perform the autopsy on the slaughtered lamb," Moses wished and conveyed. "I really love studying anatomy and dissecting flesh. But Lord, if we all eat from the lamb that is killed at the assembly, there will not be enough meat for all the Israelites to devour!"

"You Ninny," the Lord admonished Moses, *"I specifically told you earlier that each house is to have an unblemished year-old male lamb. The assembly thing is just a demonstration on how to do the process correctly.* The lamb's head, shanks and inner organs should be roasted also. None of it must be kept beyond the next morning, and whatever is left over must be burned up *or else I'll be burned up because My' sacred instructions had not been fully followed. Do you now fathom My' instructions?"*

"I never ate a lamb's spleen or pancreas before," Moses admitted. "I can't wait to partake of the sumptuous feast."

"This is how you are to eat it," the Lord continued *His' dissertation.* "First, put it in your mouth. With your loins girt, *and make sure no vestal virgins check out your shriveled-up tender' loins while you're doing this,* with sandals on your *smelly* feet and *with* your staff *(not your penis)* in hand, you shall eat *like those that are in 'flight'.* It is the Passover of the Lord."

"Do You' mean I have to pretend I'm a flying angel or an eagle in flight passing over the house when I eat the roasted spleen or pancreas?" Moses asked the Lord. "That stringent requirement seems to exceed the limits of my imagination."

"No you foolish weirdo' Dummy," the Lord chastised his dull but amusing listener. "For on the same night I *and My' Angel* will go through Egypt, striking down every first born of the land, both man and beast, and executing judgment on all the gods of Egypt-I, the Lord! *By eating in 'flight' I meant on the lam to Canaan during the mass get-away."*

"You are going to kill all of the first born males of the Egyptians all by Yourself'? Moses gasped. "What a holocaust that will be!"

"No Moses you droll ignoramus, I don't get My' hands dirty or bloody doing such animalistic business," the Lord replied. *"I'll shrewdly assign an Angel of Death as My' hit-man or henchman to perform the gruesome bloody executions."*

"I know a lot of Hebrew priests that are sinners and pedophiles," Moses informed the Lord. "Could I put their names on the Lord's hit list?"

"*No Stupid!* The blood on the doorposts and *on the* lintels will mark the houses where you *(Israel)* are. Seeing the blood, I *(My' hit-man Angel of Death)* will pass over you. *Get it Moses, the first Passover'. Pretty neat, eh?* Thus, when I *(My' hit-man Angel of Death)* strike the land of Egypt, no destructive blow will come upon you," *(the Israelites).*

"I wonder if Pharaoh will have a similar hit man out too to neutralize Your' Angel of Death?" Moses anxiously asked the Lord', who was too preoccupied formulating His' own complicated Passover strategy to listen to and evaluate His' worshiper's pertinent question.

"This day Moses, shall be a memorial feast for you," *the Lord cheerfully predicted.* "All your *messed-up* generations *in the future* shall celebrate this feast with pilgrimage to the Lord, as a perpetual institution. For seven days you must eat unleavened bread *so that when the time of crisis comes, you can 'rise' to the occasion eating leavened bread."*

"Will there be any penalties for violating this unleavened bread instruction?" Moses fearfully asked. "For example, will people's reproductive organs and buttocks fall off if they forget to honor Your' particular directions."

"For seven days you (*the Israelites*) must eat unleavened bread," the Lord insisted. "From the very first day you shall have your houses clean of leaven, and whoever eats from the first day to the seventh shall be cut off from Israel *and shall be shunned, banned and humiliated in public squares wherever clan-ish clandestine Hebrews congregate."*

"I hope You' are the One Who' is going to deliver these austere demands to the volatile Israelites," Moses pleaded. *"Those ingrates might deliberately take me for the first lamb and brutally slaughter me on an altar of sacrifice."*

"Moses," *the Lord calmly lectured,* "on the first day you shall hold a *big* sacred assembly *in a rented Egyptian' school' auditorium*, and likewise on the seventh. On these days you shall not do any sort of work, except prepare the food that everyone needs. *Do you comprehend My' words?*"

"Oh great!" Moses balked and sulked. "Over six hundred thousand Hebrews and I have to find a hall big enough to accommodate them all and then prepare food for six hundred thousand hungry vultures. Lord, I need a few major miracles to alleviate my anxiety right now!"

"Moses, keep then this custom of the unleavened bread," *the Lord frankly warned.* "Since it was on this very same day that I brought your *rank* ranks out of the land of Egypt, you must celebrate this day throughout your generations as a perpetual *mental* institution."

"Lord, do You' think I have old age' senility or dementia or something?" Moses strenuously protested. "You just told me that same damned thing a minute ago."

"Well then Moses, if it's not worth repeating, then it's not worth saying in the first place, that's what I always heard My' pal Zeus say," the Lord dictated to His' captive audience of one.

Seeing that Moses had been properly reprimanded, the Lord continued with His' remarkable lecture. "From the evening of the fourteenth *unnamed* day of the first *unknown* month until the evening of the twenty-first *unnamed* day of this *unknown* month you shall eat unleavened bread *until it comes out of your nose and ears*. For seven days *My' dear prophet*, as I had said, no leavened bread may be found in your house."

"But Lord, all of the Israelites hate unleavened bread and unfortunately I love to chew and swallow leavened bread!" Moses shouted. "Why must You' always give me these ridiculous impossible assignments to complete on Your' own hostile and uncooperative primitive people? Learn how to put up with their harassments and their chronic complaining Yourself'!"

"Anyone," the Lord said, "*be he (masculine by preference and also by Hebrew chauvinism) a resident alien with a valid work permit or a bona fide native with false I.D.,* who eats leavened food shall be cut off from the community *and also from the ever-growing gay and lesbian community* of Israel. *That man will have fresh skin shaved from his head and sewn onto his penis to effectively publicly un-circumcise the violator."*

'I wonder what will happen to women?' Moses pondered but did not have the courage to ask the Lord.

"I remind you Moses," the Lord finished, "nothing leavened may you eat, *for leavened food is reserved exclusively for My' personal consumption.* Wherever you dwell, you *(Israel)* may eat only unleavened bread. *How many times must I tell you these rigid stipulations? You got the simple message you itinerant Simpleton?"*

Moses called all the *senile and feeble* elders of Israel and said to them, "Go and procure lambs for your families, and slaughter them *(the lambs, not the families)* as Passover victims."

"But we like ham, pork, fish, veal, chicken and steak instead of lamb' meat!" the crowd yelled in opposition to Moses' plea. *"Can't we have tuna fish instead of smelly lamb?"*

"Then take a bunch of hyssop *(a branchy plant)* and dipping it in the blood that is the basin," *Moses told the antagonistic crowd,* "sprinkle the lintel and the two doorposts with this *ordained holy* blood."

"Charlatan! Cannibal! Savage! Idiotic Asshole!" all of the *senile elders and other assembled senile Hebrews yelled up at Moses on his makeshift stand to show their dissatisfaction with his intolerable commands that had originated from the Lord.*

"But none of you shall go outdoors until morning," *Moses spoke from the rickety makeshift wooden platform above the obnoxious rowdy crowd.* "For the Lord will go by, striking down the *targeted* Egyptians. When He' sees the *lamb's* blood on the lintels and on the two doorposts," Moses yelled as loudly as he could, "the *inspired* Lord will 'pass over' that door and not let the destroyer *(His' fearful Angel of Death' hit-man)* come into your houses to strike you down!"

"Liar! Fake! Fear-monger! Jerk off! Religious freak! Demented Asshole!" the Israelites belligerently and boisterously hollered. "Let's change our religion! Let's change our religion and our nationality!" they began chanting. The passionate crowd was rapidly transforming into a wild mob.

"You shall observe this as a perpetual ordinance for yourselves and your descendents*!" Moses hoarsely screamed at his very vocal and restless audience.* "Thus, you must also observe this rite when you have entered the *designated* land *of Canaan* the Lord will give you as promised."

"*Kill the dirty bastard! Hang the old prick from a tree! Cut his shriveled testicles off!*" *the crowd fanatically yelled up at poor aged Moses.*

"When your children ask you," Moses went on, 'what does this rite mean'?" you shall reply, "This is the *glorious* Passover sacrifice of the Lord, Who' passed over the houses of the Israelites in Egypt. Then He' struck down the Egyptians but spared our houses *and our outhouses'."*

"*Bull' shit! Horse' shit! Chicken' shit!*" *the crazy crowd hooted while shaking their fists up at the beleaguered Moses, who nearly fell from the vacillating and rocking rickety wooden platform on which he was standing.* "We like leavened bread that rises because we get more erections when we eat it!" *the screaming men hysterically boomed like raving lunatics.*

Then a giant thunderbolt descended from the sky and scared the shit out of everybody, including the already petrified Moses. The people instantly became silent and uncommonly respectful. They bowed down in worship, and the *intimidated* Israelites went and did what the *resolute* Lord had commanded Moses and Aaron.

At midnight the Lord 'slew' *(actually, His' hit-man Angel of Death wielded and utilized the sword) a whole slue* of Egyptian first-born in the land of Egypt. *The victims ranged* from the first-born of the Pharaoh *seated* on the *grass' hopper* throne to the first-born of the prisoner in the dungeon, as well as the first-born of the *innocent* animals *that had no souls or consciences to worry about. A lot of Egyptian aristocratic inheritances were ruined and altered by the actions of the Lord's berserk Angel of Death.*

The anonymous Pharaoh arose in the night, *lost his first hard-on in three months, and so did all of his anonymous servants and the anonymous servants' anonymous servants wake up and lose their firm erections also.* There was a loud wailing throughout Egypt, for there was not a house without its dead *victims. The ruthless Angel of Death equalizer was mighty active and busy on that particular unnamed night of that particular unknown month of that particular unknown year.*

During the *hectic* night *the aggrieved anonymous* Pharaoh summoned Moses and Aaron and said, "*You two pricks are fucking-up my whole kingdom!* Leave my people at once, you and the *crazy fucked-up* Israelites *can exit* with you!" *Pharaoh conceded.* "Go *into the hot sultry eastern desert* and *even* worship *a ship if you want to do that. I just don't care or give a damn anymore! I don't give a shit about anything except my own ass and dick!* Worship the Lord as you said," *the Pharaoh screamed like a psycho*. "Take your *flockin'* flocks, too, and your herds, as you demanded, and be gone; and you will be doing me a *massive* favor *by even taking your prostitutes, concubines, whores, homosexuals and harlots east to Canaan (which is west of Eden) with you!"*

The Egyptians *likewise had contracted enough* previously *unknown venereal diseases from foreigners and aliens*, and so they urged the people *(the Israelites)* on, to hasten their departure *and journey far away* from the land. They thought that otherwise they would die *from rampant new diseases in the land such as herpes, vaginal warts and excessive jock rot.*

The *already confused* people *(Israelites)* therefore, took their 'dough' before it was leavened *and also seized the dough and bank deposits of their' civilized Egyptian masters, taskmasters, nobles and neighbors*. They kept the *gold and silver coins they had pilfered hidden under the* unleavened dough in their kneading bowls wrapped in their cloaks on their shoulders.

The Israelites, *after the Lord's impressive thunder and lightning' bolt'* demonstration, did as Moses commanded: they asked the Egyptians *for going away presents*, articles of silver and *additional* gold and clothing. *Then they stealthily purloined what was denied them by their benign neighbors and former masters and tolerant taskmasters.*

The Lord indeed had made the Egyptians so well' disposed toward the people *(Israelites)* that they let them have whatever they *fuckin'* asked for *or had randomly stolen, just to get rid of the unwelcome arrogant barbarian Neolithic shepherds once and for all.* Thus did they *(the Hebrews)* despoil *the anonymous Pharaoh and his pompous anonymous* Egyptian' aristocrats.

Chapter Thirteen
"Consecration of First-born"

The Lord spoke to Moses, *who was awakening from a deep slumber and was wishing that another human besides Aaron would approach him for conversation in that Moses was the only human the Lord sought out to discuss contemporary Hebrew matters.* The Lord said *to the still drowsy Moses,* "Consecrate to Me' every first born that opens the womb among the Israelites, both of man and beast, for it belongs to Me'."

Moses thought, 'I think I drank too much red wine last night and am still drunk as the Lord. How could all men screw women and then come from the same womb? And all animals too coming from the same pussy as the people' happens to be absolutely and absurdly impossible? This jargon You' have stated is at its finest moment totally insane! This has to be some kind of perverted nightmare!'

But then Moses remembered the powerful lightning bolt from Heaven that nearly singed the asses of all the Israelites, so he tried to interpret another meaning to the Lord's peculiar "one cunt for all Israelites and all animals' theory."

Moses stepped outside his clay house and all of the Hebrews simultaneously stepped outside of their clay houses in rhythm specifically to listen to his extraordinary "ordained bullshit." Moses said to the *bleary-eyed* people, "Remember this day on which you came out of Egypt, the place of slavery *and the place of a better life than that which exists in Canaan, which is where the fuck we're heading,*" he began his illogical discourse. "It was with a strong hand *with many trump cards including ass-searing lightning bolts that the Lord will bring you away from here.*"

Everyone in attendance moaned, groaned and yawned as Moses continued his impromptu early morning address from his elevated rickety wooden stand. "Nothing made with leaven bread must be eaten *on our arduous journey into the desert, so all you men will not be able to have and sustain erections and screw around while our minds should be concentrating on walking across hot sultry eastern desert sands.* The day of your departure is in the month of Abib, which is not on any calendar anywhere in the whole fuckin' known world so don't ask me even a word about it."

"Get to the point! Get to the point! Get to the fuckin' point!" six hundred thousand Israelites all chanted simultaneously without any rehearsing ever being done. "A bib is what a damned child wears around its neck!" they all laughed and cackled.

Moses then said, "Therefore, it is in this month that you must celebrate this *righteous* rite. After the Lord, your God has brought you into the land of the Canaanites, *there might be some serious bickering and possibly even conflict arising,*" Moses warned. "*As you know the Canaanites all hate our guts and are aware that we want to steal their worthless desert property from them just like Abraham, Isaac and Jacob had attempted to confiscate it but failed in their unheralded but noble endeavors.*"

The crowd was becoming more restive as they finally understood what the hell Moses was telling them. A few boos and jeers could be detected originating somewhere in the back, around two miles away from the wobbly wooden makeshift speaker's platform Aaron and Moses had rudely constructed for such auspicious oratorical occasions.

"Also," continued Moses to the restless throng, "the Hittites, the Amorites, the Hivites and the Jeb-bushites all live in Canaan, *and those four crazy tribes all despise our arrogant asses too! And as you all know, they are descendents of the dreaded Ass-searians.* The Lord had sworn to your fathers, *none of which were Abraham, Isaac and Jacob,* He' would give you a land flowing with milk and honey!" *Moses shouted down to the crazed Israelites from his wobbly makeshift wooden platform.*

"Not milk and honey! You mean piss and shit! Piss and shit! Piss and shit!" *the angry rabble hostilely chanted as creative word substitutions were used for delicious milk and honey.*

Moses raised his hands to encourage silence as a loud peal of thunder echoed in the distance. Everyone quickly became respectful again out of fear of being electrocuted from lightning bolts descending from Heaven. "For seven days you shall eat unleavened bread *and not get any significant erections,* and on the seventh day shall also be a festival to the Lord, *where you can make up for the week of sexual abstinence by screwing anybody and everybody as often as you want!*"

The men in the rabble all hooted 'boisterously', and the women all cheered 'girlsterously'.

"Only unleavened bread may be eaten during the seven days, and no leaven and nothing may be found in all your territory," *Moses informed his assembled listeners for the second unnecessary time.* "So men, make sure that you jerk off and ejaculate getting your *rocks off at least twice before we leave Egypt for the long trek to Canaan!"*

"Jerk off! Jerk off! Jerk off!" the crowd all raucously yelled at Moses in a wild clamor.

"On this day you shall explain to your son, 'This' is because what the Lord did for me when I came out of Egypt. *That's why both you' and I are avid jerk offs'!"*

The unruly crowd went nuts and threatened to transform into an out-of-control mob. Again, Moses raised his hands and thunder rolled and then boomed in the distance. Silence had again been established.

"Therefore *you hick dunces*, you shall keep this prescribed rite *of frantic and intense masturbation* at its appointed time from year to year *in remembrance of our historic passage from Egypt into Canaan!*"

The disorderly crowd jumped up and down with joy and again cheered wildly and ecstatically. Finally they all settled down and became quiet as Moses raised his hands to signify that more thunder and perhaps destructive lightning bolts would be forthcoming from the ominous-looking dark-clouded heavens.

"When the Lord your God has brought you into the land of the Canaanites, *you will no longer be in Egypt,"* Moses explained to the confused assembly that knew or cared nothing about geography. "He swore to give you and your 'forefathers' Canaan, *even though most of us have only one fucked-up father and not four.* You shall dedicate to the Lord every son that opens the womb," *Moses sanctimoniously preached,* "and all the male firstlings of animals shall *also* belong to the Lord *because getting laid and disposing of first-born animals are to be our top priorities instead of you imbeciles intensely jerking off seven straight days every year to commemorate our momentous forthcoming trek!"*

The five or six hundred thousand Israelites leaped up and down and enthusiastically applauded Moses' statements. *Even the hundred thousand horny homosexuals in the throng were aroused by the orator's remarks since "getting laid" meant to them "getting it on" with another one of their own sex.*

"Every first born of an ass you shall redeem with sheep, *so every time one of you asses has a damned 'kid' first' born,"* Moses *cavalierly pontificated,* "redeem the little first-born sucker with a sheep. If you do not redeem it, you shall *be obligated to* break its neck *at breakneck speed."*

The very aroused crowd saw much merit in Moses' effective rhetoric and all yelled, "Let's get laid! Let's get laid! Let's get laid!" in unison. Finally peals of thunder loudly rumbled and rolled in the distance and everyone returned to some semblance of public decorum.

"If your son shall ask you later on, 'What' *the fuck* does *all* mean?' You shall tell him, *'Girls aren't allowed to ask important questions, but son, I'm happy that you have casually inquired,"* Moses related to the throng. "With a strong hand *having many aces in it* the Lord brought us out of Egypt, the place of slavery. When the *anonymous* Pharaoh refused to let us *(the Israelites)* go, the Lord mercilessly and vindictively killed every first-born in the Land of Egypt, every first born of man and of beast. *So son, be proud to be a Hebrew and to have your pecker circumcised,"* Moses instructed the receptive crowd to tell their male children. *"It simply means that when you are jerking off those seven consecutive days of commemoration, you should remember that you can get laid all you want the rest of the year round!"*

The throng of six hundred or so thousand gleeful Israelites went absolutely bananas and was on the verge of going berserk. A bolt of lightning descended out of the dark-clouded sky and knocked a tower from the top of a nearby abandoned building. Everyone that was celebrating again shut the hell up.

"That' is why," *Moses continued to the now somewhat reticent assemblage,* "I sacrifice to the Lord everything of the male sex that opens the *community* womb, *where all future generations of men and animals will mysteriously pop out of. Perhaps women will no longer become pregnant and have to carry children because of this wonderful new community womb, I really don't know that particular detail yet since the mysterious community womb has not been created or experimented with,"* Moses related and confessed.

The women in the crowd all excitedly cheered about the prospect of freedom from bearing children with having the new community womb, while the selfish avowed lesbians in the throng didn't give a shit (and never did) about the joys of motherhood and of the necessity for human reproduction.

"Let this then be a sign on your hand and as a pendant on your forehead: with a strong hand the Lord brought us out of Egypt," Moses lectured the large congregation from his wobbly rickety wooden platform. "And if you think that our religion is about love, forgiveness, respect for others, compassion, sympathy, not killing, not stealing and not coveting our neighbors wives or goods, you are *absolutely and positively wrong!"* Moses screamed. *"Our religion is all about circumcision, stealing Canaan from the Canaanites, eating unleavened bread, fearing curses and mass destruction and getting our dumpy asses the hell out of Egypt!"*

Now, when *the anonymous* Pharaoh let the people *(Israelites)* go, God did not lead them by way of the Philistines' land, *since that intelligent itinerary would have been too easy of a shortcut to Canaan.* That was the nearest *logical route, in addition to the Lord believing that the chosen people should sacrifice, suffer and have their balls busted and their' tits deflated at every conceivable opportunity.* He *(the Lord)* thought, 'The *cowardly* people might change their minds and return to Egypt rather than fight newfound enemies *that were actually old adversaries of their greedy forefathers in Canaan.'*

Instead, He' *(the Lord)* rerouted them toward the Red Sea *(which was truly blue)* by way of the *obscure* desert road, *which could never be seen because of shifting sand dunes and formidable blinding dust and sandstorms.* In battle array the Israelites *(even the women and children)* marched out of Egypt *even though they were afraid of confronting any enemies or armies on their craven roundabout journey to Canaan.*

Moses also took Joseph's *revered* bones along *so that a skeleton crew could use them as tools while working in the camp at night.* Joseph had *once* made the Israelites swear solemnly that, when God should come to them, they would carry his bones away with them. *In that way those important relics would not fall into the hands of an enemy, which happened to be every other culture that ever came into contact with the haughty Stone Age shepherding Hebrews.*

Setting out from Succoth, *where a notorious Hebrew brothel dedicated exclusively to the practice of oral sex had been established a full century before,* they *(the Israelites)* camped at Etham near the edge of the desert *that was sometimes called Allen. The Lord had always from the beginning wanted His' unsettled worshipers living 'on the edge.'*

The Lord preceded them, in the daytime by means of a column of clouds to show them the way, *the cloud funnel sort of functioning like a prehistoric steering 'column'.* At night the Lord used a column of fire to give them light. Thus they could travel both day and night, *burning their feet on the hot scorching desert sand during the day and getting bitten on their toes and asses by venomous desert snakes and scorpions during the night.*

Neither the funnel of clouds *that served as a steering column* by day nor the column of fire *that appeared* by night ever left its place in front of the people, *who were all thinking, "When the fuck are we gonna' be able to jerk off again or get laid again? And the men were all regretting and saying', "I should have gotten a good blow job back in Succoth."*

Chapter Fourteen
"The Red Sea"

Then the Lord said to Moses *naturally when no one else was around to eavesdrop on the conversation,* "Tell the Israelites to turn about and camp before Pi-hahiroth between Mogdol and the sea. *That's a hot resort around these parts where the people can worship and party."*

"How many times should the Israelites turn about?" Moses innocently and candidly asked the Lord. "Once or a hundred? Please be more exact when You communicate esoteric matters to me!"

"You' Dim-witty, I meant once!" the Lord's Voice thundered down to Moses. "You shall camp in front of Baal-zephon, just opposite by the sea, *by the sea, by the sea, by the beautiful sea.* Pharaoh will then say, 'The Israelites are *wimps* wandering about aimlessly in the land *just like they had wandered about aimlessly in Egypt for centuries since the time of Abraham.* The desert has closed in on them *even though the desert hasn't moved at all since the last undocumented earthquake'."*

"Please get to the point," Moses demanded. *"I've had chronic diarrhea from eating unleavened bread ever since we left Egypt. Forgive me if I might have to make a hasty exit and swiftly lift up my robe."*

"Thus will I make *the anonymous* Pharaoh so obstinate *and so obdurate* that he will pursue them *(the Israelites) with a passion. So My' dear Moses, as you can plainly see, Pharaoh is really a pretty nice fellow, but it is I that makes him stubborn and aggressive just to bust on My' chosen people and just to make Pharaoh look like the culprit bad guy in My' seemingly meaningless script."*

"What is Your' motive for making six hundred thousand Hebrews participate in this most 'outlandish' charade?" Moses asked as his stomach and abdomen growled rather fiercely from his digestive tract's severe gastritis since he had a sprue condition and really required a gluten-free diet devoid of unleavened or leavened bread.

"Then I will receive glory through Pharaoh and all his *extensive* army, and the Egyptians will know that I am the Lord," *the supernatural Voice proclaimed from a point in the lower stratosphere.*

"I really think that You' have some kind of inferiority complex and try to transfer it to me and then on to the Hebrews," Moses

yelled up at the sky. "Then You' conveniently convert into Your' mean bully mode and kick everybody's ass for trying to block or stifle Your' selfish goals when they don't even want to do that routine in the first place!"

This *plan* the Israelites did enact. It was 'reported' *(by the United Egyptian Papyrus Press)* to the King of Egypt that 'the people' had fled. *(The Israelites were 'the people', because according to the Lord's words, the Egyptians weren't really people at all but merely anonymous sub-human beings. Only the lowly Israelites were 'people'.)* Pharaoh and his *anonymous* servants *(under the Lord's dominant influence) suddenly* changed their minds about them *(the Hebrews on their Exodus).*

"What have we done?" they (*the Egyptians*) exclaimed *all at once, as was their peculiar habit, too.* "Why have we released Israel from our service? *The damned Egyptian women are all too skinny and too hard to service!"*

So *incensed* Pharaoh made his chariots ready *(the Ruler was a very excellent mechanic, wheelwright and carpenter)* and *he 'relished' the call and* 'mustered' his soldiers-six hundred first class 'chariots' *(the King also had some chariots he used as soldiers).* All of the other chariots of Egypt were 'mustered up' *so that the Pharaoh and his army could eventually 'catch-up' to the fleeing Hebrews.*

So obstinate had the Lord made Pharaoh that he pursued the Israelites even while they were marching away in triumph *after not defeating any special enemy whatsoever. The Hebrews were proud, daft simple-minded slaves that thought they were a fancy marching army when actually they were nothing more than ragtag renegade fugitives running away from Egypt's service and from the King's laws and justice.*

The Egyptians then pursued them *(the escaping Hebrew slaves)* with Pharaoh's whole *army, National Guard, militia, archers,* horses, chariots and charioteers. The *on-a-mission* Egyptians caught up with them' as they lay camped by the sea at Pi-hahiroth, in front of Baal-zephon, *the most famous desert nightclub spot in the ancient world.*

Pharaoh was already near when the Israelites looked up *(all at the exact same time)* and saw that the Egyptians were on the march *(remember, chariots with warriors and charioteers in them are not marching)* in pursuit of them *(the Hebrews). Now, the apprehensive Israelites were stationary and just hanging out in their camp and therefore, they were incapable of being 'pursued' if they were not moving.*

In great fright they *(the cowardly slave Hebrews pretending to be soldiers while dressed in battle attire)* cried out to the Lord. And they *(the craven rabble)* complained to Moses *like real crybaby bellyachers would certainly do,* "Were there no burial places in Egypt that you had to bring us out here to *futilely* die in the desert?" *they all amazingly said at the exact same time.* "Why did you do this *treachery* to us? Why did you bring us out of Egypt?" *they all vehemently demanded.*

Moses was suddenly stricken with heightened diarrhea as a wet fart shot out of his aged asshole and then the brown liquid rolled down his right leg. The Israelites (and not the awesome Egyptian army) had therefore effectively scared the shit out of Moses.

The people were both livid and adamant, and remarkably they all chanted, "Did we not tell you this in Egypt, when we said *and then chanted,* 'Leave us 'alone', *because we all need 'a loan' desperately.* Leave us alone and let us all serve in Egypt *for the rich, kind, generous, pleasant, cultured, educated aristocrats that treated us all much better than we deserved to be treated as inferior slaves. Far better for us to be slaves in Egypt than to die in the desert boondocks way out here in no man's land and also in no-god's land.*"

Moses *wiped his fat rear end with some available pinecones and then* answered his' people: "Fear not! *Only fear the Lord!*" he began. "Stand your ground, and you will see the victory the Lord will win for you today, *for He' will fight for all of you spineless yellow-bellied unskilled cowards.* These Egyptians you will see today you will never see again," *Moses confidently predicted.* "The *mighty* Lord Himself' will fight for you *although it is not fair for supernatural beings to fight against mortal men and armies. But since the Greek Olympian gods often do this, I guess it's okay for the Lord to give it a go,*" *Moses generalized.* "All you have to do is keep still *and stay away from the battlefield, you totally depraved gutless wimps! Leave the essential combat issues exclusively up to the Lord!*"

Then the Lord said to Moses *from out of the clear blue sky*, "Why are you crying out to me? Tell the *weak and pathetic* Israelites to go forward. And you *Moses,*" *the Lord boomed down loudly even though only Moses could hear Him',* lift up your staff and, with your *extended giant* hand outstretched over the sea, split the sea in two.

Then the *wimpy, weakling* Israelites may *miraculously* pass through it on dry land."

God was not through with his presentation to His' audience of one. "But I shall make the Egyptians so obstinate that they will go in after them *(the Hebrews in the Red Sea, which has always been blue).* Then I will receive glory through Pharaoh and his *royal loyal* army, his charioteers and his chariots *(since when has a chariot been capable of giving honor and glory to anyone?).* The Egyptians shall know," *the Lord continued during His' blustery filibuster to Moses,* "that I am the Lord, *a ruthless Bully with a gross inferiority complex. I constantly need praise and glory and must get those qualities of worship from humans by fear or by force.*"

The Angel of God *(His' formidable hit-man that had already done a real number on the Egyptians back in Egypt during the Passover),* who had been leading Israel's camp *(actually and technically, a camp is generally stationary),* now moved and went around behind them *to coordinate a well-conceived sneak attack.* The *steering* column of cloud also, leaving the *fore*front, took up its place behind him *to notify the Pharaoh and his doomed army that a secret sneak' attack or something mighty fishy like that kind of perfidiousness was imminent.*

The *odd steering* column of cloud came between the camp of the Egyptians and that of Israel. But the *funnel* cloud now became dark, and thus the night came *before it was expected* without the rival camps' coming closer together all night long *since every person (including the nearly blind Moses) on both sides was awed by the relentless swirling tornado.*

Then Moses stretched out his *giant retractable* hand over the Red Sea, and the Lord *got out a gigantic broom* and swept the sea with a strong east wind *equal to the force of ten trillion human farts.* The *rotating and revolving gusts of* wind lasted throughout the night and *they had real gusto as the incredible hurricane force* gales swirled around, *magically* turning the sea into dry land.

When the water was thus divided, the Israelites marched *(the runaway slaves were still pretending that they were a well' trained army in full battle array just like the forces of the anonymous Pharaoh)* into the midst of the sea on dry land *(so it was no longer a sea).* The Red Sea was still very turbulent with all of the water like a wall to their right and another *similar* wall to their left. *So, to all you carpenters out there, that was the invention of and the very beginning of' what has become known as drywall'.*

The *dastardly* Egyptians followed in *hot* 'pursuit', *and others wore armor while each soldier was allowed only one tie 'per suit'.* All Pharaoh's horses, 'chariots' and charioteers went after them *(the Hebrews in the Red Sea' dry land' corridor). Amazingly, as stated, the empty chariots went into the sea all by themselves without any warriors inside them.*

In the night watch just before dawn the Lord cast through the *steering* column of the fiery cloud upon the Egyptian force a glance that threw it into a panic. He *(the Lord)* so clogged their *advanced civilization'* chariot' wheels that they could hardly drive, *thus giving the royal drive' 'shaft' to each wheel's axis.*

With that amazing event occurring the Egyptian charioteers all said to one another in unison, "What goes around doesn't always necessarily come around!"

The Egyptians *(all of them)* sounded the retreat before Israel, *which actually was a country on the move on its way from Egypt to Canaan.* The Lord was fighting for them *(the cowardly, wimpy Hebrews)* against the *powerful* Egyptians *because He' delighted in setting up Pharaohs and their imperial armies on His' vast worldly chessboard and then beating the shit out of the mere mortals with impressive supernatural pyrotechnics and unearthly demonstrations of awesome power.*

Then the *proud* Lord told *the speechless* Moses, "Stretch out your *magical retractable* hand over the sea, that the water may flow back upon the Egyptians, upon their chariots and *upon* their charioteers. *For I believe, Moses, that the Egyptians' horses have to be watered right now."*

So Moses stretched out his *gigantic expandable* hand over the *entire* Red Sea, and at *the appearance of* dawn the sea flowed back to its normal depth.

The *desperate* Egyptians were fleeing head-on toward the sea, when the Lord hurled them *(the surprised warriors and their technologically superior chariots)* into its midst. As the water flowed back *to its normal geographic position* it *enveloped and* covered the chariots and the charioteers, *and none of the charioteers or the chariots knew how to swim or had ever even taken a lifeguard rescue training course.*

Pharaoh's whole army had followed the Israelites into the sea *when in reality, they had had the opportunity to slaughter and butcher the technologically inferior Hebrews thousands of times on land in Egypt and also the night before on land when the runaway slaves were asleep in their camp.* Not a single *or married* soldier escaped *the catastrophe that had craftily been designed and implemented by the Lord.*

But *the pathetic Stone Age* Israelites had marched *(walked and trekked)* on dry land through *the mist and* the midst of the sea, with the water like a wall to their right and to their left, *until none was 'left', 'right'?*

Thus the Lord saved Israel *long before the Hebrews ever captured Canaan from the Canaanites and then realistically called it Israel.* Israel on that day was saved from the 'power' of the Egyptians', *who hadn't even discovered electricity yet and who' didn't give a crap what lightning was technically composed of.*

When Israel saw the bodies of the *vanquished* Egyptians lying dead on the seashore *not far from Rehoboth Beach and near Goshen far from the ocean,* they beheld the great power that the Lord had shown against the Egyptians. They *then* feared the Lord and believed in Him' and in His' *favorite* servant Moses. *For if they didn't, the wimpy Hebrews would be as good as dead just like the defeated Egyptian anonymous Pharaoh and his formidable drowned anonymous army.*

Chapter Fifteen
"At Mirah and Elim"

Then Moses and the *jubilant* Israelite *chorus* all sang this song for the Lord *to the rhythm of a popular contemporary nursery school tune:* "I will sing to the Lord, for He' is gloriously triumphant *in massacring the dirtball anonymous Pharaoh's dirt-bag anonymous Egyptian army." Then there was more poetic nonsense*:

"Horse and chariot He' has 'cast' into the sea *when He' had run out of fishing lines and poles;*

My strength and courage is the Lord, and He' has been my guiding Savior *from the scumbag perverted anonymous Egyptian Pharaoh.*

He is my God, I praise Him, *because we don't want to be drowned like the scumbag Egyptians were and we don't want fire and brimstone shooting up our asses like that horrific disaster which had happened at Sodom and Gomorrah.*

The God of my father, I extol Him' *or else, He' might visit me with floods, earthquakes, tidal waves, hurricanes or other natural and unnatural disasters beyond which our limited imaginations can comprehend.*

The Lord is a 'Warrior', *and we Israelites are puny wimpy 'worriers'.* Lord is His' name, *and vengeance is His' game.*

Pharaoh's *state-of-the-art* chariots and his *doomed* army He' hurled into the sea, *and I don't want that kind of nasty shit, happening to me.*

The elite of his officers was submerged in the Red Sea, *and those unfortunate maniacs had no long reeds to snorkel with or to breathe air situated above the sea's level.*

The flood' waters covered them *at night without any 'flood' lights around to see their dead floating bodies on the sea.* 'They' sank into the depths like 'a stone' *(like stones) or (like stones that had been professionally busted).*

Your right hand, O Lord, magnificent in power, *that could decapitate Zeus or Poseidon if You' would care that be Your' Almighty pleasure.*

Your' 'right hand', O Lord, has shattered the enemy, *so we are all so very much afraid to be identified as being sinister left-handed fools.*

In Your' great majesty You' overthrew Your' adversaries *as if they were merely attacking in toy chariots.* You' loosened Your'

Almighty wrath to consume them like stubble *on a baby's chubby ass.*

At a breath of Your' anger the waters piled up *to punish and drown the dreadful enemy, as is Your' singular style of participating in and causing spectacular mass annihilation.*

The *atrocious* flowing waters stood like a mound *of feces*, the flood' waters congealed in the midst of the sea *that swallowed up all of the hairless little-dicked Egyptian soldiers.*

The *cocky* enemy boasted *speaking as one*, "I will pursue and overtake them," *and the idiotic assholes did just that.* "I will divide the spoils and have my fill of them," *even though we poor craven Hebrew slaves on the run fleeing as foolish nomads had and have no spoils to divide or lacked any food to have given to our prospective Egyptian conquerors.*

I will 'draw' my sword *with a charcoal crayon,* and My' hand *(hey, what happened to My' other hand, the left one!)* shall despoil them *that have the worthless spoils!*

When Your' *super* wind blew, *we were all 'totally blown away' by its power.* The sea covered them, like lead they sank in the mighty waters, *and we knew that the Egyptians would finally 'get to the bottom of what was happening' to them at the gala Israelite Red Sea Jamboree.*

Who is like to You' among the gods, O Lord? *Is it Zeus, Poseidon, Hades, Apollo, Hephaestus or Hermes? Un-fog our vulnerable minds!*

Who is like to You', magnificent in holiness? *In fact so magnificent that You' have deliberately at Your' divine volition violated every future commandment that You' plan to make the humble Israelites follow.*

O' terrible in renown, Worker' of wonders *that are really abhorrent curses, holocausts, massacres, tragedies, grand felonies, catastrophes, calamities, disasters, destructions, debacles and abominations.*

When You' stretched out Your' right hand, the earth swallowed them, *which suggests that all the doomed Egyptians must have been lefties, whom You' abhorred with an extreme passion.*

In Your' mercy You' led the people You' redeemed, *but You' showed no mercy toward the fated Egyptians that were led into Your' clever trap and that were then appropriately and systematically slaughtered. Oh well, there' goes civilization back a thousand years all because of Your' dedicated enmity toward the anonymous Pharaoh and his advanced culture!*

In Your' strength You' 'guided' them, *these misguided souls, to Your' holy dwelling, here in this miserably hot forsaken eastern desert that is home to only venomous snakes and to poisonous scorpions. Can Canaan be a worse fate than this horrendous detestable wasteland?*

The nations heard and quaked, *even though nations haven't any ears or any unique Quakers living in them.*

Anguish 'gripped' the dwellers in Phillistia, *and then they all wickedly suffered from the grippe.*

Then were the princes of Edom dismayed, and trembling seized the chieftains of Moab, *who all suddenly acquired Parkinson's disease and permanent dementia while using a variety of 'salt shakers'.*

Next all the dwellers of Canaan 'melted' away *in a serious meltdown.*

Terror and dread fell upon them, *which is generally Your' easy solution to any real human problem. Sympathy is most certainly not Your' strong suit!*

By the might of Your' arm they were frozen like stone, *just like You' had done to Lot's wife back at Sodom just east of Gomorrah. And so, the noble Egyptians were really in the end, like Lot's wife, pillars of their community frozen solid like petrified rock.*

While Your' people, O Lord passed over, *the constipated ones were encumbered and unable to 'pass' anything.*

And You' *assiduously* brought them in and planted them on this *God-forsaken* mountain of Your' inheritance, *that is completely worthless and situated out here in a bleak barren desert loaded with poisonous vipers and accompanying deadly scorpions.*

The placement where You' made Your' *county* seat, O Lord, which Your' hands established *and will ultimately take away from the gentle peace-loving pacifist Canaanites.*

The Lord shall reign forever and ever, *and woe be to any fuckin' Israelite or Canaanite who tries to give Him' any relevant or irrelevant crap!"*

They *(the wimpy, craven, triumphant Hebrew slaves)* sang thus because *the anonymous* Pharaoh's horses and chariots and charioteers had gone into the sea. And the Lord made the waters of the sea flow back upon them, *drowning tens of thousands of innocent asshole victims in one horrific episode of distorted and demented Biblical history.*

The Israelites had marched *(walked and trekked like roaming nomadic mendicants and vagrants)* on dry land through the midst of the *raging* sea."

The prophetess Miriam, Aaron's *sinister* sister *(What happened to Moses, Aaron's beleaguered brother? Miriam would have to be Moses' sister too!)* took *(Borrowed or stole?)* a tambourine in her hand while the *other* women *(What was Miriam? A neuter?)* went out after her with *their* tambourines. As they danced *and frolicked about*, she *(Miriam, the sexless sinister sister of Aaron but not of Moses, Aaron's younger brother)* led them in the 'refrain': *(which all the men refrained from participating in because they were too busy jerking off and victoriously squirting sticky semen all over the raunchy desert.)*

"Sing to the Lord, for He' is gloriously triumphant, *although back in Egypt, we didn't believe that He' had a snowball's chance in Hades of pulling this big motherless battle off,"* Miriam and her chorus sang *while hopping all around like drunken robins.* "Horse and chariot He' has cast into the sea, *and what a dreadful destruction of beautiful ornate property, merchandise and meritorious Egyptian civilization that particular demolition was. We must celebrate and have a jumbo jamboree."*

Then Moses led Israel forward from the Red Sea, *which was finally truly red from Egyptian blood.* They marched *(walked and trekked like impoverished, uneducated proletarian slaves)* out to the desert of *Sonny and* Shur, *for Shur was an old rich man that owned his own private desert', that's for damned sure.*

After traveling for three days through the *lengthy* desert without finding water *(this sounds like your normal, average everyday desert)*, they *(Moses and the Israelites, a new area band)* arrived at Marah, where they could not drink the water. It was too bitter.

Hence, this *off-the-beaten path* place was called Marah', *which means, "Never stop here and drink if you want to fuckin' live!"*

As the *renegade* people *(the Israelites)* grumbled against Moses *(after what they had just witnessed with the Red Sea? Come on now! What kind of short-memory idiots are we dealing with here?)*, *intelligently* saying *(asking)*, "What are we to drink?" he *(Moses) out of* desperation appealed to the Lord.

The Lord *(Who' had not anticipated the drinking water problem)* pointed out to 'him' *(Moses) (Have you ever seen so many damned stupid pronoun-antecedent problems in all your life?)* a certain *special* piece of wood. When he *(Moses)* threw this *(the special piece of wood)* into the *toxic oasis* water, the water *(it)* became *very* 'fresh' *and cursed and cussed loudly at all of the fucked-up on-the-lam Israelites.*

It was here that the Lord, in making rules and regulations for them *(the six hundred thousand gypsy Hebrews)* put them to the test. "If you really listen to the Voice of the Lord your *all-powerful* God," He' told them *while actually speaking about Himself'*, "and do what is right in His' *all-knowing* eyes, *then you will be doing as I say but not as I do."*

"If you heed His' *(My')* commandments and keep all precepts *and forceps using your biceps,"* Moses continued while quoting the Lord's Voice, "I will not afflict you with any of the diseases with which I have afflicted the Egyptians. *I will not do this even though I have just murdered all of the moronic Egyptians that are anywhere around this desolate barren wasteland.* For I am the Lord, and I am your' healer. *Now that you have with My' divine help soundly vanquished the civilized Egyptians with barbarity and with mass destruction, it is about time that you Israelites develop some basic culture and civilization,"* the Lord suggested through Moses. "You must escape from being slaves, criminals, sinners and primitive savages and you must evolve, mature and then become culture-oriented."

"Do you hear a Voice talking to us from the sky?" Aaron asked Moses. "The Voice is making no sense at all! The Israelites don't value laws, morality or codes of ethics. All we ever do is imitate our crazy Lord when we aren't preoccupied fucking around!"

Then they *(the half million or so ragtag gypsy vagabond slaves)* came to Elim, where there were twelve *springs hanging out of an old discarded mattress.* Water was pouring out of the twelve springs *in the old rejected mattress*, and seventy 'palm' trees *with opened hands on their limbs* were *situated* there also. The Hebrews camped there near the water *wishing that they had been drowned in the Red Sea just like the more fortunate Egyptian soldiers had been.*

Chapter Sixteen
"The Quail and Manna"

Having set out from Elim, the whole Israelite community *(including the minority gay and lesbian community)* came into the desert of Sin *(just where the aforementioned gay and lesbian community belonged)* so *a person could deduct that the Hebrews were living in Sin.* The desert of Sin is *located* between Elim and Sinai *and not far from the village of Sinus where all of the natives have severe allergies. The band of wanderers arrived* on the fifteenth unnamed *day* of the second *unknown* month after their departure from the land of Egypt *(Why not just say Egypt?) Of course the reckless Israelites (none of whom were conscientious environmentalists) left trash littered and strewn all across the formerly pristine desert.*

Here *(there)* in the desert the whole *ambivalent* Israelite community grumbled against Moses and Aaron. The Israelites said to themselves *(so therefore, everybody was mumbling and muttering under their breaths),* "Would that we had died at the Lord's hand *(the Lord could easily kill anyone with only one hand)* in the land of Egypt, as we sat by our fleshpots and ate our fill of bread! But you two *degenerate assholes* had to lead us into the desert to make the whole community *including homos and lesbians alike* die of *severe* famine," *a half million voices mumbled and muttered under their foul-smelling breaths. Moses and Aaron stood there with their mouths agape being accused by their former supporters suddenly turned prosecutors.*

"They're right Moses," *Aaron confessed to his younger brother.* "There is nothing out here to eat except poisonous snakes, scorpions and each other."

"Hey, that's not such a bad idea!" *chimed in an eavesdropping gay male with horny non-cannibalistic tendencies.* "We should all eat each other!"

Then the Lord said to Moses *but to no one else in the vicinity,* "I will now rain down bread from heaven for you. Each day the people are to go out and gather their daily portion," *the Lord's Voice ordered from the sky.* "Thus will I test them, *these idiotic followers of Mine' possessing low IQs'. I want to see whether or not the simpletons follow My' easy one-step instructions or not."*

"Lord," Moses said, "in all due respect You' have Almighty' power. Why not just transport us all in a giant flying oxcart from *here to Canaan and forget about all of this nonsensical suffering, bitching, drama and grueling desert low adventure."*

"Everything to you has to be easy and unearned, you lazy unmotivated dolt!" *the Lord amply chided Moses.* "You are just as indolent as the half million or so parasitic numbskulls you represent."

"Okay, please cease the harassment and the sarcastic criticism and tell Aaron and me the remainder of Your' monstrous plan," *Moses suggested.* "My older brother has got to endure agony and misery in addition to me."

"On the sixth day," *the Lord proceeded,* "when they *(the Israelites)* prepare what they bring in, let it be twice as much as they gather on the other days, *sort of like a generous bonus being reaped."*

So Moses and Aaron, *the Lord's middle-men' brokers,* told *all half million or so of* the *constantly complaining* Israelites, "At evening you will know that it was the Lord' Who brought you out of Egypt. *This is understood even though you have all already walked several hundred miles from the Nile through the eastern desert on your own sore two feet."* Moses had more to convey to his apathetic listeners, most of whom' were still mumbling and grumbling under their foul-smelling breaths. "In the morning you *nincompoops* will see the glory of the Lord as He' heeds your grumbling *and mumbling* against Him."

"Blaberbalabbulla, blabootubafora, blalblabblabblabadub," *the* half *million showed their great disenchantment by mumbling and grumbling indecipherable slave jargon under their foul-smelling breaths.*

"But what are we *(God, Moses and Aaron)* that you should grumble against us? When the Lord gives you *decayed putrid* flesh to eat in the evening," continued and *threatened* Moses, "and in the morning your fill of *rancid stale* bread *without working for it like the freeloading welfare recipients that you are,* as He' heeds the grumbling you *reprehensibly* utter against Him', what then are we? *You'll all be punished by the Lord's wrath as your hedonistic behavior has warranted*!"

"Blaberbalabbulla, blabootubafora, blalblabblabblabadub!" *the half million dissenting grumblers and mumblers grumbled and mumbled emphatically all in a strange and eerie sort of harmonic dissonance.*

Then Moses said to Aaron, *"Our people are just as fucked-up as we are!* Go tell the whole *damned* Israelite community *including the ever-growing minority gay and lesbian community* to present themselves before the Lord, for He' has heard their grumbling *and is greatly offended."*

When Aaron announced this to the whole Israelite community, they turned toward the desert, *and said,* "Blaberbalabbulla, blabootubafora, blalblabblabblabadub!" and lo, the glory of the Lord appeared in the cloud! *(There was only one cloud in the entire blue sky within a thousand mile radius).*

The Lord spoke to Moses *(no one else including Aaron could hear His' thunderous Voice originating from the distant cloud)* and said, "I have heard the grumbling of the Israelites. Tell them: 'In the twilight evening you' shall eat flesh, and in the morning you shall have your fill of bread. *You will get horrible indigestion that will hurt ten times as extreme as what you are experiencing and grumbling about now!* Then you may know that I, the Lord, am your God'!"

In the evening quail came up and covered the camp *but no one was bird watching or even saw them except Moses and Aaron since everyone else was sleeping, fatigued from grumbling and mumbling all-day-long.* In the morning a dew' lay upon the camp *and got everybody's ass wet. And when the dew finally evaporated,* there on the surface of the desert were fine flakes like hoarfrost *(whore frost?)* on the ground, *but then Moses and Aaron eventually realized that the prodigious white flakes were actually dandruff' scales from a half million dirty, scaly Israelite scalps.*

On seeing it *(the frosted flakes on the ground),* the Israelites asked one another, *"What the fuck is this white shit sprinkled all over the damned desert?" for they did not know what their own scaly dandruff looked or smelled like.* But Moses *emphatically* told them *(the amazed traveling Hebrews on the lam),* "At least half of the white flakes is bread from Heaven which the Lord has given you to eat. *Distinguish them from the white desert sand grains and have a fabulous feast that has been generated by the Lord for Aaron and my benefit."*

"Now, this is what the Lord has commanded as *Commander-in-Chief,*" Moses declared *to the non-receptive but still hungry half million Israelites, all seeming to have severe attention deficits and irreversible learning disabilities.* "So gather the flakes *although you all are totally flaky already,"* he ascertained and maintained. "Be certain everyone has enough *frosted flakes* to eat, an omer for each person, as many of you as you are, each man providing for those of his own tent. *Hey!*" Moses exclaimed. "*How come everybody has a wet ass?*"

The Israelites did as *their aged leader had* directed. Some gathered a large amount *of white frosted flakes on the ground* and other *more fortunate* individuals a small amount. But when they measured it out by the 'omer' *(not a tentmaker),* he who had gathered a large amount didn't have too much, and he who had gathered a small amount did not have too little. They so gathered so that everyone had enough *frosted* flakes to eat *because there were not any pigs around for anyone in the camp to bring home' the bacon.*

Moses also told them *(the half million inattentive unkempt dandruff-scalped scruffy Israelites),* 'Let no one keep any of it over until tomorrow morning." *But everyone paid little or no heed to his imperative instructions and as usual, the uncooperative independent-minded fools would not listen to the essence of their elderly leader's essential words.*

When some *adult delinquents and hooligans* kept a part of it over until the following morning, it became wormy and rotten, *just like their diseased colons and anuses.* Therefore Moses was displeased with them *in that the insolent Israelite violators would again attempt to worm their way out of another self-caused rotten situation.*

Morning after morning they gathered it *(the dandruff' laced frosted flakes)* until each person had enough to eat, but when the sun grew hot, the manna melted away *and all of the oily or dry scalp bacteria were efficaciously killed by the sun's radiation.*

On the sixth day they *(the retarded dippy grumbling mumbling Israelites)* gathered twice as much food, two omers *(a measurement of grain)* for each person *and a pound of sand for dessert.* When all the leaders of the community came and reported this *deviation* to Moses, he told them *with moral clarity,* "Tomorrow is a day of complete rest, *so none of you are to take baths or massage your filthy scalps.* It is the Sabbath, sacred to the Lord, *so don't do anything to get Him' pissed-off.* You may either bake or boil manna *manana.* But whatever is left put away and keep for the following day, for that is what the Lord *has* 'prescribed', *and He's the unchallenged doctor around here.*"

When they *(the Israelites)* put it *(the manna for manana)* away for the morning, as *Commander* Moses *had* commanded, it did not become wormy and rotten *like their diseased colons and like their disintegrating anuses had become.*

Moses then *confidently* said *to his bellicose audience,* "Eat it today, for today is the Sabbath of the Lord, *and you don't want those voracious worms and that cancerous rot to rise from your colons and migrate up into your vulnerable large intestines just as we have migrated from Egypt to this God-forsaken place.* On this day," Moses continued, "you will not find any *frosted* flakes on the ground *because Aaron and I made all of you take showers last night and wash your grimy scalps with a potent vinegar shampoo.* On the other six days you can gather it *(white frosted manna flakes and hardly observable dandruff' traces),* but on the seventh day, the Sabbath, none of it will be there *because from now on the night before is now designated 'Vinegar Shampoo Night' in this happy camp of contented assholes!"*

Still, on the seventh day some of the people *that had not shampooed their scalps with vinegar the night before* went out to gather it *(the frosted flakes on the ground),* although they did not find any, *not even their own filthy and smelly dandruff' droppings.*

Then the Lord said to *His'* prime earth contact Moses, "How long will you refuse to keep My' commandments and laws? *Answer Me', for I am in a nasty mood and might shoot deadly worms into your mouth that will rot your inners straight down from your throat to your esophagus!"*

"Er, er, Lord, I already have a hungry tapeworm," Moses said and explained, "and it is already measuring the entire length of my intestinal tract right this minute."

"Take *particular* note! The Lord has given you the *sacred* Sabbath," *the hallowed forceful Voice from the sky announced.* "That is why on the sixth day He' *(I)* gives you food for two days, *you incompetent Dummy.* On the seventh day everyone is to stay home and no one is to go out *on dates, on nature walks or is to shack up with horny partners and three-somes in your pathetic and sinful over-crowded tents. Just because you're all congregated out here in this remote desert doesn't mean that you're allowed to live in Sin! That's not the type of congregation I had in mind when I sent My' people out of Egypt!"*

After that *explicit monologue-directive* the people rested on the seventh day *or else the vengeful Almighty Lord would allow them no rest or peace and quiet in their already anxiety-filled and very futile earthly existence.*

The *always morally vacillating* Israelites called this food they were sampling 'manna'. It was like coriander seed, but white, and it tasted like *bitter* wafers' made with *very tart and sour* honey.

Moses *then* said *to his reluctant followers,* "This is what the Commander-in-Chief *has commanded to his Commander.* 'Keep an omerful *(a unit of grain measurement as already defined)* of manna for your 'descendents' *climbing down ladders,* that they may see what food I gave you to eat in the desert when I brought you out of the land of Egypt *and into the lawless jungle-type desert environment that exists outside the parameters of civilization."*

Moses then told Aaron, "Take an urn and put an omer of manna in it *by manana.* Then place it before the Lord in safekeeping for your *unfaithful and dissident shit eatin'* descendents, *who won't give a flying shit about that or about anything else you'll ever try to do for them."*

So Aaron placed it *(the urn he had to earn)* in front of the commandments for safekeeping, *for there was no safe place to keep a safe and no safes around to keep something safe anywhere, and no school safeties around to guard the treasured urn.* Aaron did this as the Lord had commanded Moses, *so why didn't Moses do it as commanded by the infallible Lord?*

The *recalcitrant* Israelites ate this *wonderful* manna for forty *lousy* years, *and had the shits every damned day for the next four decades.* Finally they came to settled land, but unfortunately, it was already settled by the cantankerous Canaanites', *who all loathed and hated the Hebrews more than the Canaanites loathed and hated intestinal worms and crotch and ass rot and cheap urns filled with manna.* The *trekking* Israelites reached the borders of Canaan, *which looked exactly like the vast difficult desert wasteland they had recently traversed.*

"This is the land of milk and honey!" Moses shouted to the highly disgusted Israelites.

"Piss and shit! Piss and shit! Piss and shit!" *the half million or so listless freeloading derelicts contemptuously hollered back.*

Chapter Seventeen
"Water from the Rock"

From the desert of Sin *(where no human could stay or live too long or else he or she would never be able to sin again)* the whole Israelite community *(including the ever-growing minority gay, lesbian, homosexual, queer, faggot and dyke/butch sub-community)* journeyed by 'stages' *and also by primitive oxcarts. This happened just as the Lord directed His' epic play, His' drab scenery and His' rather mediocre actors. Finally, the entire migration* encamped at Rephidim.

Here there was no water for the people *(the disbelieving cynical Israelite ingrates)* to drink, *so they imbibed a huge quantity of beer and wine instead. As usual, they intensely quarreled* with Moses', *who was trying to lead them out of another problematic mess he had gotten them into because of the Lord's propensity for creating extensive human grief for His' amusement.*

They *(the rambunctious, impatient, skeptical, antagonistic Hebrews)* therefore challenged Moses and said *to him all together in orchestrated mockery,* "Give us water to drink *or else all half million of us will shit at least twice daily in your tent. Beer and wine give us excessive diarrhea!"*

Moses *testily* replied, "Why do you quarrel with me? Why do you put the Lord to the test? *You can't get blood from a rock!"* Then *Moses began to seriously analyze the profundity of his last stellar comment.*

Here, then, in their thirst for water' the people *(the quarrelsome and vitriolic Israelites)* grumbled *and mumbled* against Moses' *authority.* The *petulant* men were saying, "Why did you ever make us leave *the security of marvelous* Egypt? Was it just to have us die *out* here *in no man's land* of thirst *for water* with our *wailing* children and our *ailing* livestock?" *(Notice that by omission it was okay for wives, nieces, aunts and sisters to die from thirst and malnutrition).*

So *feeling threatened* Moses cried out to the Lord, "What shall I do with this *rabble You'* call people?" *(The unappreciative, bratty, sulking, pouting, bitching Hebrews were the folks he had been all-too-graciously describing).* "A little more *agitation* and they will *surely* stone me! And I can't put up with that even though my head is hard as a rock!" Moses said and grieved in anguish. "I have a terrible migraine, am hung over from drinking too much beer and wine last night with Aaron, Ben and Hur, and I feel 'stoned' already *this early in the morning!" Moses' mentioning of the word "stone" gave the Lord a magnificent idea.*

The Lord *abruptly* answered Moses, "Go over there in front of the people *standing* along with some of the *insane and senile* elders of Israel. Hold in your hand as you go 'your staff' with which you *had* struck the *Egyptian* river, *and I don't mean your long penis, either.* I will be standing there in front of you on the rock in Horeb, *but nobody including you or your preposterous followers will be able to see Me'."*

"Er, Lord, what am I to do at this rock of Horeb while I'm standing there like a fool holding my long staff in front of everybody?" Moses wanted to know. "I'm basically shy, introverted and self-conscious, You' know!"

"Strike the rock, and the water will flow from it for the people *(those complaining, ungrateful idiots)* to drink. *This Moses I promise to you.*"

This Moses did *while being hung-over with a severe migraine headache*, in the presence of the *senile and insane* elders of Israel, *who didn't know or give a shit about what the hell was happening in their midst anyway.*

The *desolate* place was called Massah and Meribah, because the Israelites quarreled there, *and using that logic, every damned place they ever visited should have been called Massah and Meribah.* The Hebrews (*including the revered elders suffering from dementia*) tested the Lord saying *and shouting*, "Is the Lord in our midst or not? *Does He' have a number two piece of charcoal with which we are to take our standardized exam'? What the fuck' are we doing here at Massah and Meribah anyway?"*

At Rephidim, Amalek *(a local legitimate land baron that despised trespassers, encroachers and intruders)* came and waged war against the Israelites', *who were invading Amalek's territory and threatening to plunder it and consequently make the peaceful local residents (his employees) their exploited slaves.*

Moses, therefore, said to Joshua *(Who the hell is Joshua in this story? Where did he come from?),* "Pick out certain men *without picking on them or their scabs.* Tomorrow you shall go and engage Amalek in battle *because I am too old and cowardly to engage in that pursuit.*"

"But Moses, I'm already married and I don't want to have 'an engagement' with Amalek or with anyone else!" Joshua vehemently protested. "Do you think I look like a charter member of the gay and lesbian sub-community?"

"*Joshua,*" Moses said and clarified, "I will be standing on top of the hill with the staff of God in my hand."

"*That's utter blasphemy you've uttered!*" Joshua yelled at Moses. "*You should be standing up on the high hill with your own damned long staff in your hand! Show more damned respect for the Almighty!*"

So finally, after much explanation and definition of terms by Moses to the alarmed Joshua, Joshua did as Moses had told him: he engaged Amalek in battle *on his first date with him.* Moses had climbed up to the top of the hill with Aaron, *Ben* and Hur, *and the four of them were still groggy and dizzy from their intense drinking session the night before when all four of the patriarchs had gotten smashed and were genuinely "as drunk as the Lord."*

As long as Moses kept his hands raised up, Joshua had the better of the fight *with Amalek*, but when he let his hands rest, Amalek *and his minions* had the better of the battle.

"*You always had trouble with erections!*" Aaron criticized his half-drunk younger brother in regard to the raising of his staff. "*Try keeping it up longer Moses!*" he said, referring to the now-supernatural magic pole.

"*That's amazing!*" Hur acknowledged to Moses. "*I wish I could raise and lower my staff over my head like that needing two hands to do it with! Hey Aaron and Ben, pass the goatskin of wine over here, will ya'!*"

Moses' hands, however, 'grew tired *along with the long fingernails they had also grown.* So they *(the drunken Aaron and the plastered Hur along with intoxicated Ben)* put a rock in place for him *(Moses)* to sit on. Meanwhile, *burping* Aaron, *vomiting Ben* and *belching* Hur supported Moses' hands, one on one side and one on the other, *because although the three were quite totally ripped from the night before, they still remembered that Moses had two separate hands on opposite sides of his body.* Remarkably Moses' hands remained steady *on his staff* until sunset. And Joshua (*without the aid of an army*) mowed down Amalek and his soldiers *in tall grass* with the edge of his sword *at the edge of a field.* Thanks to Moses' incredible long staff, Joshua was the first man in history to have single-handedly defeated an entire enemy army in combat all by himself.

Then the very demanding Lord said to Moses, "*That was quite a battle down in the valley! Let's have some more entertainment. This sort of thing is what I do for amusement and for diversion when I get bored with My' divine existence.*"

"Great battle!" Moses admitted to his Heavenly Superior. "Joshua fighting with his dull-bladed sword against Amalek and his twelve wimpy shepherds without any weapons!"

The *gratified* Lord said to Moses, "Write this down *even though your culture does not have a good alphabet yet or a quality dictionary of words and phrases*. This document will be something to be remembered, and recite it to the ears of Joshua, *one ear at a time, which means you'll have to repeat the statement on both sides of his thick head.*"

"What am I to say to our latest hero?" Moses asked his divine Mentor. "That he defeated weak mild-mannered shepherds without weapons and intrepidly mowed them down in tall grass with his dull-bladed sword?"

"I will completely blot out the memory of Amalek from under the heavens," *the Lord related to Moses*. "Even Amalek will forget about his monumental defeat!"

"Do you mean that Joshua and the Israelites will never be able to remember the nefarious Amalek and the battle Joshua had had with him and his meek wimpy shepherds?" Moses asked the Lord. "You said You' were going to blot out the memory of Amalek, didn't you?"

"No you bungling imbecile!" the Lord boomed. "I meant that Amalek won't ever remember being totally routed and vanquished by Joshua but Joshua and the Israelites certainly will!"

Moses also built an altar there *that was never again altered*. He called it Yahweh-nissi, *which means something like, "Did all of this bizarre insane bullshit really happen here?"*

Moses then said *to his drinking-buddy comrades*, "The Lord takes in hand His banner, *which angels shall carry across the sky advertising His unparalleled accomplishments*. The Lord will war against Amalek *and his puny shepherds* throughout the centuries, *although Amalek is a mere mortal and the dirty bastard will soon die*. Hey Aaron, Ben and Hur," Moses said, "Pass another full cup of red wine over here!"

Chapter Eighteen
"Meeting with Jethro"

Now Moses' father-in-law, the *honorable* priest of Midian, Jethro Reuel heard *via the Semitic gossip grapevine* of all *the wonders* that God had done for *the sage* Moses and for the *ungrateful* people of Israel. He was aware how the Lord had brought Israel out of slavery *and how He' had malevolently made them suffer walking around for weeks in the hot sultry desert of Sin, thirsty, starving and discouraged.*

So his *(Moses')* father-in-law Jethro *Reuel* took along Zipporah, Moses' *devious* wife, whom Moses had sent back to him *(Jethro Reuel) because she was an adulterous slut having numerous affairs in everyone's tent except that of Moses', who incidentally was too busy helping his people and consequently was too damned tired to screw his unfaithful horny wife.* Zipporah took along her two sons' to Midian, *who just happened to look a lot like Aaron and a little like Ben and Hur.*

One of these *offspring* was called *(not named)* Gershom, for he said, "I am a stranger in a foreign land, *and I am also a stranger in all lands. There's definitely no one in the world 'stranger' than I am."* That was the most important thing Gershom ever said in his whole damned insignificant uneventful life!

The other *more precocious son* was called *(not named)* Eliezer. For he *(Eliezer)* said, "My father's God is my helper, *just like He' has helped the Israelites be stranded in the sultry eastern desert walking on hot uncomfortable sand amidst poisonous snakes and lethal scorpions five hundred extra miles to Canaan than needed,"* Eliezer said to nobody in particular. "God has rescued me from the anonymous Pharaoh's sword when actually I was more content to stay in Egypt and be exposed to some semblance of civilization that was ten full echelons above prehistoric Stone Age Israelite shepherding."

Together with Moses' wife and sons, then, his 'father-in-law' *(who was more like a father-outlaw)* Jethro Reuel came to him *(Moses)* in the desert where he was encamped near the *ominous* mountain of God. He *(Jethro Reuel)* sent word to Moses, "I, *Jethro Reuel*, your father-in-law *in case you have forgotten who the hell I am*, am coming to you, along with your *slutty* wife and her *(not yours)* two *disillusioned delinquent jerk off* sons."

Moses went out to meet his father-in-law, bowed down before him *to avoid immediate vomiting,* and kissed him *all over his perfumed countenance.*

"Phooey!" Jethro screamed. "Did you just lick all of the infected dirty toes on your dusty smelly feet a few minutes ago, you retarded double-jointed freak! That's exactly what your despicable breath smells like!" Jethro hollered at his son-in-law Moses. "And did you lick your stenchy asshole too before giving me that disgusting unwelcome wet slobber on my lips and face? Do it again and I'll smash you a dozen consecutive times right in the kisser!"

Having *formally* greeted each other, they *(Moses and Jethro Reuel)* went into the *nearby* tent. *Jethro entered the enclosure to ascertain that Moses had washed his feet good with vinegar and that Moses had diligently scrubbed his armpits, crotch and anus with vinegar, too.*

Moses then told his *often aloof* father-in-law of all that the Lord had done to Pharaoh and to the Egyptians for the sake of Israel *so that He' could promise the Israelites Canaan and then almost kill them all in the hot sultry desert while they were taking the un-scenic route from the oral sex brothel in Succoth to there.*

"You should have stayed at Succoth at the famous oral sex brothel," Father Reuel criticized. "Succoth's located right next to Fuck-off! It's been there even before the time of Sodom and Gomorrah!"

Moses informed Jethro Reuel, "At Succoth we were 'all blown' off course all the way to Shittim, where we all suddenly and mysteriously contracted severe chronic diarrhea." Moses then recounted all of the *mis-adventurous* 'hardships' they had to endure, and then Father-in-law Jethro Reuel bluntly told Moses that there aren't any 'ships' on the desert, 'hard' or otherwise. "You must have been hallucinating and seeing mirages out in the hot sultry eastern desert due to dehydration," the priest of Midian told his fatigued and disoriented son-in-law.

"Did the Lord come to the Israelites' rescue after destroying the Pharaoh and the Egyptian army?" Jethro asked his nonplussed son-in-law.

"Yes," the baffled Moses proudly stated. "He gave us manna from heaven after nearly starving us and then water from a rock after nearly making us die from thirst, you know, the typical old shit coming from the Lord's sadistic methods of cruel and unusual suffering exclusively implemented against His' most faithful worshipers," the prophet complained. "He always nearly kills us and then He' finally relents, has a change of heart and then begrudgingly saves us. That seems to be His' weird repetitious pattern."

Jethro got an idea from Moses' rendition of events. "Blessed be the Lord'," he said *out of force of habit*, "Who has rescued His' *fickle* people from the Pharaoh and from the *attacking* Egyptians. *If it was I instead of you I would have let the bastards and the bitches starve and get bitten by vipers out in the hot sultry eastern desert.* Now I know that the Lord is a deity great beyond any other," *Jethro piously and pompously maintained.* "Your account is adequate testimony!"

"Is He' now your chief Deity?" Moses asked the chief' high priest of Midian. "Have you satisfactorily mastered the intricate process of deity elimination?"

"He's definitely gone up a few notches on my list of gods, that's for damned sure!" Jethro Reuel intimated. "I want to make the Lord more than just a local mountain God," Jethro informed Moses. "I want Him' to go big' time and be worshiped all the way from the Nile to the Euphrates. The Lord is going to be the biggest and most famous God around these parts and you and I are going to make that happen, yes sireee."

"Specifically what did you have in mind?" Moses skeptically asked Jethro, who had a reputation for being the biggest conniver and the loudest braggart in the region. "Give me some particulars to evaluate."

"The Lord took occasion of their' *(the Israelites)* being dealt with insolently to deliver the people from the power of the Egyptians. *Now is our chance to capitalize on this fortuitous news and take religion national,"* Jethro revealed. "It's a once in a lifetime opportunity I am offering you."

"Could you be more detailed in your presentation?" Moses diplomatically asked. "I feel my sensitive bowels becoming loose at the mention of any prospective business proposal. You might have to give me a prospectus on your up and coming business plan."

"Certainly," Jethro amiably concurred. "I am a priest, but still I have to keep my flocks of sheep and I must shepherd them to make just an average nondescript living," Jethro confided to Moses. "If we can take religion national, or maybe even international, you Moses and I as your useful agent and manager, then I won't have to work for a modest living as a humble shepherd any more," Jethro disclosed. "You and I could manipulate the people through fear and hope. The fools fear the unknown and they fear the Lord. We will *exploit those obvious weaknesses and have the public support us while we do nothing but exploit their vain hopes and profit (prophet) by their fears."*

"What you say has plenty of merit," Moses agreed, "because if any people ever needed to get screwed and be exploited, it's those asshole Israelites, that's for friggin' sure! Most of them are dumber than dumb and have total shit for brains!"

Then Jethro, the *ambitious* father-in-law of Moses *(Do we need to be retold and reminded?)* brought a holocaust *(in the Old Testament, holocausts were good things)* and other sacrifices to God. Aaron came with all of the feeble and senile elders of Israel, *who all thought that they were being led to an outhouse to either piss their kidneys out or to take serious dumps.* But they were *delegated and* brought by Aaron to participate with Moses' father-in-law in the meal before God.

The next day Moses sat in judgment for the people, who waited about him from morning until evening *just as the slippery Jethro Reuel had meticulously planned and conspired with Moses. Phase one of Jethro's elaborate scheme had been successfully launched.*

When his *(Moses')* father-in-law saw all that he *(Moses)* was doing for the people, he inquired *in accordance with his deliberate plot with Moses*, "What sort of thing is that that you are doing for the people? Why do you sit alone *and fart out loud* while all the people have to stand about you from morning until evening? *Don't you or they have anything better to do than to fart around and smell each other's noxious gas?"*

Moses answered his father-in-law, "The people come to me to consult God, for they believe and know that I am God's middleman power broker between Him' and them," Moses articulated to Jethro Reuel. "Whenever they have a disagreement they come to me to have me settle the matter between *or amongst* them and make known to them God's *transcendent* decisions and regulations. *These Israelites are really vain and stupid shit' heads who need constant guidance and perpetual psychological reinforcement,"* Moses indicated to Jethro. *"They must be the biggest idiots in the whole universe, well, at least in the whole local galaxy, anyway."*

"You are not acting wisely *or judiciously*," his father-in-law replied *to Moses in accordance with the fundamentals of their great scheme.* "You will surely wear yourself out, and not only yourself but also these people *(gullible vain Israelite nincompoops)* with you. Moses, the task is too heavy with you," *Jethro slyly concluded and shared.* "You cannot do it alone. *That's where I come in,"* the slick priest of Midian deftly offered Moses his greedy, opportunistic, illustrious services.

"Er, get to the point," Moses nervously requested. "I'm now the Main Man around here, but to tell you the truth Jethro it's taken a lot of zip out of me just like your daughter Zipporah used to do. How can I escape all of this crazy responsibility that is slowly but surely strangulating me?"

"Now listen to me *Moses*, and I will give you some *sagacious and shrewd* advice, that God may be with you," *Jethro Reuel coyly recommended.* "Act as the people's representative before God, bringing to them whatever they have to say. Enlighten them in regard to the decisions and regulations *that these misguided assholes so desperately need*," Jethro continued, "showing them how they are to live and what they are to do. *The smartest one among them is a stupid dolt by any accepted standard of mental measurement!*"

"But I will still be overburdened advising a half million retards and mentally challenged, emotionally deficient dumbbells just the way I am doing now," Moses told and balked to Jethro. "I see no difference between your suspect plan and what the hell I'm doing right this minute."

"But Moses," Jethro interrupted, "you should look among all the people for able and God-fearing men, trustworthy men' who hate dishonest gain, and set them as officers over groups of thousands, of hundreds, of fifties and tens," *Jethro said like an ambitious, covetous, possessed maniac.* "The whole key to my strategy is that these naïve men must be God-fearing. That means they're probably also sincere, honest and gullible and will follow our instructions without questioning our selfish motives. For as you know Moses, your integrity and my dignity can both easily fit inside the same thimble."

"Hey, I get it now!" Moses joyously and triumphantly shouted. "You and I will establish and set up a massive religious bureaucracy, with layer upon layer of honest and God-fearing church officials and priests governing for us," Moses elatedly noted. "You and I could be away fishing in Mesopotamia or vacationing to Crete or Thebes or Lesbos and everything will be working like clockwork in our vast corporation during our many absences!" Moses exclaimed.

"Moses, let these men *(bureaucrats and priests and priests that are bureaucrats)* render decisions for the people in ordinary cases. More important cases should be referred to you *and to me for judgment,* but all the lesser cases the priests and the bureaucrats can settle *all by* themselves. *Money will be gained to finance our enterprise through donations and contributions to us in the Lord's supreme Name. What perfection Moses! We will have deftly initiated the perfect scam!"*

"We will both be rich without working hard at all for our abundant shekels!" Moses observed and laughed. "You will no longer have to tend your sheep for a living and I will no longer have to listen to the Hebrews' trite bullshit!"

"That's right, Moses," Jethro acknowledged. "You and I will both be shepherds, but not of sheep. We will be shepherds of people, the dumb and gullible Israelites', who will gladly pay us handsomely to sustain our luxuries and hedonistic habits, just to avoid the Lord's wrath, the superstitious idle dunces," Jethro Reuel confided to his receptive son-in-law. "Moses, that's why we need layers of God-fearing bureaucrats to serve as a buffer between us and the fucked-up Israelites!" the high priest of Midian persuasively lectured. "Those asshole lunatics with kill the religious bureaucrats before they can ever get to us!"

"Jethro, I'm really glad that you visited me with this extremely intelligent corporate structure idea," Moses thanked his visitor. "It sure beats work, and it will be easy to organize and put into action. Our comfortable lifestyle will be guaranteed by the weak-minded Israelites' fear of God and their hope for a better future. What an ingenious idea that is thoroughly disingenuous! Your admirable alacrity is to be commended!"

"Thus Moses, your burden will be lightened, since they *(the new and honest God-fearing bureaucrats and priests that will govern the God-fearing Israelites in the novel religious corporate business model) will bear it for you.* If you do this, when God gives you orders you will be able to stand the strain," Jethro attested, "and all these *dumb-ass* people will go home satisfied *with empty pockets. Ha, ha, ha!"*

"Jethro Reuel rules!" Moses yelped and boomed. "But remember Jeffy baby, I'm the big CEO of this tax-exempt religious corporation and you're just the puppet President."

Moses followed the *sound* advice of *Jethro Reuel* his father-in-law and did all that he had suggested. He picked out able men from all Israel and put them in charge of the people as officers over groups of thousands, of hundreds, of fifties, and of tens. *This is why in most church hierarchies' "denominations" stands for different religious sects and orders in the overall organization as well as the levels of moneys in the governments' distribution of legal tender bills or coins. The bottom line of 'organized' (corporate) religion is that it is all about "denominations" of money, just like the day-to-day practice in any other ordinary large business.*

They *(the honest and gullible bureaucratic officials and priests)* rendered decisions for the people in all ordinary cases. The more difficult 'cases' *of wine, beer, sex and perfume* they referred to Moses *and to Jethro*, but all of the lesser *quantities of wine, beer, sex and perfume* they settled *and divvied* among themselves.

Then Moses bid farewell to his *imaginative* father-in-law *without even seeing or talking to his slutty pig wife and his two degenerate sons.* Jethro then went off to his own country, *forgetting that he had come to the Israelite camp with his daughter Zipporah and with her sons Gershom and Eliezer, inadvertently leaving them behind among the God-fearing but totally fucked-up imbecilic Israelites.*

Chapter Nineteen
"Arrival at Sinai"

In the third *nameless* month after their *(Moses and the Israelites')* departure from the land of Egypt, on its first *name*less day, the Exodus came to the desert of Sinai, *near the famous twin mountains, Mt. Sinai and its neighboring "sneezing mountain" commonly known as Mt. Sinus.* After the journey from Rephidim to the *barren* desert of Sinai, they *(the wandering Hebrews)* pitched camp, *which was in antiquity an advanced stage of hurling and throwing tents back and forth.*

While Israel was encamped here (*there*) in front of the *immense twin*-mountain*s, Moses went up Mt. Sinai by mistake searching for grass to wipe his running nose and his running ass he had gotten while mistakenly scaling up Mt. Sinus.* Then the Lord called to him and said, "Thus shall you say to the house of Jacob, tell the Israelites: 'You have seen for yourselves how I *have* treated *(killed, massacred and drowned)* the Egyptians and how I bore you up on eagle wings and brought you here to Myself'."

"You think that having calluses all over my feet from trekking across the hot desert for hundreds of needless miles is an 'uplifting' experience?" Moses yelled up to the visible mountaintop. *"If You' think having all of the Israelites grumble and mumble about my weak leadership is being 'airborne' like an eagle up here to this mountain I am climbing,"* Moses bitterly said, *"then Your' Almighty vision must be horribly impaired just like mine is!"*

The indefatigable Lord (as usual) ignored Moses' protests. "Therefore *Moses,"* the Lord then continued, "if you hearken to My' voice and keep My' divine covenant, you shall be my special possession."

"Oh great! That's really quite splendid!" Moses screamed at *the sky before wiping his dripping nose with his right hand. "I was just a slave of the Egyptians and now You' want to make me Your' special possession! I should have died in ultimate joy being blown away back in Succoth before I ever knew anything about shitty Shittim. Oh Lord, just one more erection please before I perish! I plead for just one more erection!"*

"Moses, you *(you and the lackluster Israelites)* are dearer to Me' than all other people, though all the earth is Mine'," the Lord *obtusely* answered.

"Nobody else wants to have anything at all to do with You'," Moses related to the all-knowing Lord. *"The other more civilized*

civilizations avoid these two deserted mountains like they avoid overcrowded leper' colonies."

"Moses, I overheard your conversations with Jethro Reuel and I liked what you two nimrods had discussed," the Lord admitted. "You shall be to Me' a *widespread* kingdom of priests, *a bureaucratic holy nation with lots of successive middle-management layers.* That is what you must tell the Israelites, *but scrupulously disguise it as hope, religion and fear of God."*

So Moses wiped his leaking nose again and then went and summoned the *feeble and senile* elders of the people. When he set before them all *that the bisexual pedophile Jethro Reuel and the Supreme Lord* had ordered him *(Moses)* to tell them *(the feeble and senile elders),* the people *(the elders)* all answered together, *"We don't give a shit anymore about either living or breathing,"* they all chanted in unison. "Everything the Lord has said we will do. *Of course, in spite of our gross senility, we still realize that all of this illogical bullshit is actually coming from you and from that notorious faggot pedophile Jethro Reuel!"*

Then Moses brought to the Lord the response of the people, *leaving out the important part about "that notorious faggot pedophile Jethro Reuel."*

The Lord also told him *(the sneezing Moses),* "I am coming to you in a dense cloud *since you and your head are always dense with your mind in a thick fog.* When the people hear Me' speaking with you, they will always have faith in you also. *They will be 'mistified'! Ha, ha, ha! 'Mistified'! Get it Moses! They will be absolutely mystified"*

When Moses then had reported to the Lord the response of the *pathetic apathetic* people, the Lord added *all of the equation's details with His' mental calculator.* "Go to the people and have them sanctify themselves today and tomorrow. Make them wash their garments *and their stenchy rear ends,"* the Lord imperatively commanded Moses. "Be ready for the third *nameless* day. On the third *nameless* day the Lord will come down on Mt. Sinai before the eyes of all the *sneezing* people *being affected by the germs from Mt. Sinus.* Set *proper* limits for the people all around the mountain, *and make sure the idiots don't wander off outside the cordoned off area."*

"Can't You' just get the Canaanites to worship You' instead of the uncooperative Israelites?" Moses grumbled and mumbled to the cotton-like clouds. "You always come out of the clear blue sky and then ruin my miserable day by making it more miserable than it was a minute before!"

"Tell them, *(the Israelites), the Lord said,* "take care not to go up the mountain, *for I will give you all vertigo and you will clumsily tumble and somersault down to the ground in a massive human landslide.* The people are not even to touch the *sacred* mountain's base, *so I thought I would touch base with you on that off-limits' base matter.*"

"*Are there any other relevant instructions?*" Moses asked in a very peeved voice. "*The people down below and I both agree it was better being slaves of the Egyptians than to be what You' describe as Your' special possessions!*"

"If anyone *dares* touches the mountain, 'he' *(Women weren't 'anybody' according to the ancient prehistoric Hebrew oral and oral sex tradition)* must be put to death *(women weren't even worthy of execution).* No hand shall touch him *(the base male violators who dare to touch the base of the sacred mountain).* He must be stoned to death or killed by arrows. Such a one, man or beast, must not be allowed to live. *If provoked by disobedience I'll turn into a gigantic burning bush and scorch all the violators into embers!*"

"*Holy Smokes Lord!*" Moses exclaimed with one of his favorite responses. "*But the men and the beasts would rather ascend Mt. Sinus and sneeze and cough to death than climb up Your' wretched mountain!*" Moses squawked. "*They would rather choke during a painful allergy attack than ascend up here to the wasteland summit of Mt. Sinai!*"

"Only when the ram's horn resounds *giving the all clear sign* must they go up the mountain," the Lord added. "*That is My' new directive*!"

Then Moses came down from the mountain *(Mt. Sinai, situated next to Mt. Sinus)* and had them *(the Israelites)* sanctify themselves by washing their garments *and by wiping their foul dirty asses.* He warned them *(the horny men),* "Be ready for the third *unnamed* day. Have no intercourse with women, *but you may imagine that you are still in Succoth and getting blown away while receiving some good head from the highly-skilled ladies practicing their indispensable trade there'."* Moses, however, said nothing to the disenfranchised women, who all wished that the nuisance patriarch had been staying in Fuck-off.

On the morning of the third *nameless day* there were peals of thunder and lightning *(lightning peals?)*, and a *dark* heavy cloud *formed* over the mountain, and a very loud trumpet blast *was heard that even aroused the multitude of strumpets abounding in the Israelite camp.* All of the people in the camp trembled *from being overly aroused.*

But Moses led the people out of the camp to meet God, and they stationed themselves at the foot of the mountain, *for the mountain had only one leg.*

Mt. Sinai was all wrapped in smoke, for the Lord came down upon it with fire, *thinking that if He' destroyed His' native home, it was no big deal. He would just rebuild it or simply move to neighboring Mt. Sinus and wear an oxygen mask.* The *billowing* smoke rose from it as though *wafting* from a furnace and the whole mountain trembled violently, *imitating the base Israelites stationed at its base, who were also trembling from being overly aroused and excited.*

The trumpet blast grew louder and louder *and everyone heard it loud and clear.* While Moses was speaking, God was answering him with thunder *in thundering words spoken in short but effective one-word sentences.*

When the Lord came down *(floated)* to the top of Mt. Sinai *all of the Israelites came down with the flu from being too exposed to Mt. Sinus*. The Lord summoned Moses to the top of the mountain *(Mt. Sinai)* and Moses went *(how about climbed or clambered?)* up to Him'.

Then the Lord told Moses, "Go down and warn the people not to 'break through' toward the Lord in order to see Him'. *I don't want the Israelites to have any major 'breakthroughs' or they might invent science and technology, become too cynical and then not believe in the Lord.* Otherwise, many of them will be struck down *as I kick their mangy butts really good!"*

"Why did I have to climb this steep ugly mountain to only learn that I must then clamber down it?" Moses typically complained. "You could have had the courtesy to thunder those trite words down to me!"

"The priests, too, who approach the Lord must sanctify themselves, *especially that perverted pedophile and reputed child molester Jethro Reuel!"* the Lord commanded. "Otherwise, I will vent My' anger upon the priests *and smoke them good with an accurately tossed lightning bolt!"*

Moses said to the Lord, "The people cannot follow me up to Mt. Sinai for You' Yourself' warned us to set limits around the mountain to make it sacred."

"I was just testing you to see if you remembered My' supreme instructions," the Lord indicated to Moses. *"I wanted to see if you were paying attention to My' words of splendor! Does that answer your dumb mortal question?"*

'Long live the next Pharaoh,' Moses secretly thought. *"May he and his army stay away from the unpredictable Red Sea! The Lord is reputed to have a new Air Force consisting of fifty destructive Angels of Death!"*

The Lord *then* repeated *to Moses*, "Go down now! *(Descend Mt. Sinai, which you had just climbed like a silly old fool while you almost had a massive cardiac arrest!).* Then come up again with Aaron. But the *middle-management* priests and the people must not break-through to come up to the Lord. *For any major 'break-throughs' might lead to freedom of thought and then to the development of science and technology,"* the Lord conveyed to Moses. *"The Israelites might then discover new false gods and contraptions to worship. I will then have to vent my anger upon them and upon any major 'modern break-through' they might discover or invent."*

So Moses went down the mountain to the people and told them this, *but the people would rather listen to each other farting from the diarrhea they had contracted back in Shittim.*

Chapter Twenty
"The Ten Commandments"

Then God delivered to Moses *what the leader of the Israelites described as The Ten Demandments, which later became known as* the *more user-friendly* Ten Commandments:
I, the Lord, am your God, Who' brought you out of the *condemned* land of Egypt, that place of slavery, *and you were professionally led to a hostile hot sultry eastern desert where you almost starved to death. I mercifully took you and your dregs out of slavery in Egypt so that the Israelites could be My' special exclusive possessions."*

"Is there really a distinction as to the various types of slavery?" Moses sincerely requested knowing. "Is Yours' any better than the Pharaoh's?"

The Lord looked upon Moses "with deaf ears." Then He' said, "You shall not have other gods besides Me' *Moses, for I am THE LORD of the universe that dwells as a lonely Hermit on this remote desert mountain hundreds of miles away from any remnants of civilization.* You shall not *idly* carve *dolls or* idols for yourselves in the shape of anything in the sky or on the earth below or under the waters beneath the earth," *the Lord distinctly commanded. "If you do those naughty bad things, I will quickly become very envious and resentful and then visit you and the hapless Israelites with such mass destruction you cannot imagine."*

"So what else is new?" Moses countered. "It all sounds like the same old past rot simply repeated in the present and in the future! Try to be a little more original next time."

"You shall not bow down before them *(the false god-idols)* or worship them," the Lord said. "For I am the Lord your God, and I am a jealous God, inflicting punishment for their' *(the inconsistent Israelites')* fathers' wickedness on the children of those' who hate Me', *right* down to the third and fourth generation."

"Now why or how could anyone down here on earth possibly hate You'?" Moses responded with a degree of indignation and sarcasm. "Especially all the living Egyptians and the accursed Israelites and the innocent Canaanites', who all wish that You' would permanently move to another world somewhere far from this repugnant earth that You' claim to have created!"

The unruffled and undeterred Lord was so engrossed in His' own sensational rhetoric that He' was unaware of Moses saying anything at all. "But bestowing mercy down to the thousandth generation, *if men still have sperm and women still manufacture eggs in that distant era*," the Lord *emphatically* stated, "on the children' who love Me' and keep *My' Demandments, er, I'm sorry there Moses*, My' Ten Commandments *I shall bless and favor*."

"Exactly, what are these new Demandments, er, Commandments?" Moses laconically asked. "*I hope they aren't too severe or Draconian! I mean, it's bad enough that the Israelites now lead a Spartan existence without much in the way of material comforts!*"

"You shall not take the Name of the Lord your God in vain *no matter how frustrated you become at My' casually playing power games with your meaningless lives*," the all-powerful Voice stated. "For the Lord will not leave unpunished him' who takes His' *(My')* name in vain."

"*I know a half million Israelites' who are doomed to immediate extinction by Your' current threat!*" Moses answered the Lord. "*You' have been cursed and cussed by Your' chosen people many more times than You' have cursed the Israelites and the Egyptians with plagues, suffering and illusionary 'hard ship' mirages in the hot sultry eastern desert.*"

"Moses, remember to keep holy the Sabbath' day," the Lord reminded *his thoroughly confused listener*. "Six days you may labor and do all your work, but the seventh day is sacred and belongs to the Lord your God."

"*That's when Jethro Reuel and I can cash in big on the seventh day donations and contributions,*" Moses confessed to the Almighty Lord. "*We can become filthy rich without working, a foolproof fantastic pyramid-scheme that even the new anonymous Pharaoh would envy!*"

"No work may be done then either by you *down by the bayou with Homer (a future Greek) and Jethro (priest of Midian)*. Your son or daughter may not work, or your male or female slave *or sex slave of either sex may not work either,*" the Lord sternly lectured. "No work shall be done by the beast or by the *legal or illegal* alien' who lives with you, *even if you regard your ugly slutty wife as a beastly alien.*"

"*I don't think these new rules are going to set too well with the average Israelite's psyche,*" Moses sincerely replied shaking his head side to side to illustrate his obvious displeasure and doubt. "*The people don't even like Jethro Reuel's rules let alone these new ones established by You' nowhere near a bayou!*"

"They aren't rules!" the Lord bellowed. "They are laws! My' personal Commandments!" He' thundered with menacing authority. "In six *magnificent* days the Lord made heaven and earth, the sea and all' that is in them."

"Why do You' keep talking about Yourself' and Your' various achievements in the third person' Voice when You should be speaking to me in the first person?" Moses criticized. "How are the Israelites going to master fundamental grammar and communications' skills when You' keep abusing the language almost as effectively as You' have abused the Hebrews since the time of Abraham?"

"But on the third day, He' *(I)* rested," *the Lord proceeded as He' described an event from the distant past.* "That is why the Lord has blessed the Sabbath' day and has decided to make it holy! *Now at least I have named one day of the week for all to be able to know its identity."*

"That proves that You' too have limitations if You' had to rest after creating the earth and the sea after six days of labor," Moses perceptively recognized. "You' too are not quite as immortal and invincible as You' Lord have portended and pretended to be! It seems that You' too have Your' limitations!"

The Lord proceeded with His' eloquent repertoire in spite of Moses' justified objections. "Honor your father and your mother that you may have a long life in the land that the Lord, your God is giving you," *the Voice emphasized.* "Honor them no matter how much they may have used and abused you in the past!"

"Yeah!" agreed Moses, *"just like the Israelites have to pay homage and servitude to You' for mercilessly busting our stones and deflating our women's tits for all these hundreds of years since Abraham 'erred' and took his family out of Ur. How much more travail can we endure?"*

"You shall not kill *or imitate the way that I took care of the Egyptians, the entire population of the earth during the time of Noah, the spectacular destruction of Sodom and Gomorrah and the brutal massacre of the previously invincible Egyptian army crossing the Red Sea."*

"You shall not commit adultery, *and I am still investigating into other perverted sexual behavior such as but not limited to pre-marital sex, the licentious deportments of the gay and lesbian community and sexually active teenagers having wanton sex with married adults."*

"You shall not steal, *especially after you confiscate the land of Canaan from the Canaanites as I have continually promised Abraham, Isaac, Jacob and now promise you and the illiterate and loathsome Israelites."*

"You shall not bear false witness against your neighbor, especially when I happen to be your neighbor. *The only exceptions are when your neighbors happen to be the conniving Canaanites, the insane family of Amalek or the berserk relatives of Egyptian aristocrats. Then in those special cases' bear all the false witness you want."*

"*In addition Moses*, You shall not covet your neighbor's *(Israelite's)* house, *but if your neighbor is a Canaanite, a follower of Amalek or an Egyptian, become instantly prejudiced and burn the damned residence to the ground if you so desire."*

"You shall not covet your neighbor's *(Israelite's)* wife, *but if your neighbor is a Canaanite, that cad Amalek or a crazy Egyptian, do anything you want to your neighbor and to his good-looking wife.* Do not covet his male or female slave, nor his ox or his ass *or his male or female slave's ass*. Do not covet anything else *(goods)* that belongs to him *(an Israelite), but if your neighbor is a Canaanite, Amalek or a dastardly Egyptian, then kindly ignore the sacred principles associated with this last Demandment, er, I mean Commandment."*

When the people *(the ingrate, self-centered Hebrews)* witnessed the *grand finale* thunder and lightning' *demonstrations*, the trumpet blast and the mountain smoking *a gigantic marijuana joint*, they all feared and trembled *simultaneously just like they all always spoke and chanted at the same time*. So they *(the easily astounded Israelites)* took up a position much farther away and said to Moses *all together from a mile distant*, "You speak to us, and we will listen. *We don't want to be blasted with lightning and instantaneously electrocuted into another unknown dimension by our unpredictable and erratic-behaving' Supreme Lord.* Or else we shall die, *which on second thought, might be a blessing and the correct solution to the immediate problems associated with living!"* all half million or so desert-dwellers and meanderers recited together to Moses in a discordant chorus from a full mile away.

Moses answered the *frightened moronic* people, "Do not be afraid, *you petrified stupid assholes!* God has come to you only to test you *(your mettle)* and put His' fear upon you, lest you should sin *and enjoy yourselves for the first time in your hideous condemned* boring lives. I've concluded that God wants to determine if you all have 'heavy mettle'!"

Still the *apprehensive* people remained at a distance, *not knowing who was crazier, Moses or their' Lord thundering away inside a dark rain' cloud on the horizon.* Moses then approached the cloud where God was, *and the New Age patriarch was virtually in a trance.*

The Lord told Moses, "Thus shall you speak *to My' chosen people,* the *lame-minded* Israelites: 'You have seen for yourselves that I have spoken to you from Heaven', *which presently is all Mine' and not a place that I wish to share with you' lowly Israelites dead or alive right now. Truthfully', the Lord said, 'Heaven is too good for idiots of low ilk such as yours!* But I warn you, do not make anything to rank with Me'; neither gods of silver nor gods of gold shall you make for yourselves'."

"*It sounds like You' are a little too paranoid about experiencing competition,*" Moses challenged. "*Slightly neurotic and jealous too, if I may add!*"

"An altar of earth you shall make for Me' *that shall never be altered.* "Upon it you shall sacrifice your holocausts, *for as you' know Moses the Lord likes and values holocausts here in the Old Testament. That, however, may drastically change in the future.* Sacrifice your peace offerings too, your' sheep and your oxen *and your 'oxen-morons'! Sacrifice everything that you deem worthwhile to Me!" the Lord haughtily declared.* "In whatever place *or temple* I choose for the remembrance of My' name I will come to you and bless you."

"*Your blessings are really much like wicked curses,*" Moses injected into the rather interesting exchange, "*and if the Israelites and I could have our druthers, we would prefer to be cursed rather than be blessed 'by You' on any bayou. Then some good might result from the curse you would be administering.*"

"If you make an altar of stone for Me'," *the Lord interrupted the almost delirious New Age patriarch,* "do not build it of cut stone, for by putting *(a human)* tool to it you *therefore* desecrate it. *I really don't desire to see man develop tools, machines and weapons that might rival My' supremacy over the primitive post Stone Age pastoral shepherding Israelites. That's why I had a problem with the Egyptians. They had civilization, science and technology!*"

"*Anything else to discuss for me to consider Boss?*" Moses gingerly inquired.

"Yes, *as a matter of fact there is* Moses," the Lord replied. "You shall not go up by steps to my altar, on which you must not be indecently uncovered. *Whatever you do Moses, watch your damned step!"*

Chapter Twenty-one
"Laws Regarding Slaves"

"These are the rules you shall lay before them *(the erratic, erotic, neurotic Israelites) regarding new and used slaves,"* the Lord', Who' *fully endorsed the institution of slavery, advocated to* Moses. "When you purchase a *new or used* Hebrew slave, *feel his biceps and kick his shins to inspect and determine his general fitness,"* the Lord advised. "He is to serve you for six years, but in the seventh year, he shall be given his freedom without cost *or obligation and with no money down and no easy monthly payments to make,"* the Lord said.

"So, let's get this straight right from the get go," Moses reviewed. "It's perfectly all right for Hebrews to have other Hebrews for slaves for seven years max'. So Hebrew slavery is only a temporary seven-year condition, sort of like a seven-year itch," the patriarch keenly observed and concluded.

"That is correct," the Lord concurred. "If he *(the slave)* comes into service alone, he shall leave *his obligation* alone; if he comes with a wife, his wife shall leave with him after seven years, *if they could still tolerate one another and coexist'*, which as you know isn't always the case."

"That sort of makes sense and seems to be somewhat fair," Moses granted. "Hebrew slaves shouldn't have to slave their whole lives for others, even if the others happen to be self-righteous Hebrews."

"But if the slave's master gives him a wife and she bears him 'sons or daughters' *(he can't have both),"* the Lord prescribed and mandated, "the woman and children shall remain the master's property and the man shall leave alone *his master's house as a bachelor again*."

"Wow! What a fringe benefit to the male Hebrew slave population!" Moses replied. "He can screw around for seven years like there's no tomorrow, have scads of kids and then get off the hook without any family debts or responsibilities anchoring him down when he leaves town. And the master has more slaves to serve him just for allowing his Hebrew male slave to screw around and reproduce all he wants! It's a win-win situation for the former slave and also for his former master!"

The Lord had a corollary to his law, however. "If then the slave declares *with good intention,* 'I am devoted to my master and my wife and children; I will not go free,' his master shall bring him to

God *(Me', the One Who's talking to you right now)* and there, at the door or doorstep, he shall pierce his ear with an awl. *This symbol of permanent slavery he shall keep as a slave forever, even though his ears will rot right off his pathetic body after a few unknown months when he's in the grave."*

"No Hebrew' slave in his right mind will go for such a silly deal," Moses stated. "If he (the emancipated Hebrew slave) chooses his wife, kid and master over freedom and liberation from financial obligations, then that slave indeed deserves to be a permanent slave the rest of his freakin' life."

"When a man sells his daughter as a slave," the Lord *expounded and* continued, "she shall not go free *after seven* years as male slaves do, *for males will always have preferential treatment in My' religion, just like the scenario which exists among the Israelites in their non-slave existence.* But if the master' who had destined her for himself dislikes her, he shall let her be redeemed *as if the slave girl were a cheap bargain coupon in a bizarre bazaar."*

"Lord, pardon the awkward expression," Moses said, "but that's all pretty kosher. The master decides the fate of the female slave', who is not given a viable choice like the privileged male slave has. That is pure unadulterated chauvinism, plain and simple. I am very happy and delighted to see that the Lord like myself' is a dedicated chauvinist!"

"But Moses," the Lord provided, "The master has no right to sell her *(the Hebrew slave girl)* to a *pagan* foreigner, since he has broken faith with her. If he destines the slave girl to his son, he shall then treat her like his daughter, *who also is anyway treated as if she were a slave."*

"So technically speaking," Moses surmised and reported back to the Lord, "she' is still a slave even though she isn't classified as a slave. Pretty nifty religious propaganda to be propagating, I must admit!"

"If he *(the master or the son of the master who might also be a son-of-a-bitch)* takes another wife, he shall provide her *(the Hebrew slave girl who must slave her life away whether she is an official slave or not)* food, clothing, or her conjugal *sex* rights *with the master. Even lowly male and female slaves have to enjoy themselves once in a while."*

"What if those three specified things (food, clothing and conjugal sex rights) are not supplied by the master?" Moses requested.

"If the master does not grant her these three *necessary* things," the Lord added, "she shall be given her freedom absolutely, without *any* cost to her. *But the chances of that happening are nil and not, and nil left town. And Moses, there are other applicable laws besides those of slavery that a good Hebrew must honor,*" the Lord elaborated. "Whoever strikes a man a mortal blow must be put to death."

"If that be the case," Moses said, *"You' Lord should have died at least a million times already for what You' had administered to the Egyptian army, to the flood victims of Noah's time and to the victimized residents of Sodom and Gomorrah."*

"These particular rules and laws pertain only to the Israelites, and I am exempt from them by virtue of Divine Rights," the Lord insisted. *"What happens to foreigners and to resident sinners are separate issues and immaterial to the subject being discussed*! He (*a legitimate Israelite*), however, who did not hunt a man down, but caused his death by an act of God, *may flee to an overcrowded place' which I have set apart for this purpose, even though I have no idea where that overcrowded place might be."*

"Then acts of God are exempt from punishment just like God is exempt from making amends because of His' Absolute Divine Rights," Moses generalized. *"You appear to have all angles covered."*

"Let's say *now Moses for argument's sake that* a man *deliberately* kills another after maliciously scheming to do so *like I had done with the Egyptians and with the sinning citizens of Sodom and Gomorrah and the other immoral violators during Noah's era,"* the Lord professed. "Then you must take that evil man even from My' altar and *immediately* put him to death. Whoever strikes his father and mother should be put to death by My' law *with you as my Sheriff and Aaron, Ben and Hur you shall marshal as your chief posse' deputies to enforce My' martial punishment."*

"Well Lord, what about cursing and kidnappers?" Moses inquired.

"Whoever curses his father or mother shall be put to death *no matter what the father and mother had done to inspire the insolent verbal reaction,"* the Lord said. "And a 'kidnapper,' it doesn't matter whether he sells his *young* victim *while he is sleeping or napping* or still has him when caught, *that violator* shall be put to death."

"These strange rules will be easier to enforce than I first thought," Moses attested, *"because Your' new no-nonsense laws*

will have already killed off over half the Israelite half million population."

"When men quarrel and one strikes the other with a stone or a fist," the Lord related to Moses, "not mortally, but enough to put him in bed *with a hot water bottle on his skull,* the one' that struck the blow shall be acquitted. *Of course, this judgment is* providing that the other man can get up and walk around *and then dance* with the help of his staff *and a team of certified nurses*."

"That's more than fair," Moses automatically agreed. "It's okay to injure someone but not okay to kill him. Arguing or quarreling in public or in private should have its built-in punishment like losing a valued relationship, and getting injured ought to teach one of the quarreling parties a strong lesson."

"Still Moses," the Lord stipulated, "he *(the winner of the fight)* must compensate him *(the bedridden and wounded loser of the altercation*) for his enforced idleness and provide for his complete cure *or recovery*."

"So in effect, the winner is punished and has to compensate the loser," Moses observed and verbalized, "and the loser is punished by public disgrace and embarrassment for losing the brawl and by sustaining his physical injury. Both parties will probably never quarrel (at least with each other) again!"

"When a man *(master)* strikes his male or female slave with a rod *(even a lightning rod during a fierce thunderstorm),* and the slave dies under his hand, he shall be *punished for electrocuting the slave or for beating him or her to a pulp,"* the austere Lord demanded. "If however, the slave survives for a day or two, he *(the sadistic master)* is not to be punished, since the slave is *merely* his own property *and had not been mortally wounded at the time of the conflict."*

"That's really very just," Moses assented. "It's perfectly fine to beat slaves into near death without killing them, but if you kill them, then you must pay the token price of justice."

"When men have a fight and hurt a pregnant woman," the Lord rambled on, "so that she suffers a miscarriage, but no further *bodily* injury, then the guilty one shall be fined as much as the woman's husband demands of him."

"How often does such an event ever happen?" Moses asked. "I've never heard of such a thing ever occurring? This absurd example You've advanced seems like major trivia happening somewhere else in Asia Minor to me. The only thing the Israelite men would be quarreling about would be bragging rights over who had knocked-up the female slave!"

"Regardless," the Lord said in a distinct contrary tone of voice, "the guilty one should pay a *token minimum* fine in the presence of *partial or impartial* judges. But if injury ensues, you shall give life for life, eye for eye, tooth for tooth, hand for hand, foot for foot, *breast for breast, penis for penis,* burn for burn, wound for wound and stripe for stripe."

"So then, it's acceptable to fight, argue and hurt one another," Moses concluded, "but if you seriously maim someone, slave or otherwise, then you probably will have to pay a fine or endure a token penalty. And fines for hurting and maiming slaves are far less than fines for hurting and maiming non-slaves. It all seems quite plausible now!"

"When a man *(master)* strikes his male or female slave in the eye and destroys the use of the eye," *the Lord told Moses,* "he shall *not make a 'spectacle' out of himself but instead* let the slave go free for compensation for the eye."

"Great!" Moses exclaimed. *"If you don't like a slave, blind him in one eye and get rid of the bothersome jerk off!"*

"If he *(the volatile, sadistic master)* knocks out a tooth of his male or female slave," the Lord insisted, "he shall let the slave go free in compensation for the tooth. *This law shall apply until dentistry is eventually developed."*

"Then if you really hate a slave," Moses reckoned, "hit him or her repeatedly in the eye and not in the damned mouth! It's all perfectly clear now. People have lots more teeth than they have eyes!"

"When an ox gores a man or a woman to death," the *'oxenmoron'* must be stoned *and rocked right out of this world,"* the Lord maintained. "Its flesh may not be eaten, *for the ox did a malicious thing, and Israelites would naturally acquire the evil aggressiveness of the belligerent ox by eating its contaminated flesh.* The owner of the *plaintiff'* ox, however, shall go unpunished."

"What if the ox had a gory history of goring prior to killing the gored man or the gored woman?" Moses alertly asked. "Should I then take the proverbial bull by the horns and have the ox stoned immediately?"

"If an ox was previously in the habit of goring people and its owner, though warned," *the Lord explained,* "and if it then kills a man or a woman *(slaves could be gored by a crazy maverick ox without any penalties resulting),* then *obviously* the *aggressive* ox must be stoned. But the *beast's* owner must also be put to death, *whether he was 'stoned' during the brutal and gory attack incident or not."*

"Are there any alternatives to that rule, or is it inflexible?" Moses asked the unusually garrulous Lord.

"If, however, a fine is imposed on the owner *by the partial or impartial judges*," the Lord divulged to Moses, "he must pay in ransom for his life whatever amount is imposed on him, *usually the cost of the ox's beef times two squared,"* the Lord mandated. "This law also applies if it is a boy or a girl *(but not a slave boy or girl)* that the *villainous* ox *viciously* gores."

"*My favorite sandal color is oxblood!*" Moses remembered and stated out of context to the Lord. "But what happens if the ox decides to gore a slave and not attack and mutilate a regular-type privileged Israelite?"

"If the ox gores a male or female slave," the Lord said after a moment of deep contemplation, "the *unfortunate* owner *of the berserk maverick ox* must pay the *lucky* owner of the slave thirty shekels of silver, and the ox must *then* be stoned *if it hadn't been already."*

"*Are there any other major rules that You'* would like to expound upon?" Moses asked the Lord. "It's getting way past my bedtime."

"Yes," the Lord affirmed. "*This one happens all the time.* When a man uncovers or digs a cistern and does not cover it over again," *the* Lord said to Moses, "and should an ass or an ox *or a team of oxen or a lot of asses* fall into it, the owner of the cistern must make good. He must restore the value of the animal *or animals* to its owner," *the Lord insisted.* "The dead animal or animals, however, he may keep *and barbecue for a family picnic."*

"*Civilized countries do not have or need such ridiculous primitive shepherding laws,"* Moses told the Lord. "They don't have all of these prehistoric and antiquated pastoral situations involving oxen, donkeys, sheep, goats and both animal and human asses. Why can't we be as modern as, let's say, Egypt is?"

"Moses," the Lord said, "when one man's ox hurts another's ox so badly that it dies, they shall sell the live ox and divide the money as well as the dead animal among themselves," *the Lord indicated.* "But if it was known that the ox was previously in the habit of goring its owner, the owner *(although badly gored)* must make full restitution, an ox for an ox; but the dead animal he may keep *to roast at a large family picnic."*

"Lord, can't we just stop being a backward society and acquire the rudiments of culture and science?" Moses boldly requested. "Why must we always have regress instead of progress?"

"Moses," the Lord continued rambling instead of commiserating, "when a man steals an ox *but not by 'oxident'* or a sheep and then slaughters it, he shall restore five oxen for the one ox, and four sheep for the one sheep. *But don't ask me how I came up with those preposterous equations!*"

"But Lord, what about science, culture and technology?" Moses demanded.

"*Those advanced things are for other civilizations and for other civilizations only!*" the Lord finished.

Chapter Twenty-two
"Social Laws"

The Lord was in an extraordinarily loquacious mood and would not release poor Moses from His' custody and from His' divine influence. So the trapped and cornered New Age patriarch had to suffer (against his will) through a long symposium of the Lord's perfunctory dialectic. The versatile Lord now switched His' focus from long-standing agricultural problems to contemporary social issues.

"If a *greedy* thief is caught in the act of housebreaking and beaten to death," the Lord began, "there is no bloodguilt involved. But if after sunrise he is thus beaten, there is bloodguilt. He must make full restitution."

"*How can the thief make full restitution if he is beaten to death, bloodguilt or no bloodguilt?*" Moses inquired. "*That's completely illogical and unfeasible?*"

"Don't sweat the small stuff!" the Lord's Voice admonished. "If he *(the ambitious thief)* has nothing, he shall be sold to pay for his *brazen* theft."

"*But Lord, what if the thief is not a slave?*" Moses raised the possibility. "*Does he then become a slave if he has no money to compensate the home' owner? Aren't we getting into uncharted territory here?*"

"Stop asking such difficult and asinine questions!" the Lord chastised His' only listener. "If what he stole is found alive in his possession, be it an ox, an ass, or a sheep, he *(the thief)* shall restore two animals for each one stolen."

"*But Lord, how could the thief steal somebody's ass that is already attached to a person's body?*" Moses seriously asked. "*And what if the thief steals something that is not alive like a piece of jewelry or a pieces of gold?*"

"*The Lord proceeded with His' tedious discourse despite Moses' meritorious analysis of its apparent weaknesses.* "When a man is burning over a field or a vineyard, if he lets the fire spread so that it *then* burns in another's field," *the Lord lectured to Moses,* "then he must make restitution with the best produce of his own field or vineyard."

"*Lord, how could a man be burning over his field?*" Moses wondered out loud. "*Shouldn't he be burning inside his field, and furthermore, why should the man be burning. Why doesn't he just roll in the field and put the fire on himself' out?*"

"If the fire spreads further *than expected,*" the Lord maintained in a *not-too-pleased Voice,* "and catches on to thorn bushes, so that shocked grain or standing grain or the field itself is *eventually* burned up, the one' who started the fire must *be moral* and make full restitution."

"Well Lord, I too would be all burned up if someone either intentionally or accidentally started a fire in one of my fields," Moses innocently remarked, "and it was no wonder that the grain was shocked to see the fire heading its way!"

"Moses, here are some other ideas I have been assessing," the Lord disclosed. "When a man gives money or an article to another for safekeeping and it is stolen from the latter's house, the thief, if caught, must make twofold restitution. If the thief is not caught," the Lord persisted *in His' explanation,* "then the owner of the house shall be brought to God to swear that he himself' did not lay hands on his neighbor's property."

"Well Lord," Moses said, "it looks like You' are going to have a full agenda of cases on Your' docket every day with a big slate of minor criminal cases thrown in to boot. I think that most large thefts are wonderful. I call them 'grand larcenies'! Is humor absent from Your' stilted personality?"

"Moses, in every case of dishonest appropriation, whether it be a *dumb* ox or a *stupid* ass involved," *the Lord insisted,* "or a sheep or a garment or anything else that has disappeared where another claims the thing is his, both parties shall be present before God. The one whom God convicts *through His' agents* must make two-fold restitution to the other."

"We're soon going to have plenty of convicted convicts without good convictions, that's for damned sure," Moses acknowledged. "But then again, Your' agenda is going to be loaded with all of these petty crimes and major felonies being committed twenty-four hours a day. Every court and every partial or impartial judge is going to be overwhelmed with backlogs!"

"Moses," God said, "I have more important things to do than to judge petty human matters. It is you and your bureaucratic religious delegates that will be the ones' who will be hearing all these trivial cases, not I," the Lord firmly answered. "You are My' official representative on earth, remember?"

"Somehow Lord, I am either forgetting to remember or remembering to forget," Moses smartly responded. "Either way Your' rigid directions are virtually impossible to implement."

"Moses, let's say a man gives a *stupid* ass, a *dumb* ox, *or as you say 'an oxen-moron'*, or a sheep to another for safekeeping," *the Lord related.* "If it dies, is maimed or is snatched away without anyone witnessing the fact, the custodian should swear that he did not lay hands on his neighbor's property. The owner must accept the oath and no restitution is made."

"Lord, it would be a whole lot easier if every thief stole property that was an inanimate object," Moses attested. *"Living animals cause problems everywhere. Objects, on the other hand, do not die and are less of a problem to resolve in a justice system. So Lord,"* Moses persisted, *"get the Israelites out of this antiquated Neolithic shepherding economy that's going nowhere and get the Hebrews involved in Bronze Age mining, metallurgy and big time construction! Then we wouldn't have such pedestrian lowlife problems such as petty burglaries and animals dying while they are being stolen or transported!"*

"But if the custodian is really guilty," *the Lord continued while paying Moses little heed,* "he must make *full* restitution to the owner. If the animal has been killed by a wild beast *or a crazed wildebeest*, let him bring it as evidence, and he need not make restitution for the mangled animal."

"Insurance would be a good industry to establish," Moses *constructively suggested,* "but I am not sure if it would be so profitable in an obsolete shepherding society that tolerates so much theft, bickering and so much beastly animal husbandry among cantankerous senile elders and among mercurial-tempered shepherds and uneducated greedy animal farmers. The Israelites always seem to value hostility over reason."

"Moses," *the Lord's Voice continued from the sky after clearing His' throat,* "when a man borrows an animal from his neighbor, if it is maimed or dies when the owner is not present, the man must make restitution."

"Why would anyone want to lend their animal to their neighbor?" Moses *perceptively realized and asked.* *"That's really ignorant and inviting lots of problems to occur. The guy who lent the animal deserves to get it maimed or killed for being so naïve and foolish!"*

"I disagree with your evaluation," *the Lord's Heavenly Voice growled.* "If the owner was present, then he need not make restitution. If the animal was hired, it was covered by the price of hire."

"I say that dumb people always seem to have all the dumb problems that have been self-generated!" Moses commented. "Show me a dumb problem and I'll show You' at least one dumb person causing it!"

"Moses," the Lord said, "when a man seduces a virgin' who is not betrothed, and lies with her, he shall pay her marriage price and marry her. If her father refuses to give her to him," *the Lord theorized and commanded,* "he must still pay him the customary *trading* price for virgins."

"Lord," Moses said, "there is no going-rate-price for virgins because there aren't any virgins under the age of thirteen out there among the lustful Israelites. The only virgins out there anywhere are residing in Canaan, Egypt and Greece."

"You shall not let a sorceress live *that pretends to be a virgin*," the Lord ruled and declared. "There is nothing wrong with a girl being a virgin!"

"Look Lord, I have news for You'," Moses informed his Master. "No woman out there in the Israelite camp', sorceress on not, is a damned virgin. The sorceress-type women all go for the magic wand at age twelve as do the non-sorceress-type Israelite women that aren't lesbians. They all turn 'tricks' at a young age, sorceress or no sorceress."

"Moses," *the slightly aggravated Lord proceeded,* "anyone' who lies with an animal shall be put to death. *Sleeping with animals is definitely more immoral than sleeping with virgins!*"

"Lord, I know plenty of guys that have intercourse with animals, but they do it standing up without lying with the smelly beast," Moses challenged. "The senile elders have intercourse with animals all the time thinking that the creatures are their actual wives. Your whole premise on this issue is absurd and unrealistic!"

"And Moses," *the Lord ranted on without paying any attention to His' impatient listener's valid and rational objections,* "whoever sacrifices to any god, except to the Lord alone, shall be doomed *for his abomination.*"

"Lord, we the Israelites have been doomed ever since we followed You' and Your' wacky Angel of Death and the queer funnel cloud out of Egypt," Moses volleyed. "And I know many men and women that sacrifice to other gods just to get their minds off of floods, earthquakes, volcanoes, mass drowning, fire and brimstone and all the other weapons of mass destruction in Your' vindictive heart's awesome arsenal."

"Moses, you shall not molest or oppress *a legal or* an *illegal* alien, for the Israelites were once themselves *captive* aliens in Egypt. Also," the Lord continued, "you shall not wrong any widow or orphan."

"Lord," Moses objected, *"if You' ran the world correctly there would be no widows or orphans on this planet. Why can't You' simply allow all of us to live in peace, harmony, happiness and prosperity? Then You' would have all the worshipers You' want every single minute of every single day!"*

"And Moses," *God rambled on paying his follower little credence,* "if you ever wrong an orphan or a widow and they cry out to Me' *for assistance,* I will surely hear their cry. My wrath with flare up and I will kill you with the sword," *the Lord promptly threatened Moses.* "Then *as a result of your defiance* your own wives will be widows and your children orphans."

"Is that all You' know, a litany of shallow threats and warnings?" Moses balked. *"And what makes You' so sure that I have any intention of going around and molesting orphans and widows? You', dear Lord are being most presumptuous! Must might always equal right?"*

"And Moses," *the Lord persisted,* "if you lend money to one of your poor neighbors among my people, you shall not act like an extortioner toward him by demanding interest from him. *Loan sharking is absolutely forbidden*!"

"Lord, Moses angrily replied while gritting his teeth, *"what makes You' think that I am so ignorant that I would lend money to someone' who could not pay me back? If You' had created a decent world, prosperity would abound and no poor people would inhabit the earth!"*

"And Moses," *the Lord continued, further rattling Moses' cage,* "if you take your *destitute* neighbor's cloak as a pledge, you shall return it to him before sunset; for this cloak of his is his only covering he has for his entire body. What else has he to sleep in? If he cries out to me," *the Lord warned,* "I will hear him, for I am compassionate."

"Lord, if You' were truly compassionate, You' would give my poverty-stricken neighbor and me the means to gain wealth and happiness and have a whole wardrobe of cloaks to wear. You are afraid that we would ignore You' if we enjoyed success, prosperity and harmony amongst ourselves," Moses yelled to the sky at the top of his lungs. *"You thrive on exploiting all of these have-not situations that encompass the beleaguered Israelites!"*

"Moses," *the Lord continued to bust the New Stone Age patriarch's chops,* "you shall not revile God, nor curse a prince of your people."

"Lord, I am so disgusted with this whole weird conversation that I feel like regurgitating my sour guts all over the damned place!" Moses lividly screamed. "I have never reviled You', and in fact, I'm the only one that hears Your' Voice around here and cares to even talk with You' in either polite or confrontational dialogue!"

"Moses," *God's Heavenly Voice went on,* "you shall not delay the offering of your harvest and your *wine* press, *so stop all your silly whining right now.* You shall give me the first-born of your sons. You must do the same with your oxen and your sheep; for seven days the firstling may stay with its mother, but on the eighth day you must give it to Me'."

"You are absolutely insane!" *Moses bellowed at the Lord's ethereal Voice.* "You are beyond crazy! You are the most jealous, arrogant and selfish Being in the entire universe! You are making cruel and unreasonable demands! If You' want us to worship You', treat us with kindness and not take our first-borns! Be more civil and courteous to us! Show empathy and compassion to people and You' Lord will get respect and honor back in return!"

"Moses," the Lord calmly replied, "you *(the Israelites)* shall be men sacred to Me'. "Flesh torn to pieces in the field you shall not eat; throw it to the dogs!"

"Spare me Your' unprecedented insanity!" *Moses screamed as his behavior approached hysteria.* "I don't want to be anything like You' are. Do You' hear me? I don't want to be anything like You' are!"

Chapter Twenty-three
"Religious Laws"

The Lord was off on an absolute tangent and Moses was forced to listen to his Master's great wisdom pertaining to the "administration of Heavenly justice," which the Lord preached but did not practice against the Egyptian army at the Red Sea and against the world's population during the catastrophic Great Deluge and furthermore against Sodom and Gomorrah. The new Commandments and Social and Religious Laws pertained to the Israelites of Moses' time, and certainly those recent laws were actually new more morally oriented ideas of the Lord that Moses was presently being 'deluged' with.

"And Moses," *the Lord confidently orated,* "You shall not repeat a false report, *and Hebrew teachers should not give students false report cards.* Do not join the wicked in putting your hand, as an unjust witness, upon anybody."

"*I don't do any of these things under normal or even under abnormal circumstances,*" *Moses objected in his own defense,* "*but the Israelites perform the cited violations all the time. Why don't You' just go and address those hardheaded deviates instead of wasting Your' time addressing me? But quite frankly I must confess Lord that talking to them is like speaking to an unruly class of a half million boisterous and rowdy juvenile delinquents!*"

"Moses, neither shall you allege the example of the many as an excuse for doing wrong *to others,*" *the Lord indicated to His' aggravated audience of one,* "nor shall you, when testifying in a lawsuit, side with the many *perverts bent on* perverting *moral* justice. You shall not favor a poor man in his lawsuit *even though he has your sympathy.*"

"*Lord, do You' hear me?*" *Moses yelled as loud as he could.* "*I am a good man and I don't do any of these obnoxious and scoundrel things You' have enumerated. I use common sense, but the essential dilemma is that common sense is not too common among the depraved Israelites. Talk to them about Your' distorted concepts of a perfect Israel and allow me to die in peace and quiet!*"

"And Moses," *the Lord persisted,* "when you come upon your enemy's ox or ass going astray, see to it that it is returned to him *in short time.* When you notice the ass of one' who hates you lying prostrate under its burden," *the Lord's Voice proudly uttered,* "by no means desert him *in the desert before you eat dessert at home.* Help him to raise it up."

"Lord," Moses nervously answered, "all of the Israelites are my enemy because You' compel me to tell them ideas and laws they don't want to hear. All half-million of their' asses have gone astray along with their prostates that are never prostrate," Moses rankled. "I even think the women in our camp have prostates that are never prostrate, too. And if the Israelites see another's donkey lying helpless on the ground, I guarantee you they would kick each others' asses!"

"Moses," *the aloof Lord proceeded in His' meandering discourse*, "you shall not deny one of your needy fellow men his rights in a lawsuit. You shall keep away from anything dishonest. The innocent and the just shall never be put to death, nor shall you acquit the guilty. *Morality must be the basis for all justice and government*."

"Lord," Moses replied, "sometimes You' make less sense than that perverted pedophile priest Jethro Reuel does. You' have divine power. Just create better living conditions in a Utopian world and we won't need any courts, lawsuits' or tunics and robes or stupid cloaks," Moses asserted. "Give us happiness and prosperity, which are both within the realm of Your' capabilities, and none of this other crap would even have to be thought about! Trust your people's moral compasses."

"And Moses," *the Lord sternly lectured while staying on task*, "never take a bribe, for a bribe blinds even the most clear-sighted man and twists the words even of the just. You shall not oppress an alien, *even one without a proper Identification Card or one from another planet*. You well know how it feels to be an alien, since you were once 'aliens' in the land of Egypt."

"Er Lord," Moses balked, "kindly explain to me how I could possibly be more than one alien? All I know is that I am alienated from the Israelites when I attempt to implement Your' outlandish laws and decrees!" Moses hollered up to the clear blue sky. "What a mess I've gotten into? Why couldn't I have had the wherewithal to have just flipped over my basket in the Nile and accidentally drowned myself in infancy before I became an acne-faced juve'nile' river rat?"

"Now Moses," *the Lord passively responded to His' irate companion*, "for six years you may sow your land and gather its produce. But the seventh year you shall let the land lie untilled and un-harvested, just like the seventh day when you have to rest."

"I see," Moses said while reflecting seriously for a moment. "The seventh year is to be the Sabbath year just like the seventh day *is to be the Sabbath. The land must rest every seventh year just like the people rest once a week. But Lord,"* Moses said *after realizing something rather salient, "the basic trouble is that the Israelites would rather sow their wild oats than to sow their lousy crops in the field!"*

"Moses, I say leave the land untilled and un-harvested, that the poor among you may eat of it and the beasts of the field may eat what the poor leave behind," *the Lord conveyed to his mortal student*. "So also shall you do *Moses* in regard to your vineyard and your olive grove."

"Lord," Moses demonstrably complained, *"haven't You' noticed that we are a half-million refugees looking for suitable land to till and raise our flocks and none of us have any damned vineyard or olive groves? And besides,"* Moses argued in a trembling voice, *"if the poor wait every seven years to pick an un-harvested field clean, they would all die the other six years while waiting to eat something. Lord, don't You' fathom the message I am sending here!"* Moses exclaimed and attempted to communicate. *"That's why the poor become burglars and robbers and even steal from the blind! Poverty creates and promotes crime! Get rid of poverty and there will be little crime to have to worry about and there would then be no need to implement the futile bureaucratic administration of justice!"*

"And Moses," the Lord suavely continued, "for six days you may do your work, but on the seventh day you must rest, that your ox and your ass must always rest," *the Lord reiterated for at least the fourth time*. "In that way the son of your maidservant and the *illegal and legal* alien may be refreshed. Give heed to all that I have told you."

"Lord, You' need a sharp reality check!" Moses alleged. *"You're really completely out of it! The Israelites rest their asses every day of the year and not just on the seventh day. That's why our society is going nowhere fast. Our people lack ambition, education and culture,"* Moses firmly believed and professed. *"Give us those social tools and I predict that we will rival any civilization on the face of the earth!"*

The Lord deftly *and conveniently* changed the subject. "Moses, never mention any other god *but Me'*; it shall not be heard from your lips."

"Don't you get it?" Moses yelled up to the clear blue sky. *"Your' people switch to worshiping other gods from other cultures because those other cultures have better working and living*

conditions and better science and technology than we do. The Israelites are basically still living in the post Stone Age era, and when we see how well other societies live and what they have, we try to adopt their gods to give us the exact same things those other more prosperous societies have," Moses said. *"You' make us feel inferior to other civilizations because we indeed are culturally and technologically inferior and must continuously be nomadic in order to survive! And yet according to Your' cavalier standards we must be so proud and arrogant when simultaneously feeling inferior!"*

The Lord was adamant about getting His' main points across to His' incensed listener. "Moses, three times a year you shall celebrate a *splendid* pilgrim feast to Me'. You shall keep the feast of Unleavened Bread. As I commanded you," *the Lord's Voice stated*, "you must eat unleavened bread for seven days at the prescribed time in the month of Abib, for it was then that you came out of Egypt. *Make sure all of the Israelites wear 'a bib' during Abib, according to our strict Biblical traditions. And also,"* the Lord told Moses, *"no one shall appear before Me' empty-handed not wearing a bib during Biblical Abib."*

"You have absolutely gone off the deep end!" Moses ranted. *"Your people are starving and poor, and You' do nothing about it! Instead You' demand that they all eat unleavened bread' which nobody has because of us being itinerant desert wanderers and now You' want us to honor You' during a weeklong' feast when we have nothing to thank You' for except grief, suffering, poverty, aggravation and misery,"* Moses futilely argued. *"How could I possibly convince the already militant Israelites that grief, suffering, poverty, aggravation and misery are the hallmarks of human existence?"*

"And in addition Moses," the Lord replied, *"you shall keep the feast of the grain harvest with the first of the crop that you have sown in the field. And finally comes the feast at the fruit harvest at the end of the year, when you gather in the produce from the fields,"* the Lord insisted to Moses. "Thrice a year shall all your 'men' *(women and children don't seem to matter, as usual)* appear before the Lord."

"Lord, You' are without a doubt the most difficult Individual I have ever met and conversed with," Moses accused, *"and I believe that You' are the source of all the Israelites' many grievances and difficulties. We have no fields of grain or orchards and also no groves or vineyards to have abundant fruit and produce,"* Moses raged on. *"You have made us suppliants, humble poor migrant*

slaves traveling en masse from Egypt to who knows where! And now You' are going to cause more trouble by making me persuade the pathetic and apathetic Israelites that we must take Canaan away from the Canaanites! No way! Your crazy demands are too unattainable!"

"Moses," the Lord implored, "you shall not offer the blood of My' sacrifice with leavened bread. Nor shall the fat of My' feast be kept overnight until the next day," *the Lord instructed His' principal disciple.* "The choicest first fruits of your soil you shall bring to the house of the Lord, your God."

"Lord, the Hebrews claim that the unleavened bread makes their penises limp and that it also makes them sexually impotent besides giving them chronic diarrhea," Moses related. *"And You' spend all of Your' majestic time and effort inventing silly meaningless insignificant things like using unleavened bread during feasts and ceremonies and offering You' choice fruit that none of us have because we are simple roaming shepherds passing through desolate deserts and unproductive land! Your' demands are too excessive and egocentric for the picayune pedestrian Israelites to honor!"*

"And Moses," *the Lord's Voice continued,* "you' shall not boil a kid in its mother's milk."

"Lord, do you think for one second that such a matter is in any way relevant to Your' people? Survival is what they all have on their minds! Not trivialities like kids being boiled in their mother's milk! Get real!"

"See Moses, I am sending an angel before you, to guard you on the way and bring you to the place I have *especially* prepared," *the Lord informed His' latest patriarch spokesman.*

"I hope it is the Angel of Death that You' used against the Egyptian first-borns," Moses said, *"so then the Israelites will not have to fight the Canaanites in hand-to-hand combat according to Your' convoluted script and Your' misguided prescription! If we fight the Canaanites, we get our asses bashed in! Let the Angel of Death dispose of the Canaanites."*

"Moses, be attentive to him *(the angel)* and heed his *wise* voice," *the Lord recommended.* "Do not rebel against him, for My' authority resides in him. If you heed his voice and carry out all I tell you," *the Lord intimated to Moses,* "I will be an enemy to your enemies and a foe to your foes."

"Thanks a lot!" Moses complained in a thoroughly disgusted tone of voice. *"The Israelites don't need any more enemies and we*

certainly don't need any more foes! What we really need are friends and allies! We are now aliens passing through strange lands and we are about to alienate other more settled peoples and make them hate us more than the Egyptians had!" Moses yelled up to the clear blue sky. "All of this so that You' can give us Canaan that still belongs to the docile Canaanites! If You' want new worshipers, then You' are going to have to earn them on Your' own!"

"Moses," *the determined Lord said,* "my angel will go before you and lead you to the Amorites', *who practice illicit and immoral love,* the Hittites', *who smack anyone in the legs that wears leotards including themselves,* and the Perizzites', *who all act like parasites. You will also come into contact with* the Canaanites, the Hivites and the Jeb-bushites', *who generally want to be governor of everywhere.* I will wipe all of these groups out."

"Here we go again," Moses replied shaking his head in disagreement. "More conflict with other people. The world must hate us and we must feel alienated from the world and hate it, all because You' demand our blind allegiance to Your' arbitrary laws, customs and rules! What a crock! Why don't You' promise the Egyptians Canaan instead of tantalizing the Israelites with the worthless land?"

"And Moses," *the Lord's Voice advanced,* "therefore, you shall not kneel down in worship before their gods, nor shall you make any idols like their gods," *the Lord preached.* "You shall demolish their idols and smash their sacred pillars *and assassinate their pillars of the community.* Only the Lord your God shall you worship!"

"More equivocating bull!" Moses objected. "The Israelites will worship these strange gods because they represent human growth and economic progress and prosperity. You have nothing to offer these new people except pain, grief, destruction and emotional anguish," Moses cried out. "Which do You' suppose they will choose? When given the option who do You' suppose the Israelites will choose in the end?"

"Then Moses," the Lord continued in an unaltered and unaffected Voice, "I will bless your food and drink, and I will remove all sickness from your midst. No woman in your land will be barren or miscarry, and I will give you a full span of life."

"Why don't You' simply do those wonderful deeds 'before' we have conflict with these tribes rather than as a reward after we systematically slaughter and butcher them?" Moses debated the Lord's position. "Wouldn't that approach be more intelligent and feasible?"

"Moses, I will have the fear of Me' precede you, so that I will throw into panic every nation you reach," *the Lord predicted.* "I will make all your enemies turn from you in flight, and ahead of you I will send hornets *(plagues)* to drive the Canaanites, Hittites and Hivites out of your way."

"Oh, a really great solution!" *Moses defiantly yelled.* "The Hivites will probably now become 'Hiveites' with all the hornets left over from the Egyptian pestilences pestering them! And these Hivites already have bees in their bonnets in regard to the Israelite migration into Canaan, at least that's the latest buzz around here. Why must You' Lord want everyone on earth including the Israelites to fear Your' temper and Your' out-of-control wrath!" *Moses hollered up at the clear blue sky.* "Must You' always be exceedingly vindictive and threatening! Have You' ever heard of the words kindness, love and peace?"

"Now Moses, not in one year will I drive them all out before you, or else the land will become so desolate that the wild beasts *will learn and master arithmetic* and multiply against you," *the Lord declared.* "Instead, I will drive them out little by little before you, until you have grown numerous enough to take possession of the land."

"Here You' go again with the threat of violence routine!" *Moses dejectedly argued.* "We are nothing more than migrating slaves invading and claiming territory that is not rightfully ours. And Lord, Your' incomparable advance man, the formidable angel is going to infest these innocent people with plagues and the like so that we can then take over a plague-infested land that You' had promised to Abraham, Isaac and Jacob!" *Moses ranted.* "What a lot of hypocritical propaganda this entire scenario amounts to!"

"Moses, I will set your boundaries from the Red Sea to the sea of the Philistines, and from the desert to the river," *the Lord mapped out to His' chief human follower.* "All' who dwell in this land I will hand over to you to be driven out of your way."

"Lord, I need friends and cohorts and not new enemies," *Moses maintained.* "You' are deliberately causing new conflict and unnecessary drama and trauma in our lives!"

"And finally Moses, you shall not make a covenant with them or their gods. They *(the Canaanites, Hivites, and Amorites)* must not abide in your land, *for I want to control everything that happens after our occupation and be the Main God directing all activities and receiving all the glory, wealth and adulation,"* the Lord angrily revealed to His' shocked key apostle.

"If You' were a human," Moses nastily stated, "You' would be declared legally insane! And don't try telling me that psychiatry is only for humans!"

"And Moses, I say that they *(the Canaanites, Hivities, and Amorites)* must not abide in your land *(which is now their land)* lest they make you sin against Me' by ensnaring you into worshiping their *false* gods."

'That allusion You' have just described Lord doesn't seem like such a bad idea after all!' Moses considered but did not say.

Chapter Twenty-four
"Ratification of the Covenant"

Moses himself was told, "Come up to the Lord, you and Aaron, with Nadab, Adihu, and seventy of the *most feeble, senile* elders of Israel. You shall all worship at some distance, *for surely, the closer you come to Me', the more most of you will suspect some smoke and mirrors' chicanery,"* the Lord's phantom Voice advised His' chief aide. "But Moses alone *(that's you, Dummy I'm talking to)* is to come close to the Lord. The others shall not come too near or *I shall instantly disintegrate them into dust.* And the people shall not come up at all with Moses *(that's you again, you Dummy, the one I'm talking to while I am also talking about you).*

When Moses came to the people and related all the *bewildering* words and *complicated* ordinances of the Lord, they all answered *(as was their impolite and bad habit)* with one voice, *"Those insane words sound so fucked-up* that we will do everything that the Lord has told us. *Let's all behave ourselves for now or else we'll all have our asses savagely seared with fire and brimstone!"* the half-million dolts chanted.

Moses then *meticulously* wrote down *(although writing hadn't even been invented and perfected by advanced civilizations yet let alone used by the post Stone Age Hebrews)* 'all the words of the Lord', *even the many words the Lord did not say to him up on Mt. Sinai.*

Rising early the next morning, *Moses knew exactly what to do with his erection. Moses' very firm erection gave him an idea as he exercised his meat to exorcise area demons from the very troubled Israelite camp.* He then 'erected' at the foot *and at the heel* of the mountain an altar and twelve pillars for the twelve tribes of Israel, *without even consulting with the heads of the twelve 'tribes' and without even listening to their rancorous diatribe.*

Then having sent certain young men of the Israelites to offer holocausts *(good things back then)* and sacrifice young bulls as peace offerings to the Lord, Moses took half of the *bulls'* blood and put it in large bowls *with which the men could wash their faces.* The other half *(of the blood)* he splashed on the altar *and all around the vicinity, atrociously defacing, trashing and vandalizing the entire area with graffiti in the form of smeared bull's blood.*

Taking the book of the covenant, he *(Moses)* read it aloud *(Moses was illiterate, and so was everybody else in that region way back then)* to the people', who *defiantly* answered him, *"Read us pornographic sex stories instead and then we'll later listen to your fucked-up religious bullshit!"*

And Moses appropriately answered the zany idiots in the throng, "Listen to my words and agree with their meaning or else the Lord will make you piss from your ears and then shit out of your noses after your nostrils turn to anuses."

"All that the Lord says, we will heed and do," *the intimidated people recited all together. "We don't want smelly shit coming out of our nostrils!"*

Then he *(Moses)* took the *bulls'* blood and sprinkled it on the women*'s breasts and on the* men*'s penises* and said, "This is the blood of the covenant' which the Lord has made with you in accordance with these *divine* words. These words of His' concern *firm women's breasts for easy sucking and also concern the importance of bloody male circumcision in all basic Hebrew religious teachings."*

Moses then went up *(climbed up Mt. Sinai)* with Aaron, Nadab, Abihu and the seventy *most feeble senile* elders of Israel', who only clambered up the steep mountain *because Aaron had told the already disintegrating elders that they had died and were now ready to climb up to heaven, which they were doing.*

Under His' feet *(the Lord's feet, and it is imagined that He' had ten toes too!)* there appeared to be *(which is different than "appeared")* sapphire tile-work, as clear as the *cloudy* sky itself. Yet He' *(the mercurial Lord or His' twin' temperamental angel)* did not smite these chosen Israelites *because He' at first thought they were visiting civilized Canaanites that had come to worship Him'.* After gazing on God, they could still eat and drink *since the Lord had not surgically removed their lips, mouths and tongues with his dreaded sharp double-bladed sword.*

The Lord'*s Voice* said to Moses, "Come up to Me' on the mountain top and, while you are there, I will give you the stone tablets, *but make sure you don't swallow them like medicine tablets,"* He' ordered. "On these tablets I have written the Commandments intended for your instruction, *so it really doesn't matter that none of you know how to read, let alone write or scribble. Your descendents will be able to decipher My' message centuries from now,* for the Commandments have been written in stone and cannot be erased."

So Moses set out with Joshua', *who only went up onto the mountain of God to hide from Amalek and his barbarous men, who were still out to expire his ass even though they were lowly shepherds.* He *(Moses)* had told the *seventy feeble senile* elders, "Wait here for us until we return. Aaron and Hur *and Ben* are staying with you, *you incontinent fools, to change your diapers and to clean your' slobbering faces with the smelly dirty diapers that they will have changed.* If anyone has a complaint, let him refer the matter to them (*Aaron, Ben and Hur*)', *who will have all of you on pins and needles and in diapers until I return from my important Summit Conference with the Lord."*

After Moses had gone up *(climbed and clambered the precarious ridge)*, a *dark dense* cloud had covered the mountain *peak*. The glory of the Lord settled upon Mt. Sinai, *and all of the Israelites at the base of the mountain and all of the seventy feeble senile elders of Israel yelled simultaneously, "What the fuck's happening? If this is an omen signifying the end of the world we can finally all rejoice!"*

The thick cloud covered it *(Mt. Sinai's summit for the Lord and Moses' Summit Conference)* for six *consecutive* days, *and as usual, the directionless Israelites were in a fog all week long.* On the seventh day *(the Sabbath)* He' *(the Lord hidden in the cloud)* called out to Moses from the midst of the cloud. To the *astonished* Israelites, the glory of the Lord was seen as a consuming fire *blazing* on the mountaintop.

But Moses *easily* passed into the midst of the mist *(the stationary dark cloud that was acting like a stage curtain)* as he went up (*ascended*) the mountain, and there he stayed for forty days and for forty nights *glad that it wasn't raining all that time without an ark or an aquarium to stay in.*

And the seventy feeble and senile elders kept repeating over and over again for the forty days and forty nights, "When are we to die? Where's the ladder to heaven? What the fuck's happening? When are we to die? Where's the ladder to heaven? What the fuck's happening? Where's our stairway to Heaven?"

Chapter Twenty-five
"The Table"

This is what the Lord then said to Moses, "Tell the Israelites to take up a collection for Me' *because I really need opulent gifts and donations from the starving half-million poverty-stricken derelicts.* From every man you shall accept the *extravagant* contribution that his heart prompts him to give. *It's not easy being loved by such a ragtag multitude!*"

"Lord, every man wants to give You' absolutely nothing!" Moses testily returned. "They are former slaves without property or valuables that have been just released from Egyptian bondage and the vagrants have nothing to offer You' even if the poor creatures were crazy enough to really desire offering You' anything in their possession!"

The irrepressible implacable Lord acted as if Moses had said nothing at all. "These are the contributions you shall accept from them: *I would prefer* gold, silver, and bronze pieces and objects. *I will also accept* violet, purple and scarlet yarn, fine linen and goat hair, rams' skins dyed red, and tahash *(porpoise)* skins and acacia wood. *You might also consider donating* oil for the light; spices for anointing oil and for the fragrant 'incense' *that will make you more incensed than you presently are;* onyx stones and other gems for mounting on the ephod and the breastplate," *the Lord enumerated.* "*All these nice items should also be respectfully included in your solemn tribute to Me' your God.*"

"Lord, the Israelites are a conglomeration of lowlife paupers," Moses stated. "We are slave people wearing tawdry robes, the descendents of humble shepherds on the lam looking for a new home, and we are at odds with the other people of the world that all hate us and our avarice!" Moses valiantly emphasized. "These gifts that You' require are presently owned by kings, priests and by wealthy aristocrats. Coincidentally, they are also the items that we had been given by the Egyptians and the items that we had stolen from the Egyptians before "Your' Commandment, 'thou shall not steal' had been instituted. These gifts currently in the hands of the Hebrews are presently our only source of money exchange and bartering."

"They *(the people)* shall make a sanctuary for Me'," *the introverted Lord's Voice stated,* "that I may dwell in their midst *and not in their mist.* This Dwelling and all its furnishings you shall make exactly according to the pattern that I will now show you," *the*

Lord instructed Moses. "When I become weary of living up here alone on this desolate Mt. Sinai, then you can have the honor of carrying Me' around in this container I shall now describe to you."

"You want to live in a box?" Moses indulgently laughed. "If I were You' Lord, I would prefer to live up here all alone on Mt. Sinai rather than reside in a silly portable carton. The Israelites will be the laughingstock of the whole world when others learn that we carry our God around in a box!"

"Moses," the Lord said, "I assure you that this will be no ordinary box I am about to describe. You shall make an ark of acacia wood, two and a half cubits long, one and a half cubits wide and a half cubit high."

"Is Your' precious ark going to be a small scale model of Noah's ark?" Moses chuckled in his amused state of mind. "Should we make it waterproof and place hand-made animal figures inside, two of each species?"

"Moses," the Lord *testily* added, "plate it (*the box in the shape of an ark*) inside and outside with pure gold, and put a molding of gold around the top of it, *too*. Cast four gold rings and fasten them on the four supports of the ark, two rings on one side and two rings on the other."

"Pardon me and my ignorance Lord," Moses said, "but this is sounding more like a four-ring circus with every new word that You' say. You are the funniest stand-up comedian I ever heard, and I've been to some of the biggest and best clubs in Egypt when I was supposed to be existing and subsisting as a humble slave, thanks to a small allowance that the anonymous Pharaoh had conferred upon me!"

"Then Moses," the Lord proceeded with His' mental blueprint, "make poles of acacia wood and plate them with gold. These poles you are to put through the rings on the sides of the ark for carrying it *around*."

"Pardon me again Lord," Moses interrupted, "but why can't You' have one of Your' Ark-angels build you this new traveling ark? You or they could have it built in a jiffy through magic and sorcery but we Israelites will find such a task almost an impossibility because of the valuable materials involved and because of our lack of applicable technology as far as construction and craftsmanship is concerned."

"The poles must remain in the rings of the ark and never be withdrawn, *or else you will have to face and receive the consequences," the Lord specified.* "In the ark you are to put the Commandments that I will *personally* give you."

"I'm glad to hear that we must carry You' and Your' Commandments around in the ark with the poles through the rings in the ark's side and not with the poles suspended through the rings in our noses," Moses criticized and cackled. "That would be very painful and humiliating indeed!"

"And Moses," the Lord promptly continued His' well orchestrated dissertation, "you shall make a propitiatory of pure gold, two cubits and a half long, and *exactly* one and a half cubits wide."

"That expensive propitiatory sounds rather propitious for You', but not too propitious for the already beleaguered Israelites," Moses injected into the lively exchange. "This ark might become subject to arson or vandalism from Your' half-million non-affluent people."

"And Moses," the Lord went on while not paying any attention to His' prophet's comical statements, "make two cherubim *(three dimensional angel models)* of beaten gold for the two ends of the propitiatory, fastening them so that one cherub springs direct from each end. The cherubim shall have their wings spread out above, covering the propitiatory with them, and they *(the celestial angels)* shall be turned toward each other."

"Lord," Moses said rather vehemently, "You' had better hire artisans from more advanced civilizations to perform this highly skilled craftsmanship for You'. I suggest that creative Egyptians or Greeks would be best qualified to fulfill Your' structural expectations."

"This propitiatory that I have just mentioned," the Lord interrupted Moses, "shall be placed on top of the ark. In the ark itself you are to put the Commandments that I will give you. I will meet you there, from above the propitiatory, between the two cherubim *situated* on the Ark of the Commandments that I wish you to give *as My' gift* to the Israelites."

"It would be easier to turn an ounce of feces into a ton of gold than to perform this impossible project!" Moses forcefully protested. "You want me to have the unstable Israelites sacrifice everything they own to build this confounded ark and then You' desire to give it back to them as Your gift? What a nightmare! The ultimate nightmare!"

"And besides that Moses," the Lord persisted, "you shall also make a table of acacia wood, *and here is the Table of Contents*. The table *of contents* should be two cubits long, a cubit wide, and a cubit

and a half high. Plate it with pure gold and make a molding of gold around it *but make sure the molding never gets moldy or caked with mildew.* Surround it with a frame, a handbreadth high, with a molding of gold *that never gets moldy or caked with mildew* around the frame."

"Lord, I definitely need at least five secretaries to remember all of this information and all of Your' un-inspiring bureaucratic statistics," Moses stated with regret in his tone of voice. "Why the hell was I ever born?"

"And Moses," the Lord further stipulated, "you shall also make four rings of gold for it and fasten them at the four corners, one at each leg, on two opposite sides of the frames as holders for the poles to carry the *already described very heavy* table *of contents.*"

"The people of Israel cannot afford such a shrine for You' or for any other god in the whole universe!" Moses angrily yelled and protested. "You Lord have the power to make us successful and prosperous! Do it, and then we'll give You' any damned homage that Your' Almighty heart and soul desire!"

"These poles *designed* for carrying the table *of contents* you shall *also* make of acacia wood and plate with gold," *the Lord conveyed to His' thoroughly distraught listener.* "Of pure gold you shall make its plates and cups, as well as pitchers and bowls for pouring libations. On the table you shall always keep *Showtime* Showbread set *especially* before Me'."

"Damn it!" *Moses screamed in opposition to what his ears were hearing.* "Hire competent Hephaestus (the lame Greek god of metallurgy) to complete this colossal Herculean work assignment for You'!"

"You shall keep a lampshade of pure beaten gold," *the Lord stated, ignoring Moses' apparent frustration and angst.* "Its shafts and branches with its *ornate* cups and *elaborate* knobs and *gaudy* petals should be springing directly from it," *the ecstatic Lord dictated.* "Six *dainty* branches are to extend from the sides of the lampshade, three *dainty* branches on one side, and three *dainties* decorated on the other."

"Are there any qualified psychiatrists in Heaven?" Moses challenged his Master. "You need professional help, desperately! Is there a God Study Team up there in Heaven?"

"On one branch there are to be three *ornate* cups, shaped like almond blossoms, each with its *elaborate* knobs and *gaudy* petals, and also for the six *dainty* branches that extend from the *all-important* lampshade," *the Lord prattled on in a very serious tone of*

Voice. "On the shaft there are to be four *ornate* cups, shaped like almond blossoms, with their *elaborate* knobs and *gaudy* petals, including an *elaborate* knob below each of the three pairs of *dainty* branches that extend *directly* from the *ornate* lampshade. Their *elaborate* knobs and *dainty* branches shall so spring from it that the whole *appearance* will form but a single *magnificent* piece of pure beaten gold."

"*Forgive my intrusion into Your' Almighty trance,*" Moses angrily countered the familiar but mysterious Voice, "*but can't You' just terminate me right here and now with an errant lightning bolt or have a mountain crag swallow me up and crush me in its powerful jaws? It would be easier selling saltwater to veteran ocean fishermen than to even begin this hoax of an undertaking. Kill me now! I demand that You' do it right this minute!*"

"*And Moses,*" the Lord's Voice instructed from His' self-induced trance, "you shall make seven *splendid* lamps for the table *of contents* and so set up the *splendid* lamps that they shed light on the space in front of the *magnificent* lampshade. These, as well as the trimming shears and trays, must be of *lustrous* pure gold. *Men lust for pure gold, and that's why I call it lustrous,*" the Lord said as an anecdotal sidebar. "Use a talent of pure *lustrous* gold for the *magnificent* lampshade and for all the *magnificent* accompanying appurtenances."

"*Lord, Your' expensive ark is going to bankrupt our treasury, no doubt about it!*" Moses squawked. "*We hardly have one talent in our coffers now, and we certainly do not have the requisite engineering 'talent' to manufacture this incredible ark and table that You' so dynamically have described in entirely too much detail!*"

"*And Moses,*" the Lord's booming Voice lectured from His' hypnotic-sounding self-induced trance, "see that you make them according to the *exact* pattern shown *to* you on the mountain."

Chapter Twenty-six
"Tent Cloth, Walls and Veils"

"*Moses,* the Dwelling *(the Ark of the Covenant) itself you shall make out of sheets woven of fine linen twined and of violet, purple and scarlet yarn,*" *the Lord directed His' most disinterested listener,* "*and* also *don't forget to have cherubim embroidered on them.*"

"*But Lord, I am color-blind,*" *Moses testified to deaf ears, "and I can't even tell the damned difference between redheads and brunettes. Have some empathy for my plight and have pity on me!" Moses vainly pleaded in vain.*

"The length of each *sheet* shall be twenty-eight cubits, and the width *precisely* forty cubits; all the sheets shall be the same size and five of the sheets are to be sewn together, edge to edge, and the same *requirement* for the other five," *the Lord instructed His' suddenly lethargic pupil.*

"*Lord, we don't even have one tailor in the whole slum-like Israelite camp to properly measure the prescribed lengths and widths that You' have uniquely specified,*" *Moses argued to no avail. "Please import some highly qualified specialists from Egypt and Crete to do Your' bidding, if they could understand Your' outrageously arcane and nebulous directions.*"

"*Moses,*" *the highly focused Lord articulated,* "make loops of violet yarn along the edge of the end of the sheet in one set, and the same along the edge of the end sheet in the other set. There are to be *exactly* fifty loops along the edge of the end sheet in the first set," *the Lord proudly delineated,* "and fifty loops in the edge of the corresponding sheet in the second set, and so placed that the loops are directly opposite each other."

"*Must I courteously remind You' my dear Creator, that You' could just wish for such an ark to appear, and it would manifest itself before Your' very eyes in an instant without any human labor involved,*" *Moses debated. "And I'm inclined to believe that You' are enamored with such trite trivialities such as loops, cups, stitches, petals and branches that You' ignore the fact that Your' people, the same people You' are making these unreasonable demands upon, are poor, unskilled and screwed-up-in-the-head former shepherds turned slaves turned pissed-off nomads.*"

"Then Moses," *the Lord's Voice lectured from His' tunnel-vision trance,* "make fifty clasps of gold, with which to join the two sets of sheets, so that the dwelling forms one *harmonious* whole."

"Lord, please make me a sinful pagan right this instant," Moses maintained in an extremely perturbed voice. "If any Canaanite or Jeb-bushite god made similar demands on those tranquil tribes, the people would then come to this mountain and give You' a tumble until they eventually would find out that You' are a spoiled brat going through some troubling indefinable stage of divine adolescence. Those pagan gods are saints when compared to Your' tyranny!"

"Also Moses," *the Lord continued with absolute certainty,* "make sheets woven of goats hair, to be used as tent' covering over the Dwelling. Eleven such sheets are to be made. The length of each sheet shall be thirty cubits, and the width four cubits. All eleven sheets shall be of the same size."

"Lord, In all due respect," Moses expressed, "the foul Israelites will steal the sheets and roll around in them with their girlfriends, wives and then with their harlots, many of whom are their girlfriends and their wives," Moses cleverly answered. "And the mentally challenged Hebrews only think and care about survival and about base biological pleasure: eating, having sex and taking royal dumps. That is the biography and the biology of each one of them."

"Moses," *the all-too-focused Lord enunciated,* "sew five of the sheets, edge to edge, into one set, and the other six sheets into another set. Use the sixth sheet double at the front of the tent. Make fifty loops along the edge of the end of the end sheet in one set," *the Lord announced to Moses,* "and fifty loops along the edge of the end sheet in the second set. *It just so happens that I like the number fifty.* Also, before I forget, Moses," *the Lord didactically added,* "make fifty bronze clasps and put them *separately* into the loops, to join the tent into the whole."

"I cannot tolerate any more unnecessary frustration and vexation," Moses declared. "You make the word' 'picayune' seem like it's the word' 'gigantic'! Please Lord, immediately make me into a feeble senile elder of Israel so that I could be looking for a ladder ascending to nowhere while believing that I had just died. Please permit me to die before my bladder, balls, anus and brain all explode at the same time."

"And Moses," *the Lord added,* "there will be an extra half sheet of tent covering', which shall be allowed to hang down over the rear of the Dwelling."

"The rascally unsavory Israelites will want to wipe their behinds with this extra half sheet of tent covering once they hear it's 'for the rear' of the ark," Moses theorized and articulated.

"Likewise," the invisible Lord said from His' deep mystical trance, "the sheets of the tent will have an extra cubit's length to be hanging down on either side of the dwelling to protect it."

"Lord, You' are God!" Moses marveled. "Why must You' or Your' portable box-house need to be protected from anyone or anything? This is definitely a conundrum of the greatest magnitude! You're going to need more than sheets for protection, that's for damned sure!"

"And Moses," the Lord's Voice uttered from His' lengthy hypnotic trance, "over the tent itself you shall make a covering of rams' skins dyed red, and above that, a covering of tahash *(porpoise)* skins *on purpose*."

"There You' go again with Your' obsessive/compulsive demands," Moses strenuously objected but without any evident success. "You just can't get away from this rams and skins' shepherding agrarian culture stuff! The only way the Israelites are going to advance culturally and scientifically is to imitate the Bronze Age Egyptians and Greeks," Moses explained to no avail. "Shepherding is not where it's at!"

The Lord was still in His' self-induced trance, but Moses dared not leave His' Almighty company and be castrated or made into a dickless leper for inciting the Lord's reputed nasty temper should He' decide to exit His' weird prolonged stupor.

"And Moses, you shall make boards of acacia wood as walls for the *indicated* Dwelling," the Lord rambled on. "The length of each board shall be ten cubits, and its width one and a half-cubits. Each board shall have two arms *but no elbows, wrists or fingers*. The two arms shall serve to fasten the boards in line. In this way the boards of the Dwelling are to be made."

"You know what I think!" Moses yelled at the Lord's Voice in the sky, trying to break His' Voice's deep meditation. "I think You are a frustrated architect or engineer and that You' are taking Your' frustrations out on me and the Israelites. Why don't You' simply appoint that perverted pedophile Jethro Reuel to supervise this nutcase project? Like most priests he's usually indolent and taking advantage of the labors of others."

"Set up the 'boards' of the dwelling as follows *so that you don't get bored with this special enterprise I'm identifying*," the Lord suggested. "Twenty boards are to be on the south side, with forty silver pedestals under the twenty boards, so that there are two pedestals under each board at its two arms," *the long-winded Speaker' demanded to His' subordinate.* "Twenty boards are to be on the other side of the Dwelling, the north side, with their forty silver pedestals, two under each board."

"Are You' ready for the lunatic bin or what!" Moses screamed as loud as he could. "If I turn the ark half-way around, the north side becomes the south side and obviously the south side becomes the north side, so east side, west side, all around the ark's block and so on!" Moses angrily replied. "Why didn't You' my excellent Lord simply say 'make both sides identical' and then describe only one side to me?"

"Six boards are to be to the rear of the Dwelling to the west, and two boards for the corners at the rear of the Dwelling," *the Lord enumerated and specified.* "These two shall be double at the bottom, and likewise double at the top, to the first ring. That is how both boards in the corner are to be made," *the Lord described in detail to His' chief aide.* "Thus there shall be in the rear eight *identical* boards, with their sixteen silver pedestals, two pedestals under each board."

"Excuse me Lord," Moses barked back, "but the argumentative Israelites are going to criticize You' for being petty and arrogant. Only an avowed ogre would make outlandish dimensional demands as You' are doing now," Moses argued. "This is more torture than being burned to a crisp at the 'stake' or being burned at the hamburger!"

"Also Moses, make bars of acacia wood," *the Lord prescribed in His' seemingly endless trance-like state.* "Five bars are to be made for the boards on one side of the Dwelling, five for those on the other side, and five for those at the rear toward the west, *assuming that you do not turn the ark around, either ninety or a hundred eighty degrees. But if you turn it, make sure you turn the ark three-hundred and sixty degrees so that the ark is then situated exactly where it had been in the first place.*"

"Lord, please give me a list of the ten easiest ways to commit suicide!" Moses insisted. "What You' are describing for the Israelites to construct is genuine madness to the tenth degree times twenty!"

"The center bar," *the Lord expounded,* "at the middle of the boards, shall reach across from end to end. Plate the boards with gold, and make gold rings on them' as holders for the bars', which are also to be plated with gold. Moses," *the Lord's Voice said from*

Its' very deep trance, "*and* you shall erect the Dwelling according to the *niftily designed* pattern shown you on the mountain."

"Lord, I have a pounding headache that won't quit!" Moses informed the Deity', "and my skull can no longer contain my expanding swollen brain!" *the unfortunate prophet expressed to the Lord, Who' was still in the trance-like state.* "I don't know how much more of this anguish my failing heart can endure?"

"You shall have a veil woven of violet, purple and scarlet yarn, and of fine linen twined with cherubim embroidered on it," *the Lord disclosed for the second time.*

"I know you think I am a dunce," Moses humbly said, "but remember that I am Your' creation made in Your' image. So what does my limited intelligence say about You'?"

"Moses, the veil is to be hung on four gold-plated columns of acacia', which shall have 'hooks', *just like the first paragraphs of good papyrus newspaper articles have hooks.* The hooks of gold shall rest on four silver pedestals," *the Lord methodically outlined,* "and then hang the veil from the clasps."

"If there were a decent olive tree nearby," Moses speculated out loud, *"it would be wise for me to hang myself from it instead of hanging silly veils from fancy clasps and hooks. Whatever happened to social justice? Your' great Mind is too enthralled with ceremonial nonsense! We need more substance and less form here!"*

"Moses," *the Lord continued without regarding his prophet's complaints,* "the Ark of the Commandments you shall bring inside, behind this veil', which divides the holy place from the holy of holies. Set the propitiatory on the Ark of the Commandments in the holy of holies."

"Give me a break, will Ya'!" Moses objected. *"Can't You' at least find me a decent garage or a storage building to park and lock this new-fangled ark in?"*

"And Moses," *the invisible Lord stated in an unwavering Voice,* "outside the veil you shall place the *table of contents* and the lamp stand, the latter on the south side *(of Chicago, an ancient city not far from Biblical Philadelphia)* of the Dwelling. Place it opposite the *table of contents,* which is to be put on the north side *(windy-city side of Chicago where bears and their cubs are reputed to hibernate*).

"Should I vomit, barf or puke?" the greatly irritated Moses criticized. *"Please turn me into a dead porcupine or some kind of rotting desert road kill!"*

"Moses," the Lord slowly uttered, "for the entrance of the tent, *make it very entrancing.* It should be a variegated curtain of violet, purple and scarlet yarn and of fine linen twined, *and if you mess around with the purple drapes, then it's definitely going to be curtains for you!"*

"Oh please, I can't wait to mess with the drapes!" Moses satirically commented. "And it is going to be purple, the color of kings! What a royal travesty Your' project is becoming!"

"And in regard to the ark," the Lord's Voice summarized, "make five columns of acacia wood for this curtain. Have them plated with gold, with their hooks of gold. Then cast five bronze pedestals for them."

"Drop me down a deep cesspool because I feel like crap!" Moses prayed to Heaven for deliverance from the Lord's comprehensive and excessive non-negotiable demands.

Chapter Twenty-seven
"The Altar of Holocausts"

Moses noticed a lengthy pause in the Lord's unbelievable oration, more of an intermission than a caesura, so he stepped to the side of the mountain peak to take a much-needed leak. As Moses squirted urine during his lengthy whiz, he glanced down through the cloud mantle and observed Aaron, Ben and Hur dragging feeble and senile elders of Israel from ledges on the sides of steep cliffs. The hapless senior-senior-citizens were attempting to climb non-existent ladders to Heaven. Then Moses noticed that he was pissing into the face of an elder with his outstretched arms reaching up to Heaven for escape from this miserable life and deliriously begging for the Lord's invention of salvation.

When Moses finished relieving himself, he thought, 'This shit up here on the mountain might go on for a whole forty days and for forty nights. Please Lord', transfer me immediately from the Ark of the Covenant back in time to Noah's Ark during a savage typhoon. I need requiem from this horrible mental abuse I am encountering and even sea sickness and nausea seem like better experiences than listening to the Lord's litany.'

Evidently, the Lord's wondrous Mind had gathered more tedious instructions for Moses to fulfill, so He' beckoned to his only loyal supporter', who reluctantly ambled back to the Lord's unimpressive mountain sanctuary. 'I wish I could 'retreat' from this contact with the Lord's Voice right now,' Moses conjectured. 'But religious retreats haven't become popular yet!'

"Moses," *the invisible Lord addressed while still in His' super-deep trance,* "You shall make an altar of acacia wood *that is not to be altered.* It should be on a square *because that is exactly what you are, 'a square'.* The square *should not be a public square but* should be five cubits long and five cubits wide."

"Lord, everybody knows that all four sides to a square are equal," *Moses rudely interrupted.* "Why didn't You' just say each side is the be five cubits in length, or simply say one side is five cubits?"

"Because Moses you fool, the square *is really a cube that* will be three cubits high!" *the Lord added.* "There are a lot of cubits in this cube!"

"Can't You' resurrect Basemath, the mother of arithmetic to listen to this headache-oriented mathematical dissertation?" *Moses suggested.* "True, I am 'a square' and I might belong in the center of *a town, but being a cube or living in one is far worse than being a damned square!"*

"Moses, *you incompetent boob*, at the four-corners' there are to be horns, so made that they spring from the altar. You shall plate it *(the altar)* with bronze."

"That sort of makes sense," Moses finally agreed with something the Lord was presenting. "When You' and Your' half million people entourage come to an intersection or crossroads, the Israelites will have four horns to blow."

"Make pots for removing the ashes, as well as shovels, basins, forks and fire pans, all of which shall be of bronze," *the Lord stipulated to His' main man. "All of these exquisite preparations are quite necessary."*

"I hope these pots, shovels, basins and forks all 'pan' out for You'," Moses jested, inserting a bit of levity into the monotonous mediocre conversation. "Please finish Your' monologue before I have kidney failure."

"And Moses," *the Lord stated,* "make a grating of bronze network for it. This is to have four bronze rings, one at each of its corners. Put it down around the altar on the ground. The network," *the Lord said,* "is to be half as high as the altar. *How simple can we get?"*

"I see," Moses laughed, as he was a bit giddy from mental fatigue and from sheer emotional exhaustion. "If You' create another massive flood, and water rises, we can catch fish in the net. Or, the net could be used to capture criminals vandalizing the altar. Clever thinking Lord, I must credit You', very clever thinking, indeed!"

"Moses, you shall also make poles of acacia wood for the altar, and plate them with bronze. These *durable* poles are to be put through the rings, so that they are on either side of the altar when it is carried. And Moses," *the Lord further explained,* "make the altar itself in the form of a hollow box, just as it was *carefully* shown you on the mountain."

"Are you sure You' don't want me also to construct a mental hospital for me, Your' only real follower and advocate?" Moses objected. "This entire enterprise is beyond ludicrous and beyond absurd when one considers the deplorable plight and the terrible suffering of the impoverished Israelites. The least You' could do is to provide me with a set of blueprints."

"And Moses," *the Lord proceeded without delay in His' delivery,* "you shall also make a court for the Dwelling, *but not a* tennis court or a court of law. On the south side the court should have hangings a hundred cubits long, woven of fine linen twined, with twenty columns and twenty pedestals of bronze," *the Lord specified*, "and the hooks and bands on the columns should be of silver."

"This project is so crazy that the Israelites will do it because they will instinctively know that it has originated from the emotionally volatile and eccentric Lord!" *Moses returned*. "Do You' want me to rebuild Sodom and Gomorrah too while You' are at it? Can't I just go away from this mountain to discover the location of Noah's Ark on another mountain, presumably over in Asia Minor? I could get started on an impromptu expedition from Mt. Sinai to Mt. Ararat right now!"

"Moses, on the north side there shall be similar hangings, a hundred cubits long, with twenty columns and twenty pedestals of bronze, and the hooks and the bands on the columns shall be silver," *the Lord dictated to His' thoroughly disgusted and very bored listener.*

"Lord, all You' had to say to me was that the north side is to be identical to the south side!" *Moses indicated to deaf ears.* "Please learn and practice word' efficiency. Please stop all this damned verbal overkill!"

"And Moses," *the Lord lectured and further described*, "on the west' side of the *aforementioned* court, across the width of the court, there shall be hangings fifty cubits long, with ten columns and ten pedestals."

"Well now, at least we got away from the hundred cubit dimension on the north and on the south sides," *Moses noted and sarcastically said.* "Don't You' know any reliable building contractors in Egypt or in Greece? What about getting in touch with Pyramids Incorporated?"

"The width of the court on the east' side shall be fifty cubits," *the Lord outlined for Moses.* "On one side there shall be hangings to the extent of fifteen cubits, with three columns and three pedestals. On the other side, *Moses,* there shall be hangings to the extent of fifteen cubits, with three columns and three pedestals. *My instructions couldn't be any easier or simpler*!"

"Can't we have public hangings of Jethro Reuel and Amalek instead of these silly ceremonial court hangings?" *Moses cynically asked.* "I know a half million Hebrews that would gladly volunteer to be lynched rather than to participate in this grandiose ludicrous

167

project that You' have deliberately designed to satisfy Your' insatiable ego!"

"Moses, at the *grand* entrance to the *entrancing* court there shall be a variegated curtain, twenty cubits long, woven of violet, purple, and scarlet yarn and of fine linen twined," *the Lord related to his totally fed-up, weary follower.* "It shall have four columns and four pedestals."

"No wonder why You' only want me and nobody else up here listening to the details of this most horrible endeavor," Moses boldly criticized. *"By now, the belligerent and covetous Israelites would have rebelled and torn this whole sacred mountain apart with their strong bare hands."*

"All of the columns around the court shall have bands and hooks of silver, and pedestals of bronze," *the Lord elaborated on his glorious description.* "The enclosure of the court is to be one hundred cubits long, fifty cubits wide, and five cubits high. Fine linen twine must be used, and…"

"And the *friggin'* pedestals must be made of bronze," *Moses finished the Lord's thought while shaking his head back and forth in absolute disgust.*

"Moses, stop being so downright sarcastic!" *the Lord sternly admonished His' chief disciple.* "All the fittings of the *worthy* Dwelling, whatever be their use," *the Lord paused while finishing His' thought,* "as well as all of the tent pegs of the court, must be of bronze."

"Aren't there going to be any lamps involved somewhere?" Moses asked. *"There must be lamps associated with this great boondoggle somewhere?"*

"Yes Moses, I am glad that you have reminded Me' of that important lamp detail," *the Lord commended.* "You shall order the Israelites to bring you clear oil of crushed olives, to be used for the light, so that you can keep lamps burning regularly. *In that way Moses you can light up their lives.*"

"I see, the lamps are needed so that the Israelites can be vigilant during week-long-vigils to You'. But I am afraid, Lord," Moses said, *"the malicious-minded Israelites will become vigilantes after one day of this preposterous vigil tedium that You' insist we must perform in Your' honor."*

"Moses, I warned you about the dangers of your using sarcasm," *the Lord again threatened His' chief aide.* "Although it required nine months to make you, you can be eliminated in less than a second."

'Oh please brain,' Moses pondered, 'manufacture some more sarcasm so that I may escape this totally unbearable mean cruel world!'

"Now Moses," the invisible Lord's Celestial Voice uttered from His' deep trance, "Aaron and his sons shall maintain them *(the manufactured and assembled items)* before the Lord in the meeting tent, outside the veil' which hangs in front of the Commandments. This shall be a perpetual ordinance for the Israelites throughout their *accursed* generations."

"*I can't wait for the grand unveiling!*" Moses sarcastically remarked. "With ordinances like this one, war and conflict seem like viable alternatives for the Israelites to pursue against the hostile Canaanites and also against the ruthless Jeb-bushites!"

Chapter Twenty-eight
"The Priestly Vestments"

The Lord must have thought that Moses was an ambidextrous angel capable of fulfilling all of His' Ark of the Covenant requirements in a matter of minutes, for He' persisted in transmitting a whole slue of even more comprehensive specifications to the New Age patriarch. Moses however, was wishing that he were a gay transvestite leper rather than being the Lord's "Main Man" and exclusive "go-for" (gopher). 'I'd rather be a deviant queer on another man's 'Honey-do List' than have to listen to this ceaseless pomp and circumstance,' the fatigued old patriarch imagined and considered.

"Moses, from among the Israelites have your brother Aaron together with his sons Nadab, *A-little-dab, Will-doo-ya',* Abihu, Eleazar, Ithamar *and any other stray punk delinquent kids* he might have brought to you, so that they may be My' *official dedicated* priests."

"Wow!" *Moses exclaimed and ejaculated without ejaculating. 'At last the Lord is getting to my father-in-law Jethro Reuel's comprehensive plan to have layers of bureaucracy between the secular masses and the Lord. Now we will be able to extort money from the not-too-bright Israelites without working and tending sheep and goats,' Moses selfishly surmised. 'If I can only suffer through the Lord's forty-day and forty-night' long speech without committing suicide, I'll be able to become rich and live off of the toil of the stupid God-fearing Hebrews.'*

"For the glorious adornment of your brother Aaron', *who has a grotesque-looking body that should remain wholly covered at all times,* you shall have sacred vestments made," *the immortal Speaker precisely indicated.*

"Vestments can cover-up a lot of sins," Moses readily admitted, "especially on Aaron' who should be attending a fat farm instead of pulling down feeble and senile elders of Israel from imaginary ladders leading up to Heaven. Aaron definitely deserves a better fate than that even though my older brother is both gross in appearance and in deed."

"Therefore Moses," *the Lord announced from his deep trance-state of divine meditation,* "to the various expert workmen whom I have endowed with skill, you shall give instructions to make such vestments for Aaron. These special robes will set him apart for his sacred service as My' *appointed high* priest *and they will also make*

Aaron a candidate for assassination from rowdy atheists, non-believers, homosexual Israelites and militant apostates."

"What about Aaron's punk juvenile delinquent kids?" Moses inquired of the Lord. "And don't they have better expert artisans in Egypt, Crete and Greece than those rank amateurs that abound among the illiterate and ignorant transplanted Israelites? Did You' give those superior craftsmen in Egypt, Crete and Greece their illustrious skills like You' had given to the inferior non-existent Hebrew expert artists and tradesmen?"

"These are the vestments they *(the inferior Hebrew craftsmen and artisans)* shall make. *They shall make* a breast-piece, an ephod, a robe, a brocaded tunic, a miter', *which is to kill termites and other bothersome insects with* and a sash. In making these sacred vestments' which your brother Aaron and *his punk juvenile delinquent* sons are to wear serving as My' priests, they *(the artisans)* should use gold, violet, purple and scarlet yarn and fine linen. I promise you Moses that the Israelites will be mightier than the combined strength of all the termites in Canaan!"

"That's really neat! Quite exquisite!" Moses concurred in his assessment of the Lord's stellar decree. "If Aaron and his punk sons had to make their own priestly costumes, they would never do it, not because of lack of skill but from possessing an improper work ethic, bad attitudes and little initiative," Moses agreed. "But God-fearing artisans will surely make those required vestments in a Goshen or Succoth second."

"The ephod," *the Lord rambled on,* "they *(the cooperative God-fearing artisans)* shall make of gold thread and of violet, scarlet and purple 'yarn', *and that's no tall yarn I am telling you,"* the Lord joked from his deep contemplation. "These *colors* should be embroidered on cloth of fine linen twined," *the Lord instructed Moses.* "It *(the ephod)* should have a pair of shoulder straps joined to its upper ends *for the wearing of adorable shoulder pads by Aaron and his punk derelict sons."*

"Lord, if You' may forgive my uncouth impudence," Moses apologized, "but I think You' are being a little too keen on ceremony and on the appearance of opulence than you are on vital moral issues such as truth, honesty, justice and the Israelian way. But on the other hand," Moses shrewdly added, "I guess religious bureaucracy and religious ceremonial trappings and extravagant wardrobes go hand-in-hand. It's sort of a cultural symbiosis being brilliantly implemented here."

"Now Moses," *the Lord further emphasized,* "the embroidered belt on the ephod shall extend out from it and, like it, be made of gold thread, of violet, purple and scarlet yarn, and of fine linen twined."

"Wow!" Moses gasped in exclamation. "The embroidered belt on the ephod might extend out all the way to the Jerusalem and to Jericho beltways. Maybe even out to the sprawling Damascus suburbs!"

"Get two onyx stones and engrave on them the names of the sons of Israel: six of their names on one stone," *the Lord directed the perplexed and bewildered patriarch. "And Moses, the other six names on the other stone, in the order of their birth, ('births' because the "princes" were not all born at the exact same time from the exact same womb, and they couldn't have been born that way anyway even if they were sextuplets times two).*

"As a gem-cutter engraves a seal," *the Lord prescribed to the still baffled Moses,* "so shall you have the two stones engraved with the names of the sons of Israel and then mounted in gold filigree' work. Set these two stones on the shoulder straps of the ephod as memorial stones of the sons of Israel."

"Lord, I know of a jeweler that has a stall in the bizarre bazaar in downtown Damascus who can easily and cheaply engrave the names onto the stones," Moses eagerly mentioned. "And I must confess that some of those sons of Israel are also dirty sons-of-bitches too!"

"Thus Aaron shall bear their names on his shoulders," *the Lord specified,* "as a reminder before the Lord, *for when considering trite human affairs outside of the Divine Realm, I do have occasional memory lapses.* And also *please take note* Moses," *the Lord offered more details to be adhered to,* "make filigree' rosettes of gold, as well as two chains of pure gold, *delicately* twisted like cords, and *then* fasten the *fancy* cordlike chains to the filigree' rosettes. *This is going to be a magnificent arrangement worthy of My' honor and glory!"*

"You most certainly are an unrivaled genius," Moses praised his martinet Master, "principally because You' have sagely transformed religion from the quality of human relationships and thus concurrently have cunningly built a host of myriad vestments, ark dimensions, table of contents and trivial details around what should be important. The really essential ideas are actually being adroitly diminished and neglected by You' and Your' shabby

contingent of incompetent priests," Moses summarized. *"What a fantastic master plan from the Master Himself!"*

"Now Moses, the breast-piece of decision you shall also have made and embroidered like the ephod with gold thread and violet, purple and scarlet yarn or cloth and fine linen,*"* the Lord quantified. "It is to be square when folded double, a span high and a span wide, *and it is to remain spick and 'span'. Do you read Me'?"*

"That's really terrific planning!" Moses again complimented the Lord. *"More trivial details to really distract the public from the true issues of human interrelationships that will promote true harmony between the Israelites and the civilized world. I can't wait to meet with Jethro Reuel and get this baby rolling from the drawing board to its actual implementation!"*

"On 'it' *('the breast-piece', let's finally get our pronouns and antecedents correct before we finish this disconcerting Wholly Book of Exodus)* you shall mount four rows of precious stones. In the first row there shall be a carnelian, a topaz, and an emerald. In the second row will be a garnet, a sapphire, and a beryl. The third row *will feature* a jacinth, an agate and an amethyst. In the fourth *jeweled* row will be a chrysolite, an onyx and a jasper, *unlike the fickle and itinerant Israelites, most of whom are vile animal-like jaspers and varmints."*

"Since my wife Zipporah is not around to 'mount'," Moses evaluated and cited, *"then I suppose I'll have to be content mounting precious jewels on a breast-piece. I hope the breast-piece is nice and firm and curvy when I feel it!"*

"These stones *are not to be broken,"* the Lord warned, *"because I don't like having My' stones broken by anyone, even if it is done by accident!* The *precious* stones are to be mounted in gold filigree' work, twelve of them to match the names of the sons of Israel', *who someday will evolve into feeble senile elders climbing invisible and intangible ladders up to the firmament,"* the Lord stated. "Each *treasured* stone is to be engraved like a*n ancient* 'seal' *or like a fat antediluvian walrus* with the name of one of the twelve tribes."

"Couldn't we instead have twelve zodiac signs of constellations like the Greeks, Mesopotamians and the Egyptians do?" Moses gallantly but vainly requested. *"Twelve tribes of Israel sounds too damned mundane and insignificant in relation to the rest of the world and to the infinite universe."*

"When the chains of pure gold, twisted like cords, have been made for the breast-piece,*"* the Lord sanctimoniously declared, "you shall make two rings of gold for it and fasten them to the two upper ends of the breast-piece. The gold cords are then to be fastened to the two rings..."

"At the upper ends of the breast-piece, the other ends of the cords being fastened in front to the two filigree' rosettes' which are attached to the shoulder straps of the ephod," *Moses aptly and effectively finished the Lord's description.* "This catalogue of nomenclature is getting pretty monotonous and predictable!"

"Moses, you can almost read My' Divine Mind!" *the Lord marveled and flattered.* "You are without a doubt the smartest individual among the half million Israelites."

"All I have to do is recognize patterns of thought that then become patterns of words," *Moses disclosed his methodology,* "and the rest is rather elementary kid stuff!"

"Now Moses," *the Lord continued His' boring inventory of tasks*, "make two other rings of gold and put them on the two lower ends of the breast-piece, on its edge that faces the ephod. Then make two more rings of gold and fasten...."

"Fasten them to the bottom of the shoulder straps next to where they join the ephod in front, just above the embroidered belt," *Moses perceptively completed the Lord's direction.*

"Moses, your obnoxious and defiant behavior is now bordering on insubordination!" *the Lord bellowed.* "One more unsolicited outburst from you and I will put you into a state of hibernation!* Now then," *the Lord persisted in his incomprehensible comprehensive analysis of His' extensive Ark of the Covenant needs*, "violet ribbons shall bind the rings of the breast-piece to the rings of the ephod, so that the *entire* breast-piece..."

'The *entire* breast-piece will stay right above the embroidered belt of the ephod and not swing loose from it,' *Moses' gifted but fearful mind completed the Lord's statement as the Speaker' imagined the exact same marvelous words.*

"Whenever Aaron enters the sanctuary," *the Lord indicated to Moses,* "he should be careful not to trip over his own feet, the blundering idiot!" *the Lord's Voice thundered.* "He *(Aaron)* will thus bear the names of the sons of Israel on the breast-piece of decision over his heart as a constant reminder before the Lord. In this *most cherished* breast-piece of decision you *Moses* shall put the Urim, *in case a Urim-nalysis is necessary.* And *also include the* Thummin, *in case Aaron needs an extra one to stick out from his right hand when hitchhiking an oxcart ride into Jerusalem, Jericho or Damascus."*

"These *items* should be placed over Aaron's heart whenever he enters the presence of the Lord," *the Speaker' eloquently and educationally explained to Moses.* "Then he (Aaron) shall always bear the decisions for the *worthless dependent parasitic* Israelites over his heart in the Lord's presence. *And if Aaron should make the wrong decision contrary to My' Divine Intention and My' Supreme Will', then zappo! Instant electrocution by lightning bolt or by lightning volt! Either way it's instant vaporizing for Aaron!"*

"Are there any further instructions?" *the physically and mentally exhausted elderly visitor to the mountain summit conference sanctuary asked the erudite Speaker.* "I need to take a long crap followed by a long nap, and I hope I never wake up."

"The robe of the ephod you shall make entirely of violet material, *because anything else would be immaterial,"* the Lord *explicitly dictated.* "It shall have an opening for the head in the center, and around this opening there shall be a selvage, woven as at the opening to a shirt, to keep it from being torn."

"I see Lord," *Moses realized and confirmed what his ears had just perceived,* "the selvage should always be salvaged regardless of the circumstances!"

"Exactly My' sentiments," *the Lord agreed.* "All around the hem at the bottom you shall make pomegranates, woven of violet, purple and scarlet yarn and fine linen twined, with gold bells between them."

"Okay Lord, the Levites will be there 'with bellbottom' robes on' when You' finally stop Your' 'hemming' and hawing," *the weary prophet characterized.*

"Moses, first a gold bell, then a pomegranate, and thus alternating all around the hem of the robe. Aaron shall wear it when ministering *ceremonies in My' honor. Please notice Moses,"* the Lord's baritone Voice said, *"I used the word 'ministering' and not 'menstruating'. But I suppose we could have a few women minstrels present during their menstrual cycles, or I could even have Aaron menstruate if I really wanted to."*

"The inclusion of women would reflect the appearance of democracy being practiced during Your' blatantly chauvinistic religious ceremony," *Moses chipped in.* "Let's attempt to disguise tyranny altogether."

"Aaron's tinkling may be heard as he enters and leaves the Lord's presence in the sanctuary, or else he (Aaron) will die!" *the Lord further elaborated.*

"Don't worry Lord, Aaron still pisses quite loudly despite his old age," Moses informed his Divine Listener. "His tinkler still tinkles quite loudly and effectively."

"I meant the tinkling of the bells on the robe you bungling blundering buffoon!" the Lord abruptly clarified.

"Aaron will tinkle on either the bells or on the robe or on both," Moses solemnly answered. "Whatever it takes to please You', Lord! He'll even empty his kidneys and whiz on his and my bare feet if You' want him to."

"Moses, you shall also make a plate of pure gold and engrave on it, as on a seal *or on a walrus* engraving, 'Sacred to the Lord!' This *very excellent* plate is to be tied over the miter with a violet ribbon in such a way that it rests on the front of the miter, over Aaron's forehead. *Make sure it is done in a violet way and not in a violent way!*"

"Lord, Aaron needs a metal plate inside his head and not on the top of his head!" Moses attested. "Maybe even two or more plates inside his cranium!"

"Since Aaron bears whatever guilt the Israelites may incur in consecrating any of their' sacred gifts," *the Lord proceeded*, "this plate must always be over his forehead *to give him foresight*, so that it may find favor with the Lord."

"Can't You' simply perform brain surgery on Aaron instead?" Moses balked. "Why give my old decrepit brother, who is about to become a feeble senile elder of Israel all of this jerk-weed responsibility? It isn't fair and it isn't kosher! Aaron is eighty-three years old going on three hundred!"

"The tunic of fine linen, Moses," *the Lord stated*, "shall be brocaded. The miter shall be made of fine linen, and the sash of variegated work."

"Sounds like Aaron and his punk juvenile delinquent sons are all going to be dressing to attend a peculiar masquerade party," Moses interrupted the Lord. "Can't we just buy or rent these gaudy awkward costumes instead of making the garish things from scratch?"

"Likewise, for the glorious adornment of Aaron's *punk juvenile delinquent* sons you shall have tunics and sashes and turbans made," *the Lord proclaimed to His' rebellious audience of one*. "With these you shall clothe your brother Aaron and his *recalcitrant offspring* sons. Anoint and ordain them," *the Lord decreed*, "consecrating them as My' priests *without any formal education, preparation, studying or special training.*"

"Shouldn't these new priests of Yours' require "special education'?" Moses questioned. "Several of Aaron's sons are virtually mentally challenged and the others certainly are physically impaired and emotionally disturbed! In fact on second thought, they're all special education material, no doubt about it!"

"Moses, you must make all the linen 'drawers' for them, to cover their naked flesh from their *tender'* loins to their thighs."

"Are You' crazy!" Moses yelled like a maniac. "Not even I wear either linen or silk underwear!"

The Lord's Voice remained unruffled, staying in Its' self-induced deep trance. "Aaron and his *wayward* sons shall wear them *(linen drawers)* whenever they go into the meeting tent or approach the altar to minister in the sanctuary, lest they incur guilt and die," *the Lord deftly summarized.* "This shall be a perpetual ordinance for him *(Aaron)* and his descendents."

"Lord," said Moses in a very perturbed and disturbed tone of voice, "the only Israelites You' will get to Your' Sabbath ceremonies are cross-dressers and homosexuals that like the idea of linen, lace and silk underwear! Lord," Moses continued, "why must You' hang out on top of desolate Mt. Sinai when You' could live in luxury like Zeus does in a marble palace over in Greece on top of Mt. Olympus? Lord, answer me, will Ya'! Lord, please answer me! Lord?....Lord?"

Chapter Twenty-nine
"Consecration of the Priests"

"This is the *right* rite you shall perform in consecrating them *(Aaron and his punk juvenile delinquent sons)* as My' *privileged* priests," *the Lord dictated to Moses.* "Procure a young bull *in heat* and two unblemished *non-rambunctious* rams. With fine flour make unleavened cakes mixed with oil, and unleavened *unwavering* wafers spread with oil and then put them in a 'basket'."

"*Oh, now I get Your' modus operandi,*" *Moses told the enthralled Lord.* "*You want Aaron and his punk juvenile delinquent sons to float the cakes and the wafers down a river in the basket You' had mentioned just like my mother had done with me on the Nile back in good old Egypt.*"

"Not exactly," *the Lord contrarily said.* "Take the basket of them *(cakes and wafers that don't waver)* along with the *horny young* bullock *and the two non-rambunctious rams.* Aaron and his *deplorable punk delinquent* sons you shall also bring to the *entrancing* entrance of the meeting tent, and there wash 'them' with water."

"*Do You' want me to wash Aaron and his punk delinquent sons with water or scrub the young bull and the two rams with water?*" *Moses asked.* "*Your use of pronouns is a little too vague and unclear to facilitate accurate direct communications. In order to facilitate more effective communications I need nouns, not stupid pronouns!*"

"Don't insult My' intelligence, or if you do, you will incur My' Almighty' wrath!" *the Lord threatened.* "You know precisely what I meant, so Moses, stop acting like a retard and stop being so unacceptably facetious!"

"*Okay Lord, You' are the Boss!*" *Moses conceded.* "*You wish for me to wash the bull and the rams and not cleanse and rinse Aaron and his punk delinquent sons.*"

"Take the vestments and *next* clothe' Aaron with the tunic, the robe of the ephod, the ephod itself, and the *all-important* breast-piece," *the Lord enunciated,* "and then fasten the embroidered 'belt' around him."

"*Well, I'm sure glad I don't have to give my older brother a belt in the mouth let alone an enema!*" *Moses injected into the zany exchange.* "*That would be grossly disrespectful. A belt around the chest and the waist makes much better sense than a belt in the mouth!*"

"Then Moses, put the miter on his *(Aaron's) pointed* head, *and next place* the sacred diadem *(crown)* on the miter," *the Lord specified.*

"*I always wanted to crown my older brother,*" Moses added, "*and now here's my chance to crown him good! I can't wait to crack open Aaron's cranium!*"

"Then take the *appointed* anointing oil *that won't disappoint you* and anoint him *(Aaron)* with it, pouring it *generously* on his head," *the Lord directed.* "Then bring forward his *(Aaron's) punk delinquent* sons also and clothe them *(the unmotivated juvenile delinquents)* with the tunics. Gird them with the sashes, and *then* tie turbans on them. Thus shall the 'priesthood' be theirs' by perpetual law, and thus shall you ordain Aaron and his *obnoxious and insolent wayward* sons *into My' priesthood.*"

"But Lord," Moses protested, "Aaron and his derelict punk delinquent sons won't be able to wear 'priest' hoods' on their heads because they will already be wearing miters and turbans. How can one wear three headpieces without looking like a fool or a local yokel simpleton?"

"*You're resourceful Moses and I am sure you'll work that particular anomaly out some way,*" the Lord promised, showing confidence in Moses' independent thinking skills. "*Where there's a way there's a will to achieve it! But as I see it Moses you're biggest obstacle that you must overcome is that you're a legend in your own mind and nowhere else!*"

The Lord paused for a moment to gauge the impact of His' last aphorism upon His' impressionable subject' and disciple. Then He' again pursued His' very tedious discourse. "Moses, I ask your noble indulgence as I proceed with My' exacting dissertation," *the Lord continued.* "Now you must remember to bring forward the *horny young* bullock in front of the *strategically located* meeting tent," *the Lord instructed His' favorite and only student.* "There Aaron and his *unruly punk delinquent* sons shall lay their hands upon its head. Then slaughter the *horny young* bullock before the Lord at the entrance to the *centrally situated* meeting tent, *and be sure to make the entire demonstration very gruesome and gory.*"

"I understand Your' impeccable logic completely," Moses told his flawless all powerful Master. "It is beautiful irony we are exhibiting and illustrating to the Israelites here. Usually a bull will gore a person in a gory fashion, but priests representing the people are goring a young horny bull in a very gory display. It is indeed gory for Your' glory!"

"Then Moses," the Lord continued from His' self-induced trance, "take some of its blood *(the horny young dead bull)* and with your finger *(you have your choice of eight along with two thumbs)* put it on the horns of the altar. All the fat that covers its inner 'organs' *and inner pianos,* as well as the lobe of its liver *and of its right ear,* together with the fat that is on them you shall take and burn on the altar."

"Oh heck!" Moses complained. *"I was hoping that I could stay and 'chew the fat' with my brother Aaron and his contingent of ornery punk delinquent sons."*

"But Moses," *the Lord insisted,* "the flesh and hide and offal of the bullock you must burn up outside the camp, since this is *and can only be characterized as* a sin' offering."

"Lord, You' must forget about all of this ceremony, vestments, animal sacrifices, superficial rituals and fear mongering," Moses suggested. *"Now if You' could think of a way to have basic sex incorporated into Your' mundane religious ceremony, then the Israelites will buy anything Your' teachings will be selling! I guarantee it!"*

The Lord pretended that He' had not heard Moses' very practical proposal. "Moses, after this you must take one of the *non-rambunctious* rams and after Aaron and his *delinquent criminal punk* sons have laid their *crummy* hands on its heads, *then immediately* slaughter it. The blood you shall take and splash all over the sides of the altar *and the rest splash onto each other's faces until all of you look like a pack of idiotic clowns."*

"But how can we appease the ever-growing number of Animal Rights' activists in attendance at the gala butchering ceremony that You' have very cunningly described as a sacrifice?" Moses earnestly asked the Lord.

"There are no 'rights' other that the 'rites' outlined in the Ten Commandments that will be carved in stone tablets and then presented to you as My' personal human code of conduct!" the Lord exclaimed from His' self-induced trance. "First I shall teach you morality and then an introduction to ethics is certain to follow a little later on."

The invisible Lord's Voice hesitated for a moment and then conveyed more complex procedures and rules to Moses. "Then Moses, *I command you* to cut the ram into pieces. Its' inner organs and shanks you shall first wash, and then put the pieces with the head. The entire ram shall then be burned on the altar, since it is a holocaust', *which is a good thing now but will be understood as an evil thing in the distant future.* This will be a sweet-smelling oblation to the Lord."

"*I beg Your' pardon Lord,*" Moses balked, "*but Your' team of clownish priests will look like a group of butchers going bonkers in front of the lackadaisical Israelites. Don't You' understand? Animal sacrifices are indicative of outdated primitive and non-civilized tribesmen and clans!*" Moses hollered in despair toward the clear blue sky. "*Why can't You' lead the befuddled Israelites into the modern world that is lived and enjoyed by Greeks, Egyptians and 'Cretans' instead of the world that belongs to the pathetic 'cretins' that we are!*"

"*After that Moses,*" the Lord narrated, "take the other ram, and when Aaron and his *repugnant* delinquent punk sons have laid their hands on its head, slaughter it. Some of its blood you shall take and put on the tip of Aaron's right ear and on the tip of his *punk* sons' right ears. Then," *the Lord orated from His' hypnotic state,* "put some blood on the thumbs of their right hands *to honor Thummin* and on the great toes of their right feet *to honor walking when Thummin' rides doesn't work.*"

"*You are more warped than a gnarled ash tree!*" Moses asserted. "*Do You' expect the Israelites to sit or stand quietly through this kind of ultra-boring exhibition? Your sacred ceremony lacks entertainment value. Show the people dancing girls and striptease artists and nudie venues and vaudeville routines and naked jugglers and they will worship You' like clockwork every Sabbath from sunrise to sunset!*"

"Then Moses," the Lord continued without heeding any of Moses' sage advice, "splash the rest of the blood on all sides of the altar. Then take some of the blood that is on the altar *before it dries and stains the bronze covering,* together with some of the anointing oil, and sprinkle this on Aaron and *on* his vestments," the Voice directed. "Next do the same to his *punk delinquent* sons and their *punk delinquent* vestments, that Aaron's sons and their vestments may be sacred."

"*This is barbaric madness,*" Moses claimed, "*absolute madness! Now You' want Aaron and his ignoramus sons to have a zany food fight with ram's blood around Your' holy altar so that they and their vestments can suddenly become sacred!*" Moses screamed at the clear blue sky. "*Even the Israelites are sophisticated enough to recognize this bizarre ceremony to be primitive and barbaric in nature. I shall 'abstain' from the staining' ceremony! It is both a desecration and an abomination!*"

"Now Moses, from this ram you shall take its fat from its fatty 'tail' *so that this fatty 'tale' becomes corpulently famous in the future,"* the Lord professed to His' completely disgruntled disciple. "I want the fat that covers the inner organs, the lobe of the liver *but not of the ear*, and its two kidneys with the fat still on them. *I also desire you to take* its *(the butchered ram's)* right thigh, since this is an *extraordinary* ordination ram," *the Lord definitively and concisely explained to Moses.*

"Your ordination ram sounds like just an 'ordinary' ram to me," *Moses observed and defied,* "but a dead and butchered ordinary ram that is the center of an 'extraordinary' and comical bloody food fight performed by a bevy of punk delinquent clowns that is all transpiring around Your' sacred altar. Lord have mercy!" *Moses yelled as he held the sides of his throbbing head.*

"Then Moses," *the Lord calmly orated from the depths of His' deep trance,* "out of the basket of unleavened food that you have set before the Lord, you shall take one of the loaves of bread," *the Voice instructed,* "one of the cakes made with oil, and one of the unwavering wafers."

"Are Aaron, his inane insane delinquent punk kids and I to then have a massive slapstick food fight that is a continuation of the corny but humorous clownish blood battle?" *the astounded Moses asked the Lord.*

"No you frivolous fool!" *the Lord snapped from His' trance-like state.* "All of those things you shall put into the hands of Aaron and his *recalcitrant* sons, so that they may wave them as a wave offering before the Lord."

"That's not such a bad idea," Moses acknowledged. "The Israelites could all stand in sections from their seats and then perform an enormous wave around the campgrounds in response to the waves being performed by Your' greenhorn priests gathered around the altar."

"Then Moses," *the Lord added,* "after you have received them *(loaves of unleavened bread, cakes and unwavering wafers)* back from their *(Aaron and his punk delinquent kids')* hands, you shall burn 'them' on top of the holocaust (*the wheat products and not their hands*) on the altar as an *aromatic* sweet-smelling oblation to the Lord."

"What!" Moses exclaimed in horror. "You want me to burn and incinerate my brother Aaron and his punk' kids on your altar? Maybe roast and sizzle his punk delinquent kids, but certainly not dear Aaron," Moses said. "But the Israelite audience will become quite ecstatic upon seeing Aaron's punk delinquent kids go up in smoke during the culmination of the ceremony and gratefully leave the misery of this troubled earth in a rather majestic and captivating blaze of glory!"

"Finally Moses," the Lord explained from His' lengthy stupor, "take the breast of Aaron's ordination' ram and *cautiously* wave it as a wave offering before the Lord. This is to be your own portion to enjoy."

"Are You' daft and delirious!" Moses screamed so loudly that several of the feeble senile elders climbing invisible ladders up to Heaven several hundred feet below snapped out of their dazes. "You want me to eat Aaron's barbecued breast at the altar and then start the Israelites into a series of waves around the open campground suddenly turning the solemn ceremony into a raucous sacrilegious religious revival?"

"Thus Moses," *the Lord passively proceeded*, "you set aside the breast of whatever wave offering is waved, as well as the thigh of whatever raised offering is raised up, whether this be the ordination ram or anything else belonging to Aaron and his *punk delinquent* sons."

"Let's get this straight!" Moses boomed. "You want the Israelites to appreciate cannibalism by having me eat Aaron and his punk delinquent sons' assorted body parts?" Moses hollered until the veins and arteries in his neck nearly burst right out of his throat. "For Your' blessed information, the Hebrews are only one level above cannibalism right now, and You' desire for us to regress back into it! What a vulgar and obscene blasphemy this whole impious holocaust is! The damned people of the future are absolutely right in their condemnation of holocausts!"

"Now Moses," *the Lord suavely lectured from His' trance*, "such things are due Aaron and his *absurd punk delinquent* sons from the Israelites by perpetual ordinance as a contribution. From their peace offerings, too," *the Lord deductively reckoned*, "the Israelites shall make a contribution, their *personal* contribution to the Lord."

"What about making a contribution to the betterment of civilization? To human dignity and to human growth and development?" Moses futilely argued. "What about making a contribution to humanity and to human harmony and to human integrity? What You' are suggesting Lord is nothing more than a contribution to Your' own unquenchable egomania!" the New Age patriarch frantically yelled at the top of his lungs.

The Lord was not at all moved by Moses' astonishment at His' exceptional audacity, and certainly not moved by his heightened emotionalism. His faceless form stood before the agitated New Age patriarch in flowing white robes that glistened from shafts of sunlight that filtered through the dense cumulus cloud that billowed around and covered the drab peak of Mt. Sinai.

The Lord remained cocooning in His' self-induced trance. "Moses, the sacred vestments of Aaron shall be passed down to his descendents, that in them they may be anointed and ordained. The *fortunate descendent (the one next in line to be barbecued and then cannibalized)* who succeeds Aaron as priest and who' is to enter the meeting tent *(unaware of his scheduled doom on the short-list sacrifice agenda)* to minister in the sanctuary will be clothed with the vestments for seven days."

"Wow! I'm sure glad that I and my sons aren't in Aaron's family," Moses offered and opined. "At least now I'll eventually die from disease or old age and not from being butchered, barbecued and eaten!"

"Moses, you shall take the flesh of the ordination ram and boil it in a holy place. At the entrance of the meeting tent Aaron and his *punk delinquent* sons shall eat the flesh of the ram and the bread that is in the basket. They themselves shall eat of these things by which' atonement was made at their *official* ordination and consecration. But," *the Lord's Voice coming from the vague form qualified,* "no layman may eat of them, since 'they' *(the food on the altar, not the laymen) are sacred.*

"This divine trick might really work and scare the daylights out of the vulgar sinning Israelites!" Moses gleefully exclaimed. "Bring Aaron and his sons back to life after watching them being barbecued, incinerated and cannibalized by each other and then finally by me. If that gimmick doesn't put the fear of God into the Hebrews, then I don't know what the hell will!"

"Now Moses," *the Lord professed from His' unconscious state existing within His' hazy-like form,* "if some of the flesh of the ordinations' sacrifice or some of the bread remains over the next day, this remnant must be burned up *or I will be truly burned up and you will quickly know about Me' being burned up when My' reprisal envelops you."*

"Yes Lord, that cause and effect commentary stands to reason," Moses agreed without questioning his Master's suspect motives or flimsy logic.

"And Moses, it *(the bread remnants)* is not to be eaten, since it is *deemed* sacred. 'Carry out' all of these orders in regard to Aaron and his *repulsive punk delinquent* sons just as I have given them to you."

"*I certainly will!*" Moses assented. "Aaron, his punk delinquent sons and I could have delicious barbecue 'carry-out' restaurants all over Asia Minor, a whole chain of thriving franchises. We will incinerate human priests like the people would naturally want us to do, and they will eat the priests in the restaurant booths or at their outdoor picnic tables," Moses assessed and reviewed. "Then You' will resurrect the eaten priests back to life, and we could turn a handsome profit the other six unknown days of the week when we are not bilking the Hebrews on the Sabbath," Moses excitedly yelled. "Our amazed restaurant customers will gladly pay an entertainment surcharge in wicker collection baskets out of fear of being devoured themselves'. What an ingenious plan You' have devised! It sounds absolutely foolproof! And to think that only ten minutes ago I had doubted Your' veracity!"

"Now Moses, seven days you shall spend in ordaining them *(the lucky descendents of Aaron that will be butchered, barbecued, eaten and incinerated by Hebrews and then miraculously resurrected)*. You shall sacrifice a *young horny* bullock each day as a sin offering, to make atonement *to Me'*. Thus also shall you anoint it in order to consecrate it."

"No sweat my sweet Lord!" Moses exclaimed with a smile. "I will gladly do these uncanny things for You' have given me hope and inspiration. After my chain of barbecue synagogue/restaurants takes off, I'll be rich and be able to live a comfortable life in Egypt or Greece until my dying days."

"Seven days you shall spend in making atonement for the altar and *subsequently* consecrating it," *the Lord demanded*. "Then the altar will be most sacred, and whatever touches it will be most sacred."

"*Who cares about a little inconvenience and sacrifice?*" Moses attested. "*I might even open a chain of 'inconvenience stores' and franchise them also along with my flourishing restaurants!*"

"Now Moses, this is what you shall offer on the altar," *the Lord prefaced, again without showing any overt emotion*. "You must have two yearling lambs as the sacrifice established for the day."

"*Of course,*" Moses compatibly agreed. "*Every successful restaurant presently thriving in Egypt or anywhere else and every fledgling restaurant chain must have a daily special listed on their menu."*

"You are to sacrifice one lamb in the morning and one lamb at the evening twilight," *the Lord's Voice emanating from the bright but nebulous form stipulated.* "With the first lamb there shall be a tenth of an ephah *(an inaccurate unit of grain measurement)* of fine flour mixed with a fourth of a hin of oil crushed olives and, as its libation, a fourth of a hin of wine."

"Lord, are You' sure You' weren't a gourmet chef before You' became Lord?" *Moses sincerely asked with admiration.* "You seem to have some excellent recipes and menus stored in Your' Lordly acumen!"

"The other lamb you shall offer at the evening twilight," *the Lord specified,* "with the same cereal offering and libation as in the morning. You shall offer this as a sweet-smelling libation to the Lord."

"Easy as leavened bread rising up in an Egyptian or Greek baker's oven," Moses laughed. *"Anything else I have to know how to execute besides unwary priests on altars in franchised restaurants?"*

"Throughout your generations," *the resplendent Lord philosophized from His' self-induced trance,* "this established holocaust *(a good religious practice back then as long as it was performed by the Hebrews and not the Aryans)* shall be offered before the Lord. The offering will take place at the *entrancing* entrance of the meeting tent, where I will meet you and speak to you."

"This exciting business proposition is even better than manna from heaven or any of Your' other strange supernatural methods," Moses said. *"Wait until I tell that perverted pedophile Jethro Reuel about this deal!"*

"There, at the altar," *the faceless Lord's form pontificated in a familiar resonant baritone Voice,* "I will meet the Israelites. Hence, it *(the meeting)* will be made sacred by My' glory. Thus, I will consecrate the meeting tent, and the *unaltered* altar, just as I also consecrate Aaron and his *punk delinquent* sons as my *surrogate* priests," *the Lord concluded and expressed.* "I will dwell in the midst *and the mist* of the *shabby and shoddy* Israelites and will be their *radiant* God *forever*."

"I'm with You' all the way on this one, Lord," Moses replied clapping his hands in glee. *"Any other editorializing You' feel that*

You' have to do before I take a healthy crap and then collapse on my straw bed?"

"They *(the shallow, sinful, baneful Israelites)* shall know that I, the Lord, am their God' Who brought them out of the land of Egypt, so that I, the *eternal and infinite* Lord, their' God, might dwell among them."

"Hooray for capitalism and long-live restaurant chains!" Moses whooped. "Who in their right mind really gives a happy hang about social justice and prudish holier-than-thou morality anyway?"

Chapter Thirty
"Altar of Incense and Oil"

Moses went and took his lengthy dump, and then the patriarch slept for a full day and next he finally returned to listen to more of the Lord's fascinating prattle. The Lord had returned to just a Voice, the outline of His' radiant form dressed in a glistening white robe was no longer visible to the optically deficient Moses', who had major trouble seeing and finding his pecker when he had to take a leak let alone viewing the Lord's mysterious outline.

"For burning incense," *the non-incensed Lord lectured to Moses*, "you shall make an altar of acacia wood, *the only cheap wood available around here until we can pilfer and use timber from the fabled Cedars of Lebanon. The incense altar shall have* a square surface a cubit long, a cubit wide, and two cubits high, with horns that spring directly from it."

"You' seem to be pretty horny with all of these horns' You' want attached to everything," Moses observed and said. "What about a rack of antlers instead?"

"Its *(the altar's)* great grate on top, its walls on all four sides, and its horns you shall plate with pure gold," *the Lord further delineated for Moses' information.* "Put a gold molding around it, *and if you dare to use any gold-plated antlers instead of gold-plated horns, you Moses will be broad-sided and 'racked' up very badly by My' legendary Angel of Death before you can ever va-moose!"*

"I promise to only use genuine rams' horns," Moses solemnly and sincerely pledged. "I feel 'behooved' to do that out of fear of being permanently exterminated by the legendary and notorious Angel of Death."

"Underneath the molding you shall put gold rings," *the Lord decided and announced.* "*There will be* two *(gold rings)* on one side and two on the opposite side, as holders for the poles used in carrying it *(the unalterable incense altar)*. Make the poles too of acacia wood," *the Lord dictated to Moses*, "and plate them *(the poles)* with *good quality* gold."

"Well Lord," Moses said with some disappointment, "since I am Your' personal 'go for', maybe we can use 'gopher' wood some day like Noah had done in constructing the original ark. And if we ever have a democratic-style election in this primitive Israelite camp, I'll be one of the first to go to the polls (sic poles)."

"This altar," *the Lord advised and directed,* "you are to place in front of the veil that hangs before the Ark of the Commandments where I will meet you."

"And that's where I will 'meat' Aaron and his retinue of obnoxious punk delinquent sons before they are butchered, barbecued, eaten and incinerated," Moses laughed and nodded his head in full agreement precisely like a mindless crazed madman would behave.

"On it *(the unalterable incense altar)* Aaron shall burn fragrant incense," *the Lord revealed to His' earth partner.*

"That makes plenty of incense' sense to me," Moses frivolously answered. *"Aaron will be burned on the main altar but he will burn incense on the unalterable incense' altar before he himself is flame-broiled and roasted for public consumption. The Israelites will learn about free enterprise after they first become consumers of Aaron and his punk delinquent sons."*

"Morning after morning, when he *(Aaron)* prepares the lamps," *the Lord related from His' mystical deep trance,* "and again in the evening twilight, when he lights the lamps, he shall *also* burn incense. Throughout your generations, this shall be the established incense offering before the Lord."

"Don't they do a similar practice in a distant land named India?" Moses asked His Mentor. *"No wonder why You' prefer incense. The terrible aroma that's given off can stink to High Heaven!"*

"On this altar you shall not offer any profane incense, or any holocaust or cereal offering, nor shall you pour out a libation upon it *unless it is libations' hour at all the local taverns and bars.* Once a year Aaron shall perform the atonement rite on its horn *on Amateur Night during the Annual Israelite Variety and Talent Show,"* *the Lord indicated to His' now avid student.*

"Aaron can really play the horn-a-plenty," Moses concurred. *"He really knows how to blow and exactly when to suck on the old horn! When he picks his nose and plays his horn, we call him 'the boogie-woogie bugle boy'."*

"Throughout your *forthcoming* generations this *commemorative* atonement is to be made once a year with the blood of the atoning sin offering," *the Lord perfunctorily stated to Moses.* "This altar is most sacred to the Lord."

"Instead of thinking about Your' glory and splendor all of the time," Moses cautiously criticized, *"every once in a while consider the problems and diseases and poverty of us little guys down here on*

earth. Incidentally, when Aaron plays the atoning horn in the upcoming talent show, may he use 'a-toning (a tuning) fork' to get the right pitch?"

The Lord also said to Moses during His' extended filibuster, "It's great being immortal and not needing any shut eye!" He' intentionally busted on His' sole apostle. "But seriously Moses," the Lord changed His' tone while still in His' extended deep meditation, "when you take a census of the Israelites' who are to be registered, each one, as 'he' *(masculine by preference and also by discrimination)* is enrolled, shall give the Lord a forfeit for his life. *This will be done* so that no plague will come upon them for being registered."

"*If a male nurse registers with you, will he then be a 'registered nurse'?*" Moses cleverly asked. "*I think and truly believe that Your' abstract obtuse census is beyond my senses.*"

"Moses, everyone' who enters the registered group must pay a half-shekel *fee*, according to the standard of the sanctuary shekel, twenty gerahs to a shekel," *the Lord related to the somewhat groggy New Age patriarch.*

"*I get it now,*" Moses elatedly cheered. "*The shekel is sort of like an admission fee to church where Jethro Reuel, Aaron and I can cash in big on the many Sabbath contributions. Smart thinking, my sweet Lord!*"

"*Moses,* this *necessary* payment of a half-shekel is a contribution to the Lord *so that I could have sanctuaries and altars' built all over Asia Minor,*" the Lord explained to the suddenly disappointed patriarch. "Everyone of twenty years *of age* or more who' enters the *cash* registered' group must give this donation to the Lord. *Then my dear Moses,*" the Lord professed, "*you can buy more gold rings, silver bells and purple drapes for Me' to have altars and sanctuaries all over Israel when the sacred and most blessed Ark of the Covenant visits those remote sectors of our yet to be conquered country currently called Canaan. I believe it is your Manifest Destiny Moses to take over Canaan!*"

"*Will everyone be pulling his fair share to subsidize this enormous religious expenditure?*" Moses honestly inquired. "*Your' sanctuaries and altars will put a great strain on our already bankrupt economy and also put a major delay on our scheduled invasion of Canaan.*"

"The rich need not give more," *the Lord outlined*, "nor shall the poor give less *than the rich*. Everyone gives a half-shekel in this *general* contribution to the Lord to pay the *cited* forfeit for their lives."

"Look Lord," Moses balked, *"first of all there are no rich people among the have-not Israelites. Everyone is dirt poor. Secondly, You' are advocating extortion. You are threatening to eliminate lives in a mass forfeit for anyone that doesn't cough up half a shekel to subsidize Your' future elaborate and ornate sanctuaries and altars all over Asia Minor!"* the chief Hebrew yelled at the clear blue sky.

"Moses, when you receive this forfeit money from the *meager motley* Israelites," *the Lord commented*, "you shall donate it to the service of the meeting' tent, that there it may be the Israelites' reminder, before the *All-Powerful, Omnipotent and Mighty'* Lord, of the *total* forfeit paid for their lives."

"This is sort of like cash in advance, insurance so to speak, but definitely very clever religious extortion in disguise," Moses deducted and shared. *"And then Lord we nail the public again when they attend the religious services and learn the fear-of-God while observing Aaron being butchered, barbecued and then consumed by his punk delinquent sons and by me, only to be reincarnated to do it all over again during the next week's performance. What unrivaled genius!"*

The Lord *then* said to Moses, "for ablutions *(the washing of one's body or a part of the body)* you shall make a bronze laver with a bronze base. Place it between the meeting tent and the altar, and put water in it. *Aaron and his sons shall use it in washing their hands, their feet their personals, and each other's personals. I'm quite serious about this particular detail, so don't even consider any prevarication or ruses."*

"Smart thinking," Moses complimented his erudite Teacher. *"A public display of nudity such as a community washroom where Aaron and his punk delinquent sons scrub each other in the open will certainly attract a congregation of curiosity seekers and horny kinky voyeurs in a hurry."*

"When they *(Aaron and his punk delinquent sons)* are about to enter the meeting' tent," *the Lord further disclosed*, "they must wash with water, lest they die. Likewise, when they approach the altar in their ministry, to offer an oblation to the Lord, they must wash their hands and feet lest they die."

"Being an anointed priest in Your' sacred ministry can be a most precarious occupation," Moses observed and concluded. *"I'm glad to be Your' chief prophet and not Your' high priest. And I*

believe that that perverted pedophile Jethro Reuel will want to transfer from the title of priest to the title of prophet if my father-in-law knows what's good for him!"

"This shall be a perpetual ordinance for him (Aaron) and his descendents throughout their generations," *the Lord finished on that topic. "This is both My' decree and My' mandate."*

"Now Lord," *Moses realized and asked,* "what' are we to do about the expensive anointing oils You' have alluded to? Where can they be obtained?"

The Lord *paused for a moment and then* said to Moses, "Take the finest spices *to spice up the rather dull ceremony. Allow young females to carry the spices to the altar. We'll appropriately call them 'The Spice Girls.' There should be* five hundred shekels of free-flowing myrrh *along with* half that amount, that is, two hundred and fifty shekels of fragrant 'cinnamon' *without any synonym. Also Moses, include* two hundred fifty shekels of fragrant 'cane' *if we are 'able'. In addition obtain* five hundred shekels of cassia-all according to the standard of the sanctuary shekel *as outlined and defined in the Dictionary of Official Biblical Customs and Sanctuary Standards, published circa five thousand BC somewhere around Ur in Mesopotamia," The Lord academically informed Moses.* "Include a hin of olive oil and *then* blend them into sacred anointing oil that should be perfumed ointment *that is* expertly prepared."

"Lord, You' are going to need a highly experienced brew-meister or blend-master just to mix these precious oils together," Moses stated. "In what library is that Dictionary of Official Biblical Customs and Sanctuary Standards should I need to do extensive research on the obscure subject? Is it in Alexandria? Is the library in Thebes? In Athens?"

"Moses, with the sacred anointing oil you shall anoint the meeting tent and the Ark of the Commandments, the table and all its appurtenances, the lamp stand and its appurtenances, the altar of incense', the altar of holocausts with all its appurtenances, and the laver with its base."

"Excuse my ignorance Lord," Moses interrupted the Master's speech, "but shouldn't the Israelites be anointed instead of all those inanimate objects being anointed. The Hebrews are the ones that need to become holy, and not the assorted tables, lamps, altars and lavers."

"When you have consecrated them *(the objects and not the people)* they shall be most sacred," *the Lord conveyed to the extremely confused Moses.* "Whatever touches them *(the blessed holy objects)* shall become sacred. Aaron and his *demented punk delinquent* sons you shall also anoint and consecrate as My' *selected* priests."

"*Lord, I truly think that a religion that values people over objects would work a lot better than what You' are erroneously proposing,*" Moses rendered his unbiased opinion. "*If it were not for the roasting and the cannibalizing of Aaron and his maverick and iconoclastic punk delinquent sons, then I don't believe that Your' ideas would fly at all with the listless and generally disinterested Israelites!*"

"*Moses,* to the Israelites you shall say: 'As sacred anointing oil this' shall belong to Me' throughout your generations *and throughout your skin and hair regenerations.* It *(the sacred oil)* may not be used in ordinary anointing of the body, nor may you make any other oil of a like mixture, *even though most of you desperately need baths or showers right this very minute!* It *(the oil)* is sacred, and shall be treated as sacred 'by you' *and even by those of you way down by the bayou.* Whoever prepares a perfume like this, even if you have a patent, or whoever puts any of this *substance* on a layman, shall be cut off from his kinsmen. Moses,*" the Lord said with heartfelt emphasis, "*we want a closed society here where no outside ideas or influences will destroy our unity, our camaraderie and My' lofty goals and ambitions.*"

"*We will never have civilization, real culture, science and technology,*" Moses regretted and muttered, "*as long as You' keep the Hebrews narrow-minded, ignorant, isolated and inbred among ourselves.*"

The Lord *next* told Moses, "Take these aromatic substances: storax', *which is not where axes are stored*; onycha and galbanum, these and pure frankincense in equal parts. Then blend them into *fragrant* incense. *Do not crush the frankincense in a stein, otherwise we'll get frankin-stein', and My' dear Moses, we don't want that monstrous thing happening!* This *new* fragrant powder, expertly prepared *by rank amateurs,* is to be salted and so kept pure and sacred."

"*That's very understandable,*" Moses concurred with the Lord's description. "*Aaron was at one time a sailor, so now he's sort of an old salt' who has the skill and the expertise to capably salt the powder away.*"

"Then Moses,*" the Lord expounded, "grind some of it *(the powder)* into fine dust and put this before the Commandments in the meeting tent where I will meet you *before you meat Aaron and his* *malicious punk delinquent sons,"* the Lord explained. "This incense will be treated as most sacred by you."

"Lord, Your' bountiful wisdom is inimitable and invincible!" Moses praised. "Glory be to You'!"

"And finally Moses, you may not make incense of a like mixture for yourselves, *patent or no patent.* You must treat it as *being most* sacred to the Lord," *the Master Teacher lectured in a monotone Voice from deep within His' incredible trance.* "Whoever makes an incense like this for his own enjoyment shall be cut off from his kinsmen'."

"Hmmm," Moses said to no one in particular, "where can I acquire the required ingredients? Being cut off from my kin as You' had said? Well, that's not such a bad idea after all. And furthermore," Moses whispered to the gentle breeze high up on cloud-covered Mt. Sinai, "what Israelite would make incense like that for his own enjoyment as the Lord had stated?" the old sage mumbled to a mountain crag, nearly falling over a cliff. "Now sex, gambling and prostitution for enjoyment, those things common vices make much more sense to the Israelites than to derive enjoyment from attempting to duplicate the special sacred oil formula of the Lord."

Chapter Thirty-one
"Choice of Artisans"

The Lord *then* said to Moses *because every other human was afraid to communicate with Him'*, "See, I have chosen Bezalel, son of Uri, *brother of Urine*, son of Hur and *Her, Cousin of His,* in the tribe of Judah. I have filled him *(Bezalel)* with a divine spirit *that is simply divine,*" the Lord's Voice proudly announced to Moses. "This skill and understanding and knowledge *that Bezalel possesses* is in every craft *imaginable.*"

"Bezalel was 'crafty' even before You' conferred all of that wonderful skill on him," Moses reminded the Lord. "But shouldn't these skills be learned and developed rather than be divinely inspired and granted? What You' are saying and have conveniently bypassed seems to be contrary to the functioning of daily reality down here on earth!"

"*I have equipped Bezalel* with *abundant* knowledge in the production of embroidery, in making things *(objects, items)* of gold, silver and bronze. *I got the idea of gold, silver and bronze from games known as 'the Olympics' that Zeus holds over in Greece at a place called Delphi,"* the eloquent baritone Voice disclosed to Moses.

"But Lord," Moses reacted, "shouldn't men learn and acquire skills to improve their lives and their environments? You are merely giving one man all of this understanding just to build and manufacture fabulous memorials and monuments to You' and to You' alone," Moses challenged. "How about helping the downtrodden Israelites? How about assisting the advancement of humanity in general? That's how You' get and keep worshipers!"

"Moses, you are being most difficult at a time when I am about to exit from My' most private and lengthy contemplation ever," the Lord threatened from deep within His' trance-like state. "Bezalel will also be very adroit in cutting and mounting precious stones, in carving wood, *carpentry*, and in every other *known* craft."

"You ought to make Bezalel artful in finding his own destiny and being successful for himself and adequately providing for his family instead of laboring day-in and day-out constructing myriad sanctuaries exclusively for Your' Almighty' Glory," Moses complained.

"As his *(Bezalel's)* assistant I have *anointed and* appointed Oholiab, *the brother of A-hol-in-won-liab*, son of Abisamach of the tribe of Dan. I have also endowed all of the experts with the necessary skill to make all the things I have ordered you to make," *the Lord confirmed to Moses*. "*These items are* the meeting *and greeting* tent and the Ark of the Covenant' *which doesn't even have to float on water. It (the singular Ark)* will carry the Commandments with the propitiatory on top of it, and all the furnishings of the tent," *the Lord reviewed for Moses' information and especially for His' own sake.*

"*Please think of the Israelites and their poor self-esteem, their weak self-concepts and their defeated crestfallen heads,*" Moses *begged the Lord.* "*Cut them (the nomadic former-slaves) a break from their unenviable plight and from their travails and they will worship You' every single Sabbath as sure as You' have made little green apples.*"

The Lord was so focused on His' next revelation that He' failed to weigh and assess Moses' arguments in defense of humanity in general and in support of the Israelites in particular. "And Moses," *the Lord prattled on,* "*you shall supervise the construction of* the table *of contents* with its appurtenances, the pure gold lampshade with all its appurtenances, the altar of incense, the altar of the holocausts with its appurtenances *and* the laver with its base," *the Voice enunciated.*

"*You're beginning to sound like a parrot!*" *Moses countered.* "*I guess you invented the echo, too!*"

"*You shall also oversee the building and manufacturing of* the service cloths, the sacred vestments for Aaron the chief priest and for his *punk delinquent* sons *serving* in the ministry, *the appointing and* the anointing oils, and the *flagrant* fragrant incense for the sanctuary. All these *truly magnificent* things they *(the flamboyant artisans, Bezalel and Company, Incorporated)* shall make just as I have commanded you."

"Men will respect and honor You' only if You' teach them how to provide for themselves instead of doing all their labor to pacify and to satisfy Your' greedy psychological needs!" *Moses articulated to his Master and Supreme Purveyor.* "Self-reliance is the best religion of all!"

The *undeterred* Lord *next* said to Moses, "You must also tell the *craven but obnoxious* Israelites *as* you *speak to each of the half million people individually,* 'Take care to keep My' Sabbaths, for that is to be the token between you and Me' throughout the generations. Therefore, you must keep the Sabbath as something sacred.'"

"Lord, a man's pride and his family and his accomplishments are what he values most," Moses protested. "If You' could somehow connect Your' message and Your' heavy didacticism with those recognizable truths, then the Israelites will worship and revere You' above all else."

"Moses, whoever desecrates it *(the Sabbath)* shall be put to death," *the Lord promised and warned*. "If anyone does work on the Sabbath, the *insidious* person must be *swiftly* rooted out of his people and then instantaneously exterminated so that I can have absolute control and authority over the remaining obedient Israelites that still fear Me'."

"Have You' ever studied the definitions of cruelty, vindictiveness, intolerance, threats and enmity?" Moses asked the Lord. "You' need to take an advanced course in 'Human Being Appreciation'. Persuasion works better than brute force. Respect works better than intense fear. Psychology works better than punishment! Have You' ever considered taking an advanced course in Anger Management?"

"And Moses," *the Lord redundantly maintained*, "six days there are for doing work, but the seventh day is the Sabbath of complete rest, sacred to the Lord. Anyone' who does work on the Sabbath shall be put to death."

"But Lord, what if all of these exorbitant work projects You' have assigned for the construction of Your' sanctuaries, Ark, and altars fall far behind schedule?" Moses nervously asked. "Would it be all right then to labor on the Sabbath for the Lord's honor and glory?"

The Lord was oblivious to Moses and acted as if the New Age patriarch wasn't even in His' presence. "So shall the Israelites observe the Sabbath," the Lord's Voice noted to His' main 'spokesman,' *who never had ever been a wheelwright as mentioned earlier in this mediocre text*. "The Hebrews should keep it *(the Sabbath)* throughout their generations as a perpetual covenant. Between Me' and the Israelites," *the Lord professed and presented in improper grammar*, "and it is to be an everlasting token *that has been established*."

"But Lord, isn't a token simply a small favor that is represented as a temporary condition?" Moses debated with His' oblivious Divine Listener. "A token is either a small remembrance or a tiny coin."

"Moses, in six days the Lord *(Who' here is speaking about Himself* in the third person while addressing Moses in the first *person, which was a very bad habit of His')* made the heavens *(Did you know that there was more than one Heaven?).* And *then He' conscientiously fabricated* the earth. But on the seventh day," *the Lord reiterated for the umpteenth time,* "He' rested at His' ease."

"*That again proves that You' have limitations too!*" Moses *exclaimed.* "*The Lord is not as omnipotent as He' would like us to believe! You had to rest after laboring six consecutive days! You got tired, fagged out!*"

When the Lord *at last* finished speaking to Moses *on the summit of majestic cloud-covered Mt. Sinai,* He' gave him two *similarly shaped stone* tablets inscribed by God's own finger *(you have your choice of ten).* "*Moses, take these two tablets, drink plenty of water and see Me' in the morning if you still have a headache from our most rewarding summit meeting!*" the Lord commanded as He' *finally terminated His' prolonged self-induced trance and completely vanished from the scene.*

Chapter Thirty-two
"The Golden Calf"

When the people *(the half million or so listless indolent Israelites)* became aware of Moses' delay in coming down from the *treacherous* mountain, *they all cheered, thinking that the patriarch had died from frostbite or had been ravaged by wild animals.* They gathered around Aaron and said to him *(all half million or so of them amazingly spoke the exact same words without the use of Idiot Cards),* "Come, make us a god' who will be our leader. As for the man Moses' who brought us out of Egypt, we do not know *or care* what has happened to him *or to his fat dumpy ass."*

Aaron *became neurotic and momentarily flabbergasted and finally* replied, "Have your wives, sons and daughters take *off their clothes* and the golden earrings they are wearing *in their noses, bellybuttons and tongues and tell them the rings really belong only on their ears.* Then take *all of* the earrings to me."

So, all the people *(a half million or so strong)* took off *their raunchy clothes and* their earrings *from all parts of their bodies* and brought them to Aaron. *But* Moses' older brother *was at the time very busy selling invisible ladders to old senile fogies and also changing the diapers of the feeble delirious elders of Israel.*

Aaron *readily* accepted their' offering *(gold body-piercing rings that were supposed to be earrings)* and he fashioned this gold with a graving tool *he had borrowed from Bezalel,* making a 'molten' calf *that quickly lost its outer skin as if it were a shedding snake.*

Then they *(the half million or so thick-headed Israelites in the camp)* cried out, "This is your God, O Israel', who brought you out of the land of Egypt *and deposited your dumb asses way out here in the middle of fuckin' nowhere."*

On seeing *the excited people and hearing* this *blasphemous chant,* Aaron built a *makeshift* altar before the calf *that had four calves on its legs behind the golden knees* and *anxiously* proclaimed, "Tomorrow is a feast of the Lord. *Let's have a big steak-out barbecue and screw everything else!"*

Early the next day the people offered holocausts and *enthusiastically* brought peace libations *piece by piece.* Then they sat down on the *dirty insect-infested* ground to eat and drink, and soon rose up to revel *and make merry, especially the radical gay faggots in attendance.*

With that *noise from the camp rising up to the top of Mt. Sinai,* the Lord said to Moses, "Go down at once to your *raucous* people', *who ought to be My' sedate worshipers.* You brought them out of the land of Egypt, but now they have become depraved *maniacs lusting for pleasure.* They have soon turned aside from the way I pointed out to them," *the Lord angrily noted,* "making for themselves a 'molten' calf *modeled after an active volcano* and then worshiping the skinless molten calf. As they are sacrificing to it they are *mockingly* crying out, "This is your God, O Israel', who brought you out of the land of Egypt!"

"But Lord," Moses said, "You' never show Yourself' to the dim-witted Israelites so they have no idea what You' look like, and as a matter of fact, neither do I! The calf is their image of what they believe Your' image ought to be," Moses stated. "Don't tell me that You' are jealous of a silly molten fake-god calf with four golden calves on its legs behind its knees that doesn't even know how to molt its skin off!"

"I see how stiff necked this people is *(My' former worshipers that have abandoned Me' because I have been callous, cruel and threatening to them)."* The Lord continued to address Moses, "Let Me' alone, then, *so that I may sulk and pout at losing a worshiping competition to an inanimate molten golden calf.* My *docile* wrath will blaze up against them *(the disobedient, naughty Israelites' (who only want to have a good time for a much-needed change of pace)* to consume them. Then I will make you a great nation."

"Your great nation is going nowhere as long as You' are only motivated by envy, revenge and spite!" Moses chided and contradicted the already antagonized Lord. "Get and stay on the right course and show more respect for the people You' desire to worship You'."

But then Moses *reconsidered the exercise of his audacity and* implored the Lord his God by saying, "Why, O Lord, should Your' wrath blaze up against Your' own people, whom You' brought out of the land of Egypt with such great power and so strong a hand *with all trump cards?* Is there more to Your' Almighty personality than retribution, threats and sundry plague visitations?"

"Moses, don't taunt Me' with your barbs," the Lord warned. "I am in no mood for frivolity or for semantics or some other antics like that."

"Why should the Egyptians say *all at once,*" Moses related, "with evil intent He' brought them *(the Israelites)* out, that He' might kill them in the mountains and exterminate them *in the desert along with the crawling bugs under their sitting asses and eliminate them from the surface of the earth? The perceptive Egyptians really had You' pegged, Lord, and their assessment was right on the money."*

"What do you suggest?" sobbed the mercurial and enigmatic Lord' Whose' sensitive, tender feelings had been hurt, deservedly so.

"Let Your' blazing wrath die down," Moses advised. "Relent in punishing Your people', who only want to celebrate something, anything, just to release their miserable frustrations. Your' idea of celebration is for them to sacrifice everything for You', a remote introverted Deity that avoids contact with all other humans except unfortunate me!"

"Should I not destroy these puny fickle non-believers?" the Lord asked His' soon-to-be exclusive prophet and doomsayer. "Counsel Me' so that I may not devastate the entire worthless population with one wave of My' hand!"

"Lord, remember Your' servants Abraham, Isaac and Jacob', whom You' affectionately called Israel," Moses reminded his on-the-edge Mentor.

Then Moses proceeded with his constructive suggestions but the Lord preempted him. "Servants are living beings," the Lord told Moses, "and regrettably Abraham, Isaac and Jacob are all dead and gone. You are now My' only true servant among the clamorous descendents of Israel."

"Remember Lord how You' swore to my forefathers by Your' own Self', saying, 'I will make your descendents as numerous as the stars *in a cloudy night's sky.* And all this land I promised *that neither I nor You' legally own*, I will give your *ungrateful* descendents as their *perpetual* heritage'."

Moses then turned and came down *(descended as opposed to fell)* the mountain with the two *stone* tablets of the Commandments in his hands, *accompanied by a herd of curious mountain goats.* On the front and the back of the *heavy* tablets were words written by God, *having drawings, graffiti and inscriptions that were engraved by God Himself'. The only trouble was that no human among the Israelites knew how to read or how to write, since everyone was illiterate because writing had not yet sufficiently developed into an alternate method of communication.*

Now, when Joshua *(who had acute hearing and a cute girlfriend)* heard the noise of the people shouting *below,* he said to Moses, "That sounds like a battle in the camp. *I hope that Amalek and his vengeful henchmen shepherds have not invaded our camp seeking retribution and looking to kick my cowardly ass and then sodomize me!"*

But then Moses answered his military chieftain, "Get a fuckin' life Joshua! It does not sound like the cries of victory, nor does it sound like the cries of defeat," *Moses clarified.* "*In fact it does not sound like cries at all. What we hear Joshua are the sounds of 'revelry', although it is well after 'reveille' when I usually have my 'reverie' before engaging in 'repartee'."*

As he *(Moses)* drew *(sketched a picture of a nude big-breasted woman)* near the *Israelite* camp, he *(Moses, because Joshua was daydreaming of the same nude big-breasted woman) lost his concentration* and *in his distraction* saw the *golden* calf and *the naked people* dancing *around it*. With that *observation,* Moses' wrath flared up *along with his already enlarged hemorrhoids.*

"Moses, don't get your bowels in an uproar!" Joshua cautioned. "That's when it's easy for someone like a midget to kick the shit out of you!"

Moses was so livid that he threw the *stone* tablets down and broke them on the 'base' of the mountain, *completely ignoring the mountain's altitude and hypotenuse and Basemath's teachings.* Taking the calf they had made, *(it is unclear here how Moses got from the base of the mountain to the center of the camp so quickly)* he *(Moses)* fused it *(the pagan calf-god)* into the fire and then ground it down to powder. *He ground the false god with his bare hands in the fire squeezing the golden calf into shreds and then into ash particles without even getting burned.* Moses then scattered the powder on the water *(a polluted stream that flowed next to Mt. Sinai)* and made the Israelites drink *the newly concocted nutritional health food supplement.*

Moses asked Aaron, *"What the fuck are you doing?* What did this people ever do to you that you should lead them into such a grave sin?"

Aaron replied, *"True, I have been a super asshole in your extended absence from the camp,"* he began. "Let not my lord be angry *with my apparent deviation.* You know well enough how prone the people are to evil, *especially when they prostrate in prayer and the guys' prostates begin to act up!* They said to me *in a peer pressure situation,"* Aaron continued, "make us a god to be our leader *that represents prosperity, pleasure and happiness, all terrific things that the Lord' abhors.* For the man Moses' who brought us out of Egypt *(he had carried each and every one of the half million Hebrews on his strong back),* we do not know or *give a flying shit* what has happened to him. So Moses," *Aaron paused to catch his breath,* "I told them *(all half million individually),* 'Let anyone' who has golden jewelry *rings and golden panties* take them off!' They gave them *(the requested articles)* to me, and I threw them into the fire, *keeping the golden panties to frenetically sniff in the interim.* Then this *inanimate* calf came out of the fire *and almost bit my fuckin' pecker off!"*

When Moses realized that, to the scornful joy of his foes, Aaron had let the people run wild *in a simulated pagan orgy,* he stood at the gate of the camp and cried, "Whoever is for the Lord let 'him' *(no women allowed)* come to me!"

All the *loyal* Levites *in their blue canvass tunics and blue canvass robes* rallied to him' *(Moses),* who was 'canvassing' the camp for supporters, and hopefully, strong athletic supporters that had the sufficient balls to back him.

Moses told the *no-nonsense law and order* Levites *in an impromptu pep rally,* "Thus says the Lord, the God of Israel: Put your sword on your hip, *and let's play 'Moses' Says' (an early form of 'Simon Says').* Every one of you, go up and down the camp *with a stern 'gait',* from gate to gate *and intimidate* and slay your own kinsmen, your friends and neighbors."

"He's an absolute maniac and as drunk as the Lord!" Joshua told Aaron. "Moses is ready for the asylum and psychology hasn't even been invented yet!"

"He's as crazy as the Lord, too!" Aaron concurred.

The Levites, *like little programmed mechanical men,* carried out the *bizarre* command of Moses, and that day there fell about three thousand of the people *that in spite of the threat of imminent death still believed in partying and having a good time while thinking about prosperity, pleasure, happiness, hedonism big tits, hairy pussies and sex.*

Then Moses said, "Today you have been dedicated to the Lord *while the slain sinners have been 'deadicated' to death.* For you were against your own sons and kinsmen to bring a blessing upon yourselves this day. *Long live the Levites, the Lord's new Secret Police!"* Moses proclaimed.

On the next day Moses said to *the half million minus three thousand'* people, *"You Levites really slay me!" he joked.* "The rest of you have committed a grave sin *while the loyal Levites have blessedly killed three thousand Israelites for partying and the loyal Levites have sent them to their graves, which incidentally have not been dug yet. According to the Lord's inflexible principles, the* punishment must always be greater than the sin or crime or the crime that is sin," Moses orated to the exasperated crowd to exacerbate their anxiety. "I will go up to the Lord, *Who' has deliberately ostracized Himself' from your vile midst by living in a remote mist,* and I will see if I am able to make atonement for your *inexcusable* sin."

So Moses went *(climbed the steep mountain)* back to the Lord and said, "Ah! *Are you a dentist! I need a tooth pulled*! *But more seriously Lord,* 'this people' *(Your' former worshipers and my former followers)* has indeed committed a grave sin in making a god of gold for themselves *and partying around it while having fun and pleasure',* which we both know are taboo according to Your' stringent doctrines and laws. If You' will only forgive their sin!" Moses pleaded. "If You' will not, then strike me out of the book You' have written *because then I won't want to be mentioned anywhere in Your' damned biography or in Your' damned boring autobiography."*

The Lord answered Moses *in convoluted grammar*, "Him' only who has sinned against Me' will I strike out of the book, *not even giving him 'three strikes and you're out' but limiting each violator to only one 'strike-out'.* Now *Moses*, go and lead the people whither I have told you. My *notorious formidable* angel will go before you," *the Lord informed his stressed-out New Age prophet.* "When it is time for Me' to punish *any deviates from My' harsh but benign rules and laws,* I will punish them for their sin. *The punishment shall always be far worse than the offense. The Levites had done the right thing by savagely slaughtering three thousand of their brethren,"* the *gratified Lord concluded and conveyed.* "They had committed no sin by killing their kinsmen for sinning against Me'."

Thus the Lord *(through His' awesome Angel of Death)* smote the people for having had Aaron make a *very simple golden* calf for them, *but for some inexplicable reason, Aaron was spared from extermination by the zealous jealous newly established Levite Secret Police.*

Chapter Thirty-three
"Moses' and God"

The Lord told Moses, "You and the 'people' *(we're getting a little too touchy and impersonal here about the insolent and hedonistic Israelites)* who' you brought up from the land of Egypt are to go from here *(Mt. Sinai, next to Mt. Sinus)* to the land I swore to Abraham, Isaac and Jacob. I swore I would give the land to their *chaste* descendents, *but somehow, things haven't worked out as I had planned."*

"Lord, many of the Israelites believe that You' have reneged on Your' hollow hallow promise because Abraham, Isaac and Jacob are all long dead," Moses countered. "But on the other hand, I have a Mt. Sinai migraine and the Israelites all have excruciating Mt. Sinus' headaches too, so we all want to get the hell out of here as soon as possible."

"Canaan will be yours despite your decadent followers' weak character and their diabolical behavior," the Lord confidently predicted to His' chief advocate. "Driving out the Canaanites, the Amorites, the Hittites, the Perizzites, the Hivites and the Jeb-bushites will not be easy," the Lord candidly admitted. "I will send My' *courageous* angel before you to the land flowing with milk and money."

"Many of the Hebrews say that the land of Canaan that You' covet is a barren wasteland that *flows with urine and feces* and not with abundant milk and honey, if I may use polite terms for the Israelites' more coarse and vulgar language descriptions," Moses returned, daring not to say the words' *"piss and shit"* in the Lord's presence.

"But I Myself' *have more important affairs to attend to* and will not go up to Canaan in your *friendly* company," *the Lord disclosed to Moses.* "I say this *bad news* because you are stiff-necked people, stubborn and obstinate, otherwise I might exterminate you if I become *'incensed'* and angered."

"Extermination is Your' *easy* solution to those that refuse to worship an egotistical Deity that sulks like a child and that bullies His' followers with threats and then with real devastation," Moses stated. "Is it no wonder that Your' adherents can be counted on less than half of one hand?"

Moses soon told the Israelites the essence of the Lord's evaluation, *and* when the people heard the bad news, they went into mourning *sickness, including the men*, and no one wore his *(or her?)*

ornaments. *In fact there was no need for any ornaments at all because no one had a lawn or a front or back yard out there in the hot arid desert. And also, there were no holiday pine trees in the hot sultry eastern desert around Mt. Sinai and Mt. Sinus for the women to hang their ornamental decorations on and for the men to hang their balls on.*

The Lord *then* said to Moses, *"Hi Moses!* Tell the Israelites: 'You' are a stiff-necked *and stiff-penised'* people'. Were I to go in your company even for a moment, I would *be tempted* to exterminate you *en masse.* Take off your *gaudy* ornaments, *trinkets and balls,*" *the Lord told Moses to inform 'their' disinterested and aberrant people,* "and then I will see *and determine* what I am to do with you."

Some of the more stubborn Israelites with severe personality disorders elected not to take off their garish ornaments because then the Lord would do nothing to anyone (violator or no violator) one way or the other. "Why give Him' a choice and a chance to act if we take off the gaudy ornaments and our balls?" they deviously whispered to one another.

Most others among the wandering tribe were fearful of the Lord's nasty temper and of His' demonstrative proclivity to rage-out against defenseless mortals for trivial reasons. So *on the journey* from Mt. Herob onward, the Israelites finally laid aside their ornaments *and the more intelligent men kept their balls hidden from public scrutiny.*

The tent', which was *appropriately* called the "meeting *and greeting* tent," Moses pitched outside the camp some distance away *from its center.* Anyone' who wished to consult the Lord would go to the meeting tent *situated* outside the *on-the-lam debris-littered* camp. *Moses only received one visitor the first several weeks of the great trek toward Canaan and that guest was Aaron' who wanted to talk about forming a business alliance with Jethro Reuel and Moses to swindle the gullible and fearful Israelites big time using religion and the fear of God's wrath as their manipulative psychological tools.*

Whenever Moses went out to the tent, the people would all rise and stand *(out of fear of execution by the unscrupulous and invisible Angel of Death)* at the *entrancing* entrance of their own tents. They would cautiously watch Moses enter his tent, *and that was a sign for everyone to avoid any and all contact with the New Age patriarch and the Lord's notorious supernatural hit-man', the fearless and undaunted Angel of Death.*

The *ominous* column of *dark* clouds would descend from Heaven and stand *guard* at the entrance while the Lord consulted with Moses *in the awe-inspiring meeting and greeting tent.* On seeing the *steering* column of clouds *seemingly* standing at the entrance of the tent, all of the *scared shitless* Israelites *would pass around toilet paper to wipe their fannies and then* would worship *incessantly out of fear of execution by the most formidable but invisible Angel of Death* (from the entrances to their own tents).

Prior to recent developments the Lord used to speak to Moses Voice to face, as one man *customarily* speaks to *and addresses* another, *but now the Lord just speaks and barks His' imperative commands with little empathy extended to His' servant.* Moses would then return to the camp *of rebels*, but his young assistant Joshua, son of Nun *and None*, would not move out of the camp *fearing that Amalek would find him out in the open and really kick the shit out of him.*

Moses said to the *omniscient* Lord, "You indeed are telling me to lead this *disorganized* 'people' *(now reduced to an unnamed mass of lowlife egotistical nobodies)* on, *but how do I know for sure that You' are not leading 'me' on?* You have not let me know whom You' will send with me," *Moses reminded the always evasive and enigmatic Lord*, "yet You' have said, 'You are My' intimate friend. Also, you have found favor with Me'. Now, if I have found favor with You', do not let me know Your' *strange* ways. In knowing you I will find favor with you. *That Lord is exactly what You' had told me."*

Moses was puzzled and perplexed when his Mentor's Voice did not answer. "Lord, what on earth or in Heaven are You' trying to say by those crazy words?" Moses asked. "What's with all this corny and fake special favor stuff? I don't need any special favors or tokens from You', believe me when I say that!" Moses remarked in a quasi-scoff. "I am certain that there will be a gigantic rope (not a string) attached to whatever minuscule deed You' ever decide to do for me. I don't need a large bulky anchor dangling from my skinny wrinkled neck!"

"Then too, this *decrepit and sickly-looking* nation, after all, is your own *itinerant* people,*"* the Lord clearly said, deftly changing the subject from small favors to Moses' explicit duty and responsibility to the insubordinate Israelites. "I Myself*,"* the Lord continued, "will go along with you to give you *necessary* rest, suggestions and advice."

Moses *angrily* replied, "If You' are not going *to Canaan Yourself*, do not make us go up from here. *We'll get our asses kicked good, Angel of Death or no Angel of Death in front of our ragtag invasion.*"

"*Are you doubting My' Divine veracity and My' Supreme authority?*" the Lord alleged and boomed. "*If so craven old man you should again speak defiantly so that I can incinerate you right on the spot.*"

"How can it be known that we, Your' *exclusive* chosen people, and I, have found *definite* favor with You', except by Your' *going on the march and accompanying us?*" Moses compromised and attested. "Then we Lord, Your' *disobedient* people and I, will be singled out from every people on *the face of* the earth. *Could someone please tell me what these words in this atrocious script actually mean?*"

"The Lord *promptly* answered Moses, "This request, too, which you have just made, I will carry out, because you have found favor with Me' and you are now My' intimate friend *and trustworthy confidante.*"

"*Don't do me any favors!*" Moses yelled in the Lord's Voice's direction. "*I don't get intimate with any homosexual man or with any Deity! I don't even get intimate with my ugly slutty wife Zipporah!*"

Then after a moment of contemplation Moses added in his "*intimate*" dialogue with the Voice, "Lord, do let me see Your' glory!"

He answered, "I will make all My' beauty pass before you, and in your presence I will pronounce *and spell* my name L-O-R-D', the One' Who shows favor to whom I will. I grant mercy to whomever I will."

"*Well Lord, since we're now on an intimate basis, what do You' really look like if You' want me to get, as You' say, intimate with You?*" Moses politely requested. "*I've never been hit on by a Deity before!*"

"My face you cannot see, for no man sees Me' and still lives," the Lord explained.

"*Are You' some kind of Male Medusa or something? Are You' Medusa's grotesque-looking brother?*" Moses inquired. "*You certainly have a Man's deep baritone Voice, so I know You' mustn't be effeminate or a perverted cross-dresser!*"

"Here," continued the Lord'*s Voice*, "is a place near Me' where you shall station yourself on the rock. When My' glory passes, I will set you in the hollow of the rock and will cover you with My' hand until I have passed by."

"Holy Lord!" Moses boisterously exclaimed. "Your secret Glory must be really awesome to see! Maybe it's best if I never see It' at all!"

"Then," *the Lord suavely said,* "I will remove My' hand *from My' Glory,* so that you may see My' back. But My' face *and My' Glory* are not to be seen *under any circumstances or else you will most certainly die!"*

Chapter Thirty-four
"Renewal of the Tablets"

The Lord', *who never was hoarse or spoke with a raspy Voice, then* said to Moses, "Cut two *identical* stone tablets like the former ones *you had smashed at the base of Mt. Sinai, you stupid fool,* that I may write *(rewrite)* on them the Commandments, which *along with drawings and graffiti* were *the moral codes of human behavior inscribed* on the former tablets you broke."

"*That's just Your' offensive style,"* Moses accused and alleged, *"blame everything You' deem wrong on me. At least I only broke Your' two stones and didn't destroy any cities or drown all the people in the world in a massive flood like Someone I know! Lord, the damage I do to anything is always minimal."*

"And Moses," *the Lord encouragingly proceeded,* "get ready for tomorrow morning when you are to go back up to Mt. Sinai, *for I have humorously led the Israelites around in the desert in complete circles for the past several weeks,"* the Lord chuckled. "On the mountain you are to present yourself *to Me'* like a good little prophet. No one shall come up with you *to the all-sacred mountain top and observe our intimacy,"* the Lord indicated. "No one is ever to be seen on any part of the mountain, and even the flocks and the herds are not to go 'grazing' there *or I might 'graze' them with an errant lightning bolt or better yet, I might even employ the old fire and brimstone method again, ha, ha, ha!"*

"I think You' are paranoid and need immediate professional psychiatric help," Moses recommended. *"Who cares if anyone sees me visiting You' atop Your' mountain? It's Your' damned mountain, isn't it? Learn to share it! Let's have a little socialism introduced here!"*

Moses then cut two tablets like the former he had broken, *and he then regretted that he had ever broken the Lord's stones.* "You can't take these stones for 'granite',"* Moses complained about his rigorous endeavor.

Early the next morning he *(Moses)* went up Mt. Sinai *wishing that he were ascending Mt. Sinus instead.* Moses was doing just as the Lord had commanded him, taking along the two *duplicate* stone tablets *that would be difficult to swallow even with ten gallons of water.*

Having come down in a cloud, the Lord, *still in a fog*, stood with him *(Moses)* there and proclaimed, *"Don't you wish you could*

213

travel in a cloud like I do and not have to climb up these steep rugged precipices?"

There was a momentary pause as Moses caught his breath. "Moses, this is the Lord *speaking*." Thus the Lord passed before him and cried out, "The Lord, the Lord, a merciful and gracious God, slow to anger and rich in kindness and *intimate* fidelity, I will continue My' plenteous kindness for a thousand generations. I will forgive wickedness and crime and sin, and Moses, I will not declare the guilty guiltless, but I will punish children and grandchildren for their fathers' wickedness."

"I am convinced now Lord that You' are absolutely warped!" Moses gasped. "You have gone off the deep end! Who's Your' shrink, that hyperactive pedophile child-molester Jethro Reuel?" Moses angrily asked. "How could You' possibly say that grandchildren are responsible for their grandfathers and for their fathers' sins? Kids will be cursed even before they are born and even before having a chance to lead good lives? How could You' be so prejudiced in Your' judgment?"

Moses was awe-struck by the craziness of the Lord's aforementioned cryptic words, so he at once bowed down to the ground in worship *of irrationality*. Then 'he' *(Moses, the pronoun king)* said, "If I find favor with You', O Lord, do come along in our company, *because I don't want to be alone with the Israelites when they get drunk and become uncontrollable. I don't trust them, and they might conspire against me.* They are indeed stiff-necked *and stiff-penised* people as You' have *aptly* described, yet Lord," *Moses begged*, "pardon our wickedness and sins, and receive us as your own *in spite of our shortcomings and our characteristic premature ejaculations', which keeps the grand total of our population and the grand total of Your' worshipers down considerably.*"

"Here then," said the Lord, "is the *convenient* covenant I will make *with you and with the Israelites*. Before the eyes of all your people *(not 'My' people' or 'our people')* I will work such marvels as have never been wrought in any nation anywhere on earth," *the Lord haughtily boasted*.

"I thought that arrogance and bragging were only grotesque human deficiencies," Moses objected and argued to no avail. "If You' Lord are going to do something great, just do it and stop promising and predicting. If this is indeed Your' script and Your' play as You' have maintained," Moses said, "then get Your' act together and don't make a scene!"

"The people among you will soon see how awe-inspiring My' deeds are that I the Lord will do by your side," *the Deity's Voice revealed to Moses.* "But *listen closely* Moses; you must on your part keep the Commandments I am giving *(re-issuing to you since you broke the first set, you clumsy and peevish pond-scum Dummy)* you today."

"Thanks a lot for the bonus!" Moses said as he graciously accepted the Lord's second set of replacement stone tablets. "I am sure that the people will honor and 'depreciate' them," he uttered, making an inadvertent slip of the tongue.

"I will drive out before you the Amorites *with their love couches,* the Canaanites *with their ferocious canines,* the Hittites *with their tawdry leotards,* the Perizzites *with their prestigious prestidigitators,* the Hivites *with their hordes of hives* and the unpredictable Jeb-bushites', *who all want to be governor over the lawless Israelites."*

"Lord," Moses marveled, "no matter how You' slice or cut it, You' want the hapless Israelites to occupy the land of those tribes that You' have fraudulently promised to my forefathers. And now You' are bragging about how You' and Your' fierce Angel of Death are going to lead the charge against these passive and non-violent tribes!"

"Take care Moses," *the Lord cautioned,* "not to make a covenant with these inhabitants of the land that you are to enter *(invade, plunder and trample),* or else they will become a snare among you," *the Lord's Voice cautioned.* "Tear down their altars and cut down their poles *and replace them with My' altars and with My' poles even though the new nation will be called Israel and not Poland.* You shall not worship any other god, for the Lord is the Jealous One, a jealous *fanatical* God is He."

"At last, words of truth from Your' lips," Moses verified. "Jealousy is Your' principal motivation followed by greed and revenge. Thank You' Lord for finally telling it like it is!"

"I told you Moses," *the Lord reiterated,* "do not make a covenant with the inhabitants of that land, *the one I promised your mentally deficient deceased ancestors.* When they render their wanton worship to their gods and sacrifice to them," *the Lord bellowed while referring to the present pacifist residents of Canaan,* "one of the foreigners might invite you to partake of their *obscene* sacrifice."

"I get it Lord," Moses stated. "You want the Israelites to have a closed society so that our only allegiance will be to Your' Glory,

215

which like Your' face, we can never look upon. Keep out distrustful outside ideas for they might corrupt our general ignorance and our decadent inbreeding. Keep us isolated from science and culture! What a ludicrous mess this is!"

"And Moses," *the Lord went on*, "neither shall you take their daughters as wives for your sons, otherwise, when their daughters render their wanton worship to their gods, they will make your *gullible* sons do the same."

"*All outsiders are evil from Your' limited perspective, and all Hebrews are destined to be ignorant of civilization and isolated from constructive outside influences. Lord,*" Moses sincerely said, "*did You' ever hear of the maxim: 'It is always easier to borrow than to invent?' That quotation simply means the Israelites will stay stupid as long as we have to depend on our non-existent technology base and upon Your' closed-minded religion.*"

"Moses, you shall not make for yourselves molten gods *with lava spewing out of the idol's mouth, nose, ears and rectum. And furthermore* you shall keep the feast of the Unleavened Bread, *even though your men complain of fewer erections from not rising properly*. For seven days at the prescribed time in the month of Abib (*our only month to date*) you are to eat the unleavened bread *with 'a bib' around your necks according to our proud Biblical tradition*," the Lord divulged. "This will symbolize how you came out of Egypt during Abib," the Lord summarized His' general instructions to His' Main Man.

'I think that possibly Jethro Reuel has corrupted the Lord's mind', Moses thought, 'and the main problem is that the Lord is all-powerful but at the same time also psychologically disturbed and requires counseling. This whole rotten scenario might spell doomsday for me and for the Israelites if I do not carefully handle Him' with kid gloves.'

"And Moses," *the Lord further lectured*, "to Me' belongs every first-born male that opens the womb among all your livestock, whether in the herd or in the flock."

"*Are You' insinuating Lord that the Hebrew' men have sex with virgin sheep and goats and not with experienced hookers, whores, prostitutes, concubines, maidservants, harlots and wives?*" Moses asked. "*Your nebulous statements need more clarification!*"

"The firstling of an ass you shall redeem with one of the flock," *the Lord stipulated*, "and if you do not redeem it *with value coupons*, you must break its neck *at breakneck speed as I have indicated to you many times before,*" the Lord ranted. "The first-born among your sons you shall redeem *with a ten percent discount and three value-added coupons."*

"You drive a hard bargain, but I guess You' have to when You' are the Lord and must somehow make chicken salad out of chicken shit as is the case with the Israelites!"

"And *in addition* Moses," *the Lord elaborated,* "no one shall appear before Me' empty-handed, *not even the poorest, destitute indigent pauper among the Hebrews.* For six days you may work, but on...."

"On the seventh day you shall rest," *Moses added.* "On that day you must rest even during the seasons of plowing and harvesting. *How many times do I have to hear this crap?*"

"How did you know what I was about to say?" the Lord wanted to find out. "Is someone holding up idiot cards for you to read off of even though you are basically illiterate?"

"I've heard Your' browbeating sermons a thousand times and have memorized all of Your' lackluster lines," Moses all-too-honestly answered. "I know Your' whole routine by heart. That's all she 'rote', ha, ha, ha!"

"*Anyway You' geriatric numbskull,*" the Lord continued, "you shall keep the feast of Weeks *since we don't know the names of any of the days except the Sabbath.* It shall begin with the first wheat harvest, and likewise, the feast at the *culminating* fruit harvest at the close of the year, *but we don't know which months those events transpire in either. So far Abib is the only month we have a name for,*" the Lord reviewed for Moses to realize and ponder.

"I think we will have invented the 'colander' before we organize a credible 'calendar'," Moses creatively jested to his unappreciative supernatural Listener.

"Three times a year all your men shall appear before the Lord, the Lord God of Israel *so that I can make the evil ones' rapidly disappear into thin air.* Since I will drive out the nations before you to give you a large territory," *the Lord outlined,* "there will be no one to covet your *worthless sandy* land when you go up three times to appear before the Lord, your God, *and I then make most of the sinful Hebrews disappear.*"

"Threats and promises, that's Your' game and I must admit that You' play it well," Moses keenly observed and praised.

"And Moses, you shall not offer Me' the blood of sacrifice with unleavened bread, nor shall the sacrifice of the Passover feast be kept overnight for the next day," the Lord prescribed.

"*Of course,*" Moses understood, "*You' prefer to eat leavened bread and leave the unleavened bread for the inferior Israelites to eat as a food of submission and as a meal of subordination,*" Moses concluded. "*You don't want to see the Hebrew' men get erections and enjoy themselves for a change for five minutes of simple earthly pleasure!*"

"The choicest first fruits of your soil you shall bring to the house of the Lord your God, and most of all," the Lord specified, "you' shall not boil a kid in its mother's milk!"

"*We've been through this dismal abysmal nonsense before Lord! No mother in her right mind would boil her own kid in her breast milk!*" Moses screamed. "*That would be an abomination of the greatest magnitude! And it seems that You' are determined to keep the Hebrews starving, poor and uneducated and then take from our use the best we have of every fruit, lamb and cherished jewelry piece,*" Moses 'plaintively' accused. "*Selfish is too modest of a term to describe Your' hungry lust for domination! That's what really should be abolished!*"

Then the Lord said to Moses, "*Although you are illiterate*, write down these words, for in accordance with them I have made my covenant with you and with Israel."

"*You're pretty big on covenants, aren't You'?*" Moses objected quite vehemently. "*What about that super big covenant you had made with Abraham about the Land of Canaan? Where's the big payoff?*"

So, Moses stayed there with the Lord the full duration of forty days and forty nights. *The Lord was pretending He' was Noah inside the original Ark all the time.* Moses *did an amazing thing for he* did not eat any food or drink any water *(although he ate water and drank food to stay alive)* as he wrote on the tablets the *immortal* words of the *timeless* covenant, the Ten Commandments.

As Moses came down from Mt. Sinai, *he had an allergic attack from germs blowing over from Mt. Sinus.* He carried the two stone tablets of the *reformulated* Ten Commandments in his hands, *so he couldn't brush or wipe the snot away from his long ugly nose.* The skin on his face had become radiant when he had conversed with the Lord, *and the nasal debris blown by the stiff wind smeared all over his cheeks and it acted like beneficial moisturizing cream making his face glow even more than it had just done by simply being radiant.*

When Aaron and the other *restive* Israelites saw Moses and noticed how radiant the skin on his face had become, they were afraid to come near him *because they all knew he might sneeze a lunger or a lung, or possibly even two lungs right into their bushy-bearded unkempt faces.*

Only after Moses called to them did Aaron and all the rulers *and yardsticks* of the community come back to him. Moses then spoke to them *in a peculiar language then known as "Mucus Semitic."*

Later on, all the Israelites *(a half million minus the three thousand that had been butchered by the ferocious Levites)* came up to him *(Moses)* and began sneezing, curiously conversing with the New Age patriarch in Mucus Semitic. Moses enjoined with them all that the Lord had told him on Mt. Sinai. *Everyone was speaking Mucus Semitic except the feeble senile elders', who' all were just speaking plain and simple Mucus.*

When he *(Moses)* finished speaking with them *(the irrational sages and elders),* he put a veil over his face *pretending to be a woman virgin.* Whenever Moses entered the 'presence' *and the gifts* of the Lord to converse with Him', he removed the veil until he came out again. *The Lord seemed big on costumes and transvestite cross-dressing.*

On coming out *of the closet, or in this case "out of the tent,"* he *(Moses)* would tell the Israelites all that had been commanded *and how great it was to finally be liberated and to finally be able to role play his true sexuality in public. Eventually the Israelites became engendered with Moses' gender preferences.*

Then the Israelites would see that the skin of Moses was radiant; so he *(Moses)* would put the veil over his face until he again went in to converse with the Lord *on sacred Mt. Sinai.*

"I wonder if Moses knows that the perverted pedophile Jethro Reuel is practicing his ventriloquism on my younger brother' patriarch by projecting his voice to sound like the Lord's baritone," Aaron said to Joshua. *"My foolish-hearted younger brother is often easily deceived by pranks and by sophisticated canards Joshua,"* Aaron elucidated, *"and certainly Moses is my most gullible brother who' is very easily duped."*

"And to think that the ignorant Israelites believe that Moses will lead us all to the land of milk and honey," Joshua answered in total disgust. *"Sounds like a lot of glorified piss and shit to me!"*

Chapter Thirty-five
"Sabbath Regulations"

Moses 'assembled' the whole Israelite community (*including the now-minority straight community*) *from a "Whole Israelite Community Kit" that Aaron had given him as a joke.* He said to them, "*Listen up, you dumb ass dunces,* this is what the Lord has commanded to be done. On six days work may be done *or else all of you will be extremely sorry.*"

"*Who the hell wants to work?*" a half million minus three thousand irate voices yelled in unison. "*Work sucks! Work sucks! Work sucks!*" the Israelites wildly chanted.

After things eventually quieted down, Moses continued, "But on the seventh day shall be sacred to you as the Sabbath of complete rest to the Lord."

"*The Lord wants us to rest for Him' too in addition to working our elbows off for Him the other six consecutive nameless days'! We don't even have adequate Rest Rooms!*" four hundred and ninety-seven thousand un-melodious voices screamed out together. "*Fuck you! Fuck you! Fuck you!*" the angry throng all chanted in unison like crazed automatons.

After fifteen chaotic minutes of vociferous protest, silence was finally again re-established by the Levites. "Anyone' who does work on that day shall be put to death!" *Moses preached from a cliff on Mr. Sinai down to the unruly Hebrew crowd.* "Lazy Israelites deserve no other fate than death!"

"*You're totally fucked-up! You suck! You're totally fucked-up!*" the almost half million shouted, jeered and chanted.

Three thousand Levites wearing heavy blue canvass robes yelled a plethora of battle cries and then dashed to the forefront with swords held over their heads. The Levite warriors stood on both sides of Moses on the dangerous mountain cliff, and the boisterous mob shut up in a hurry until it was so quiet that one could hear an almond drop.

"You shall not even light a fire, *because fires have been lit at the altar to qualify as the only legitimate fires,*" Moses told the *now* quiet but *still* restless throng. "No fire shall be lit in any of your dwellings on the Sabbath Day, *unless of course you have a chimney, and as we all know,*" Moses concluded and scoffed at his audience, "*nobody in this cheap-ass camp has a chimney or even a stove in their friggin' frigid tent.*"

Then Moses told the whole Israelite community *including the minority "straight community," which featured skinny men with big long erections,* "This is what the Lord had commanded: 'Take up a collection among you for the Lord'."

"But we are poor and have no money to give!" a feeble blind senile elder cried out from the front row. A dozen savage Levite Storm Troopers approached the poor old coot and swiftly decapitated him, putting the old cantankerous codger out of his misery once and for all. This rather shocking demonstration of violence really impacted the formerly wild mob and soon the assemblage settled down into a large courteous open-air synagogue revival-type congregation.

"Everyone," *Moses continued with outstretched arms,* "as his heart prompts him, shall bring as a contribution to the Lord, gold, silver and bronze *out of threat of being pulverized either by the Levites or by the invisible berserk Angel of Death.* Violet, purple and scarlet yarn, fine linen and goats' hair *should also be donated. In addition,"* Moses stated, *"the Lord will accept* rams' skins, and *furthermore He' will accept* 'dyed' wool *that hasn't been taken from a deceased ram for over a week so be wary of all the ramifications,"* solicited Moses. *"The Lord will be thrilled to receive* dyed red and tahash *(porpoise dyed on purpose)* skins, acacia wood and oil for the light*,"* Moses aptly relayed to the half million apathetic listeners standing before him in forced silence. "And lastly, you may contribute spices for the 'anointing oil', *which must be anointed by priests and I must emphasize that the 'anointing oil' cannot anoint all by itself. And don't forget* fragrant incense'," *Moses enthusiastically added, "just as long as it' doesn't incense the Lord, so don't apply the fragrance too flagrantly. Be very careful about that particular minute detail.* Also, onyx stones and other gems to be mounted on the ephod and on the breast-piece *will undoubtedly be gratefully contributed and gladly received."*

The crowd mumbled and grumbled in a low rumble, considered the consequences of savage and instantaneous Levite and/or Angel of Death executions, and against their will, the masses politely listened to Moses' religious propaganda and to his unyielding demands that were really the Lord's redundant unyielding demands.

"Let every expert among you come and make all that the Lord has commanded you *to manufacture and construct*: 'the Dwelling with its tent, its covering, its clasps, its boards, its bars, its columns, and its pedestals'. *Praise be the Lord,"* the chief guardian of the faith proclaimed.

Moses paused and coughed for a moment, happy and encouraged to have seen the half million or so Israelites reticent and passive. "And to the *gifted and talented* craftsmen among you," *the patriarch confidently boomed out,* "remember to manufacture the Ark of the Covenant with its poles, the propitiatory, *the pituitary*, and the curtain veil," *he reminded the inattentive but fearful artisans.* "*And what would this grand project be* without the table *of contents* and the *exquisite Showtime* Showbread, the lamp stand with its appurtenances, the lamps and the oil for the light, the altar of incense and the *non-flagrant* fragrant incense."

A distinct low mumble of "Bullshit! Bullshit! Bullshit!" could be discerned originating from the center of the large contingent of volatile Israelites. Hostile Levites shouted several frightening war cries and in an instant silence once again prevailed at the camp assembly.

"And also," *Moses proceeded from atop his hastily constructed makeshift rickety wooden stand on the mountain cliff,* "remember to include an entrance curtain for the *entrancing* entrance of the Dwelling. *Also include* the altar of holocausts with its bronze grating, its poles and all its appurtenances and the laver with its *intricate* base," *Moses lectured the now lethargic audience of disbelievers.* "And last but not least," *Moses instructed the phlegmatic artisans in the throng,* "you must also assemble and make the hangings of the court *or else the Levites will make you all hang with the hangings,"* Moses threatened, effectively imitating the Lord's swagger. "And the hangings must have columns and pedestals, *and don't forget about the vital* curtain for the court's *entrancing* entrance, the tent pegs for the Dwelling and for the court with the needed *accompanying* ropes."

When the crowd again simmered down Moses spoke once more. "*And finally my fellow dolts, all you contented artisans out there, don't forget to* include the service cloths for use in the sanctuary," *the speaker announced,* "the sacred vestments for Aaron the *high* priest *and those designated* for his *incorrigible punk delinquent* sons', who will form *the first layer* of the Lord's *bureaucratic* ministry. *And don't forget gentlemen, your' sacrifice, your work and your toil shall be rendered gratis to the Lord's honorable service!"*

When the whole disgusted and disgruntled Israelite *straight and gay communities* left Moses' presence, everyone, as his heart suggested and as his spirit prompted *and as his mind especially feared*, brought a *special* contribution to the Lord for the construction of the *essential* meeting *and greeting* tent. *They also brought stolen fabric materials* for all the services and for the sacred vestments to be worn by Aaron and his *unmanageable punk delinquent* sons.

Both the men and the women, all as their hearts prompted them, brought brooches, earrings, rings, necklaces, *amulets* and various other gold articles *they had been hording for a massive spring "Camp Close-out," the Israelites' version of a huge combination garage, attic and lawn sale.*

Everyone' who happened to have violet, scarlet, or purple yarn, fine linen or goat' hair, rams' skins dyed red or tahash skins, all brought them *to the staging area. Plenty of the men and women had goats' hair, so they asked barbers to trim their locks and tresses, even the 'old goats' among the disenchanted Israelite men.*

Whoever could make a contribution of gold, silver or bronze offered it to the Lord *out of fear of execution by the bellicose Levites.* Everyone' who happened to have *disposable* acacia wood *(something that everyone always carried around with them and bartered for wine and sex)* for any part of the work, brought it *and reluctantly donated it to the general cause.*

All the women' who were excellent spinners *(talk about gender discrimination)* danced and rotated around the camp against their wills in honor to the Lord. The excellent spinners also brought handspun violet, scarlet and purple yarn and fine linen thread, *which they spun while spinning and dancing wildly around the weird camp of gypsy sickos.*

All the women' who possessed the skill spun goat hair', *which they trimmed from the heads of all the old goats in the oddball Israelite camp. No one was exempt from the responsibility so therefore there weren't any scapegoats.*

The princes *(tribal chiefs)* brought *stolen* onyx stones and other gems for mounting on the ephod and on the breast-piece as well as *an assortment of* spices, oil for the light, *oil for the heavy, fat Israelites,* anointing oil, *appointing oil,* and *last but not least unflagrant* fragrant incense.

Every Israelite man and woman brought to the Lord such voluntary offerings *they had no use for and wished to discard as refuse as they thought best to unload the worst of their junk during this once-in-a-lifetime opportunity. They did this "rummage cleanout"* for the various kinds of work' which the Lord had commanded Moses to do *and assign.*

Moses said to the *peeved and irritated* Israelites, "See, the Lord has chosen Bezalel, son of Uri *and Urine*, son of Hur *and Her*, of the tribe of Judah, and has filled him with a divine spirit of skill and understanding and knowledge in every craft, so Bezalel, *my warmest congratulations!*" *Moses commended.* "*You Bezalel are hereby commissioned to do most of the work needed to be done all by yourself and to supervise the remaining work to which you have not been assigned!*"

The crowd let out a boisterous cheer for Bezalel', who then unexpectedly fainted while considering the great burden of responsibility recently delegated to him by Moses while speaking for the all-demanding Lord.

Moses informed the now-happy crowd, "He *(Bezalel)* will work in the production of embroidery, in making things of gold, silver and bronze, in cutting and mounting precious stones and in carving wood, along with other important crafts."

Everyone again cheered Bezalel, who was finally being revived by a team of prehistoric paramedics that were frantically slapping his face and aggressively pulling and tugging his beard. Finally, with the help of the accomplished prehistoric paramedics, Bezalel was revived, able to rise to his feet and then the overwhelmed fellow suddenly collapsed back down to the ground.

"He *(the Lord)* has given Bezalel and Oholiab, son of Ahisamach *and Thank-u-very-mach*, of the tribe of Dan the ability to teach others," *Moses yelled down from his shaky wooden platform, "but since Bezalel will be doing most of the work, all the other crap that I had alluded to won't really be necessary.*"

After the crowd stopped applauding, Moses finished his long-winded oration. "He *(the Lord)* has endowed them *with dowels* and the skill to execute all types of work *or else be executed by the murderous Levites. They know all about* engraving, embroidery, the making of variegated cloth of violet, scarlet and purple yarn and fine linen thread," *Moses informed the gleeful Hebrews, who were elated because Bezalel was going to do most of their work.* "They *(Bezalel, Bezalel and Bezalel)* also know all about weaving and all other arts and crafts," *Moses solemnly related, "but as you all now know, all of that worry is irrelevant because Bezalel will be doing most of the damned work all by himself.*"

Bezalel, who had managed to get to his feet a second time with the assistance of the militant and hardly specialized prehistoric paramedics, fainted back down to the ground. The already standing crowd (unaware of the artisan's predicament) gave the unconscious master craftsmen another standing ovation.

Chapter Thirty-six
"Tent Cloth and Coverings"

"Bezalel, therefore," *Moses told the gleeful assemblage of Israelites*, "will set to work with Oholiab *in the 'O Holy Lab'* and with all the experts' whom the Lord has 'endowed' *with dowels* and skill and understanding. *As you now know this great skill and understanding our incomparable artisans possess will be of no assistance whatsoever to Bezalel since he'll be doing most of the intricate work all by his lonesome,"* Moses reviewed. "He will execute all the work for the service of the sanctuary *or immediately be executed by the Levite Secret Police,* just as the Lord *has* commanded."

Moses then called Bezalel and Oholiab and all the other experts' whom the Lord had endowed with skill that *they wouldn't be using. This procedure was done despite the fact that the craftsmen's* hearts had been moved to come and take part in the *enormous* work *project they called the AOTCCA, or the Ark of the Covenant Construction Authority.*

They *(Bezalel and Oholiab)* received *at the "O Holy Lab"* all the *great* contributions' *(rummaged junk and old souvenirs),* which the Israelites had brought *or stolen* for establishing the service of the new *bird* sanctuary *Bezalel was delegated to build right next to the Lord's sanctuary.*

Still morning after morning the *criminal-minded* people continued to bring their' voluntary offerings to Moses, *who was amazed and said to Aaron and to Joshua, "Where's all this fuckin' junk coming from?"*

Thereupon, the experts' *who weren't executing the various kinds of work for the sanctuary because Bezalel had been assigned to perform it* all told Moses, "*Dig it Dude*! The people are bringing much more *garbage and worthless trinkets* than is needed for Bezalel to carry out the *nerve-racking* work' which the Lord had commanded us *(him)* to do."

Moses, therefore, ordered a proclamation to be made throughout the *teeming* camp, "Let neither man nor woman make any more contributions for either the Lord's sanctuary or *for the adjacent bird sanctuary because Bezalel is deluged with cheap costume jewelry and other assorted scrap material."*

So the people stopped bringing their offerings *and complained that they still had a lot of worthless junk cluttering-up their small tents that were still crammed with refugees left over from the* massive Exodus from Egypt. There was already enough *junk* at hand, in fact, more than enough *to fill a huge land dump and give it severe chronic indigestion.* Enough was there *in Oholiab's "O Holy Lab"* to complete the work *on the Ark of the Covenant* that remained to be done.

Bezalel was not one to procrastinate. The various experts' who were not executing the *enormous* work *detail watched Bezalel frantically* make the Dwelling with its ten sheets' woven of fine linen twined, having cherubim embroidered on them with violet, purple and scarlet yarn. The length of each *exotic* sheet was twenty-eight cubits and the width four cubits, *enough to dry off a large size elephant or hippopotamus's ass.* All the sheets were of the same size.

Five of the sheets were sewed together, edge to edge, *because the Lord delighted in keeping the overtaxed Bezalel on the edge of life in terms of his assiduous enterprise and very demanding work schedule.* Bezalel did the same pattern on the other side *as the other expert craftsmen watched his serious activity and laughed at his assigned monumental ordeal.* Loops of violet yarn were made along the edge of the end of the first set, and the same along the edge of the end sheet in the second set. *But the amused and laughing expert craftsmen were kept out of the Lord's inner circles or "out of the Lord's loops," so to speak.*

Fifty loops were thus put on one inner sheet, and fifty loops on the inner sheet of the other set, with the loops directly opposite each other. *The looped loop d' loop work was so tedious and so exhaustive that the beleaguered and harassed Bezalel said to Moses, "I'm so fatigued that I think I'm getting 'lupus' from all these fuckin' loops!"*

Then fifty clasps of gold were made, with which the *sheer* sheets were joined so that the *extraordinary* Dwelling formed one whole. *Then Bezalel got quite pissed' off just thinking about the magnitude of the Ark of the Covenant project that he had to complete all by himself and consequently the irritated fellow proceeded to knock Moses unconscious with a stiff right-cross and next he contemptibly stomped on the old geezer's head.*

The next day Bezalel wove sheets of goat hair into a tent over the Dwellings *for the Lord's sanctuary and for the adjacent bird sanctuary.* Eleven such *sets of* sheets were *meticulously* made. The length of each sheet was thirty cubits and the width four cubits *because Bezalel went to 'great lengths' to achieve those dimensions all by himself as his entertained idle colleagues stood in attendance and laughed at his arduous endeavor.* All eleven sheets were of the same size.

Bezalel then sewed five of the sheets' edge to edge into one set, and the other six sheets *in each set* were sewed edge to edge in another set *arrangement. So the industrious Bezalel became so frustrated from his difficult and impossible work assignment that he then stitched Moses in his tawdry robe to the inner frame of the adjacent bird sanctuary and then the master artisan perniciously administered to the startled patriarch a second black eye twice the size of the first one.*

Fifty *custom-made* loops were *fabricated and* placed along the edge of the end sheet in one set and fifty *integral* loops along the edge in the corresponding sheet in the other *matching* set. Fifty *identical* bronze clasps were made with which Bezalel *gingerly* joined the *splendid* tent *together* so that it *now* formed one *fabulous* whole. A *sturdy* covering for the tent was made of rams' skins dyed red, and above that, a covering of tahash skins *was attached. Then Bezalel became so nervous and so aggravated that he left the Lord's Ark of the Covenant sanctuary and marched over to the adjacent bird sanctuary and then swiftly kicked the already moaning Moses directly in the sensitive bird' cage' area.*

Boards of acacia wood were made as walls for the *Lord's* Dwelling. The length of each board was ten cubits, and the width one and a half' cubits. Each *finely honed* board had two arms *but no wrists, fingers or elbows to speak of.* Bezalel *then painstakingly* fastened them in line

In this *standard* way all of the boards of the Dwelling were made. They were set up as follows: twenty boards on the south side *facing Philadelphia,* with forty silver pedestals under the twenty boards so that Bezalel put two pedestals under each board at its two arms. He *skillfully* placed twenty boards on the north side of the Dwelling, with their forty *quintessential* silver pedestals, two under each board. Bezalel then *feverishly* rushed to put six boards at the rear of the Dwelling to the west, *saying to himself, "Go west old Man!" followed by "The indomitable Lord will be here with bells on!"*

Two additional boards were placed at the corners of the rear of the Dwelling *as Bezalel kept 'lumbering' back and forth with new boards.* These boards were double at the bottom, and likewise double at the top, to the first ring. That is how the boards in the corner were made, *and not even the most enthusiastic carpenter* would give two flying shits reading about the frame's complex construction.

Thus, there were in the rear *of the structure* eight boards, with their sixteen silver pedestals, and two pedestals *situated* under each board. Bezalel then made bars *of soap* and *wonderful* bars of acacia wood *and next the livid craftsman energetically performed several complicated gymnastic exercises on the newly manufactured 'parallel bars.'* Five were laid down for the boards on one side of the dwelling, and five for those on the other side, and five for those at the rear to the west.

"This is much more toil and hardship than I ever expected to do!" the irate Bezalel muttered to himself. *"I think I'd rather watch my dick fall off and then disintegrate on the ground than to do this lousy shittin' mother-fuckin' project all by myself! Is there no relief or justice in this pathetic world?"*

The center bar at the middle of the boards was made to reach across from end to end. Bezalel next *conscientiously* plated the boards with gold, and golden rings were made on them as holders for the gymnastic 'parallel bars', which were also *intricately* plated with gold gild.

Bezalel was still extremely pissed off and antagonized from his excessive labor. He angrily picked-up the one remaining board, 'lumbered' inside the adjacent nearly completed bird sanctuary, ripped a still-dazed Moses from the center post-frame that still had his robe sewn to it, hurled the noble patriarch to the ground and then shoved the long splintery board straight up the old man's fat flabby ass.

Feeling a trifle satisfied from "getting even," the expert craftsman then returned to his immense labor. The veil of the *sacred* Dwelling was *superbly* woven of violet, purple and scarlet yarn, and of fine linen twined, with cherubim embroidered on it. Bezalel assembled four gold-plated columns of acacia wood, with gold hooks *that had previously been used by camp hookers in their perverted sexual exploits,* and then four silver pedestals were *individually* cast for them.

The curtain for the *entrancing* entrance of the tent was made of violet, purple and Scarlet *O'Hara'* yarn, and of fine linen twined, woven in a *who' gives a shit* variegated manner. *Bezalel next formed* its five columns, *modeled after flimsy Old Testament papyrus newspaper columns,* with their hooks *from former hookers* as well as their capitals and their *associated* bands. These *objects* were *meticulously* plated with gold, and their five pedestals were *shaped out* of bronze.

Then the versatile Bezalel lifted his hammer over his head, marched inside the adjacent bird sanctuary, and pounded the already inserted splintery board repeatedly until it had penetrated the howling Moses' sore ass all the way up to his esophagus.

Chapter Thirty-seven
"The Ark"

Bezalel finally made the Ark of the Covenant *of shabby weak* acacia wood, *the only desert tree that grew within a hundred miles of the misery-plagued Israelite camp.* The Ark was two and a half cubits long, one and a half cubits wide, and one and a half cubits high. The insides and the outsides were *stylishly* plated with gold, and a *handsome moldy* molding of *fools*-gold was tacked around it *in a rather tacky fashion.*

Next four gold rings were cast by Bezalel *because the skilled artisan was very pissed off at the amount of time expended regarding his great travail, but then he went and retrieved the gold rings he had recently cast at Moses, who' now again was tethered to the post-frame inside the adjacent bird sanctuary.*

The four gold rings were *then* put on four supports, two rings for one side, and two rings for the opposite side, *and then Bezalel euphorically exclaimed, "Ring-a-ding-ding!"* Poles of acacia wood were *specially* made and plated with gold, *but first Bezalel tested their flexibility by using each to pole vault over the adjacent bird sanctuary.* These *(the poles)* were *then* put through the rings on the sides of the Ark, *specifically intended* for carrying it.

The propitiatory *and the pituitary lids* were made of pure gold, two and a half cubits long and one and a half cubits wide. Two cherubim of a 'beaten' *but not completely defeated* gold were made for the pair of *attractive* ends of the propitiatory. One cherub was fastened on one end *similar to Moses tethered to the main post-frame of the adjacent bird sanctuary,* the other at the other end, 'springing' *and then falling'* directly from the propitiatory at its two *flawless identical* ends.

The cherubim had their 'wings' spread out above *with their backs pointing both to the east and west wings of the Ark,* covering the propitiatory *and the complementary pituitary* with them. They *(the angels, but not Angels of Death or Hell's Angels)* were turned toward each other *symbolically guarding the Ark of the Commandments* with their *grim* faces looking toward the propitiatory *and toward the pituitary, although nothing was yet in the Ark to guard.*

The table *of contents* (*as already indicated*) was made of *worm-infested* acacia wood, two cubits long, one cubit wide and a half a cubit high. *Relatively speaking, Bezalel's dick was two cubits long and two cubits wide and no cubits high.* It *(the worm-infested*

233

wooden table) was plated with pure gold' *gild as was Bezalel's impressive golden dick.* A molding of pure gold was put around the table *but not around Bezalel's throbbing lengthy pecker.* A frame a handbreadth high was also put around it *(the table of contents),* with a molding of gold around the frame *but not around Bezalel's humungus sexual instrument.*

Four rings of gold *and the rings of Saturn* were cast for *it (the sensational table of contents)* and fastened one at each of the four *already described* corners. The rings *of Saturn* were alongside the frame *serving* as holders for the poles to carry the table, *and if no 'Poles' were around to carry the table, then naturally the Israelites would be their able-bodied substitutes if Egyptians or Mesopotamians were not available for Ark of the Covenant duty.*

These poles were made of *inferior* acacia wood and plated with gold, *and even Bezalel's extensive penis might have also been made of worm infested acacia wood, and we already know it had been generously plated with gold.* The 'vessels' *and small boats* were set on the table *of contents, so everything looked as if it were in 'shipshape' condition.* The table's plates and cups, as well as its 'pitchers', *catchers, pancake 'batter'* and *toilet* bowls for pouring libations, were of pure gold.

The *Lord's handcrafted* lamp stand was made of pure beaten gold, *for the Israelites had stolen plenty of the precious metal from the exploitive Egyptians, and now Moses was extorting the gold from the pissed-off Israelites using Jethro Reuel's "Fear of God" tactic to have the apprehensive victims cough up the valuable merchandise or swiftly and surely lose their lives.* The *Lord's special handcrafted* lamp stand', *lengthy* shaft' and *attendant* branches' as well as its *accompanying* cups, knobs and petals were springing directly from it. *However the required lamp stand's lengthy 'shaft' was not quite as long as Bezalel's mammoth gold-plated elephant-dicked hard-on was.*

Six branches extended from its *(the lamp stand's)* sides, three *fucked-up* branches on one side and three *matching fucked-up* branches on the other. On one *fucked-up* branch there were three *fucked-up* cups, shaped like *fucked-up* almond blossoms, each with its *fucked-up* knob and *fucked-up* petals. On the opposite *fucked-up* branch there were three *fucked-up* cups, shaped like *fucked-up* almond blossoms, each with its *fucked-up* knob and *fucked-up* petals, and so *on* for the six *fucked-up* branches that extended from the *fucked-up* lamp stand.

On the shaft there were four *mother-humpin'* cups, shaped like *mother humpin'* almond blossoms, with their *mother humpin'* knobs and *mother humpin'* petals, including a *mother humpin'* knob *located* below each of the three *mother humpin'* pairs of *mother humpin'* branches that extended from the *already mentioned mother humpin'* lamp stand. The *mother humpin'* knobs and *mother humpin'* branches sprang so directly from it that the whole *mother humpin' thing* formed but a single *mother humpin'* piece of pure beaten *mother humpin'* gold. Its seven *mother humpin'* lamps as well as its *mother humpin'* trimming shears and *mother humpin'* trays were made of pure *mother humpin'* gold. A talent of pure *mother humpin' gold* was used for the *mother humpin'* lamp stand and its various *fucked-up* appurtenances.

The *shit-eatin'* altar of *shit eatin'* incense was made of *shit eatin' termite and shit eatin' worm-infested* acacia wood, on a *shit eatin'* square, a cubit long, a cubit wide, and two *shit eatin'* cubits high, having *shit eatin'* horns that sprang directly from it. Its *shit eatin'* grate on top, its *shit eatin'* walls on all four sides, and its *shit eatin'* horns were plated with poured *shit eatin'* gold *just like Bezalel's shit-eatin' dick.* A *shit eatin'* molding of *shit eatin'* pure gold was put around it. Underneath the *shit eatin'* molding *shit eatin'* gold rings were placed *and situated* two on one side and two on the opposite side, as *shit eatin'* holders for the *shit eatin'* poles *for the shit eatin' Israelites* to *shit eatin'* carry. The *shit eatin'* poles too were made of *ant-colonied, termite and worm' infested* acacia wood and plated with *shit eatin'* gold. The *shit eatin'* sacred anointing oil and the *flagrant* fragrant *shit eatin'* incense were *both* prepared in their pure *mother humpin'* form by a *fucked-up fuming* perfumer.

Chapter Thirty-eight
"The Altar of Holocausts"

The altar of holocausts was made of *ant, termite and worm-infested* acacia wood on a square *that was* five cubits long and five cubits wide. Its height was three cubits, *and no one really cared about those measurements, not even the stickler Bezalel', who was seriously considering pounding a second much larger splintery board straight up Moses' already abused asshole over in the adjacent bird sanctuary.*

At the four' corners' horns were made that sprang directly from the altar, *designed by Bezalel to gore any sinner through and through after Moses or Aaron would press a secret button activating the totally lethal horns.* The whole altar was plated with bronze and all the utensils of the altar, the *hashish* pots, the *shit* shovels, the *urinal* basins, the *tuning* forks and the fire *bed*pans were likewise made of bronze.

A *great* grating of bronze network was *especially* made for the altar and placed round it on the ground *to catch fish in case of a desert flood or to snare vile sinners that the horns failed to gore.* The grating was half as high as the altar *because its propitiatory lid and its pituitary were inactive during the gratings' sporadic adolescent growth cycle.*

Four rings were cast for *the rams' horns' altar' four corners' defense* and for the bronze grating, as holders for the poles', which were made from *defective and rotting termite infested* acacia wood and plated with *inexpensive imitation* bronze. The poles were *carefully* put through the rings, *and the Lord's intricate schematic was putting poor Bezalel through the wringers.* The *artificial-bronze* poles were put on the sides for carrying the altar', *which was made in the form of a hollow box to represent the total knowledge of all the Israelites and their prolific screw-happy ancestors.*

The bronze laver, with its *cheap tinny-looking* bronze base, was made from mirrors of the women' who served at the entrance of the tent *as part of the smoke and mirrors' vaudeville magic routine of the outrageous Ark itself. The women also often used the mirrors to examine themselves and each other for random vaginal warts and for inflamed hemorrhoids.*

The court was made as follows. On the south side *opposite Philadelphia* the court had *public* hangings *sponsored by the Levite religious fanatics.* Other hangings were woven of fine linen twined, a hundred cubits long, with twenty columns and twenty pedestals of *cheesy* bronze, the *fishing* hooks and the *rock* bands of the columns being *composed* of *"Hi Ho* Silver."

On the west side there were *public* hangings *that were exclusively sponsored by Aaron and his rock band of punk delinquent sons.* The hangings were fifty cubits long with ten columns and ten pedestals, the *fishing* hooks and the *rock* bands of the columns being silver.

On the east side, *east side, all around the camp* the court was fifty *"who gives a shit"* cubits long. *No people were hung on the more moderate east side of the court. Only the victims' tits and balls were hung on the sadistic east side as reminder examples of what happens to sinners and what happens to non-contributors to the "Ark Foundation."*

Toward one side of the *Ark of the Covenant* there were hangings to the extent of fifty cubits, *and this is generally why the sacred object was called the "Altar of Holocausts," because of the huge area designated and reserved for mass hangings toward that one side.* That side had three columns and three pedestals *that served as a deluxe lynching gallows.*

Toward the other side beyond the *entrancing* entrance of the court there were likewise hangings of the extent of fifteen cubits, with three columns and three pedestals *for gallows, thus confirming the sordid morbid macabre nature of the two bleakest sides of the "Altar of Holocausts."*

The hangings *and gory lynchings* on all sides of the court were woven of fine linen twined *and quite gruesome to watch on a full or an empty stomach.* The pedestal *gallows* of *the Levite execution* columns were of bronze, while the *fishing* hooks and the *rock* bands of the columns were made of *premium "Hi Ho* Silver." The capitals were silver-plated and all of the *fancy execution* columns were banded with pure silver.

At the *entrancing* entrance of the court there was a 'variegated curtain *with various gates.* It *(the curtain)* was woven *not of 'iron' but of ultra*-violet, *infra*-purple and *hued* Scarlet *O'Hara* yarn of fine linen twined, twenty *who gives a shit* cubits long and five *who gives a shit* cubits wide, in keeping with the *architectural* hangings of the *who gives a shit* court.

There were four *who gives a shit* columns and four *who gives a shit* pedestals of *who gives a shit* bronze for it, while there *who gives a shit* hooks were *fabricated* of *Hi Ho* Silver. All of the court's *who gives a shit* pegs for the Dwelling and for its *who gives a shit royal* court around it were of *who gives a shit* bronze.

The following is an account of the various amounts of *heavy* metal used on the Dwelling', *which was still dwelling on Bezalel's tortured mind.* The Dwellings' Commandments were drawn up *with artwork and graffiti* at the command of Moses, *whom was still smarting from his brutal flogging inside the adjacent bird sanctuary that had been administered by Bezalel.* It (the Dwelling and the Commandments) was *officiated over* by the *heavy metal bronze sword carrying* Levites under the direction of Ithamar, *an emotionally disturbed punk delinquent* son of Aaron.

However, it was Bezalel, son of Uri and *Urine,* son of Hur and *Her* of the tribe of Judah that made all that the Lord commanded Moses *to construct. So actually, Bezalel had done the unappreciative patriarch a mighty big favor in assembling the Ark of the Covenant and its attendant altars and its spectacular table of contents.* Bezalel *was supposed to be* assisted by Oholiab *working together in the O Holy Lab, but* the son of Ahisamach of the tribe of Dan *had been exempted from the Lord's service by Moses' arbitrary interpretation of the Lord's Divine Will. That's the principal reason why Bezalel had beaten the living shit out of Moses in the recently constructed adjacent bird sanctuary.*

Oholiab was an *adept* engraver, an embroiderer, *an embezzler*, and a weaver of variegated cloth of *ultra*-violet, *infra*-purple and Scarlet *O'Hara* yarn and of fine linen, *but he spent most of the time during the Ark's construction engraving tattoos of naked women on lesbians' asses.*

All the gold used in the entire construction of the sanctuary *and the more popular adjacent* bird sanctuary had previously been given as an offering *(an extortion of stolen Egyptian merchandise from the overtaxed and under-worked Israelites)* amounted to twenty-nine 'talents', *enough to sponsor a century and a half of Hebrew 'talent' shows.* Seven hundred and thirty shekels were over that talent' number, according to the standard of the sanctuary shekel', *which had never been right or correct since its trial inception and ultimate implementation.*

The amount of the silver received from the *coordinated straight and gay* communities was one hundred talents and one thousand seven hundred and seventy-five *and a half* shekels, according to the standard of sanctuary shekel', *which was recklessly kept by that horny, cheating perverted pedophile priest Jethro Reuel.*

One bekah apiece, that is a half-shekel apiece, according to *the fallacious and corrupt* standard of sanctuary shekel' *report,* was received from every man of twenty years of age or more, *even the ones that had not yet entered puberty.* The number of these was six hundred and three thousand five hundred and fifty men', *half of whom had never entered puberty and all of whom were scared shitless of the fanatical zealous jealous Levites and the Lord's very dangerous Angel of Death. That's why and how the money had been so easily collected.*

One hundred talents were used for casting the pedestals *in the Israelites first annual spring' play' competition.* One talent was used for each pedestal of the sanctuary and for each pedestal of the veil *after its grand unveiling and opening.*

The remaining one thousand seven hundred and seventy-five *who gives a shit* shekels were used for making the *ornate fishing* hooks on the columns, for plating the capitals *for the court's scheduled and widely anticipated capital punishment hangings,* and for the *very expensive rock* bands.

The bronze given as an offering amounted to seventy *who gives a shit* talents' and two thousand four hundred *who gives a shit* shekels. With this was made the' *fantastic who gives a shit* pedestals at the *entrancing* entrance of the meeting *and greeting* tent, the bronze *who gives a shit* altar and the *opulent who gives a shit* pedestals around the court.

The *who gives a shit* pedestals at the *entrancing* entrance of the *fucked-up* court and all the *shit eatin'* tent pegs for the Dwelling and for the magnificent *mother humpin'* court around the Ark of the Covenant were made by *the ass kickin'* Bezalel'. *And the mother humpin' master craftsman still wanted to pulverize the shit out of the totally fucked-up patriarch, Moses.*

Chapter Thirty-nine
"The Vestments"

With *infra*-purple, Scarlet *O'Hara* and *ultra*-violet yarn' were woven *spider webs* and the service cloths *for prostitutes to use while providing their various sexual services to lines of anxious male clientele*. Also the service cloths *allotted* for use in the sanctuary *and for use in the adjacent bird sanctuary* were woven, as well as the sacred vestments for Aaron and his *incorrigible punk delinquent* son priests, as the *egocentric self-indulgent* Lord had *directly* commanded *to Moses.*

The ephod was woven of *commonplace* gold thread and of *ultra*-violet, *infra*-purple and Scarlet *O'Hara* yarn of fine linen twined.

'Who's going to wash all these damned linens?' Bezalel *thought as he feverishly stitched and sewed away towards completion of his immense task. 'Oh well, I guess it's that dumb bastard Moses' problem to worry about that. I just have to make all these crappy veils and stuff so that I can go back to my tent and screw my four kinky wives,' Bezalel concluded with a smile on his face.*

Gold *leaf* was first hammered into gold *loose*-leaf *paper* and then cut up into threads *while poor accursed Bezalel kept all of the bystanding jocular expert craftsmen 'in stitches' involuntarily exhibiting to them his great frustration.* These threads were woven with the *ultra*-violet, scarlet *O'Hara* and the *infra*-purple yarn into an embroidered pattern on the fine linen. *Bezalel took a few minutes to make for himself a fine linen twined robe', which he held up for his envious eyewitnesses' inspection and yelled out to the knot of hysterically laughing taunters, "How do you guys like these threads?"*

Shoulder straps *and shoulder pads* were made for it *(the ephod)* and joined to its two upper ends *until it was finally upended*. The embroidered belt on the ephod'*s beltway* extended out from it, and like it, was made of *tawdry, shoddy* gold thread, of *ultra*-violet, Scarlet *O'Hara* and *infra*-purple yarn and of fine linen twined, as the *materialistic* Lord had *originally* commanded Moses.

The onyx stones were prepared and mounted in gold filigree, and Bezalel took great precautions safeguarding the gems *because he didn't want to have his precious stones broken like Moses had broken the Lord's stones. The precious gems were mounted by Bezalel', who kept hopping on and off of them to protect the Lord's new family jewels.* They were engraved like seal *and walrus* engravings with the names of the sons of Israel *and the names of other sons-of-bitches* etched on them. These stones were set on the shoulder straps of the ephod as memorial stones of the sons of Israel, *most of them genuine sons-of-bitches,* just as the Lord had commanded Moses.

The *much-heralded* breast-piece was embroidered like the ephod for the sons of Israel *sons-of-bitches,* with *cheap artificial* gold thread and *ultra*-violet, *infra*-purple and Scarlet *O'Hara* yarn on *rags* of fine linen twined. It was 'square', *just like Bezalel and Moses were both squares.* The breast-piece *containing the family jewels of the sons-of-bitches of Israel* was folded in double, a 'span' high *and a river bridge* wide in its *completed* folded form.

Four rows of precious stones were mounted on it *(the breast-piece, that looked like a nice, juicy plump tit).* In the first row were a carnelian, a topaz, and an emerald *city.* In the second row *there* was a garnet, *a hornet,* a sapphire, a beryl, *and a killer bee.* In the third row was a jacinth, an *adjacent* agate, an amethyst *and a pharmacist.* In the fourth row there was a crysolite, *a cry-so-much,* an onyx, a jasper' *and a varmint. In the fifth row sat Jethro Reuel, Joshua, Aaron and Oholiab in the back of the class in the last row next to the windows.*

They *(the human 'gems', including Jethro Reuel, Joshua, Aaron and Oholiab)* were mounted in gold filigree *and pedigree* and their number was twelve, to match the names of the sons of Israel, *each a royal son of a bitch as has been extensively mentioned.* Each *precious* stone was engraved like a seal *or a walrus* with the name of one of the *primitive New Stone Age* tribes of Israel.

Chains of pure gold, twisted like cords *and like the chords of bad music,* were made for the *tit-like* breast-piece, with two gold *agreeable* filigree' *pedigree* rosetta stones and two gold rings, *a partridge and a pear tree.* The two rings were fastened to the two upper ends of the *tit-like* breast-piece. The two gold chains were then fastened in front to the two *agreeable,* filigree *pedigree* rosetta stones, which were attached *but not married* to the shoulder straps of the ephod *infested with aphids.*

Two other gold rings were made *by Bezalel* and put on the two lower ends of the *tit-like* breast-piece on the edge facing the ephod *infested with aphids.*

Two more gold rings were made and fastened to the bottom of the two shoulder straps next to where they joined the ephod *infested with aphids* in front, just above its embroidered *beltway that went all* *the way to Damascus (where all 'them-ass-kiss-ers' live). Ultra-*violet ribbons bound the rings of the *unique tit-like* breast-piece to the rings of the ephod *infested with aphids*, so that the embroidered belt*way that stretched all the way to them ass-kiss-ers in Damascus* did not swing loose from it *like a loose swinger would do.* All of this *the really pissed* Bezalel did just as the Lord had *expressly* commanded Moses to do.

The *bitchin'* robe of the *bitchin'* ephod was woven entirely of *bitchin' ultra*-violet yarn, with a *bitchin'* opening *like a vagina* in its *bitchin'* center like a *bitchin' pussy* opening of a *bitch's* shirt. *The bitchin' robe' was decorated* with *salvaged* selvage *and cleavage* around the *bitchin'* opening to keep it *(the bitchin' robe)* from being torn.

At the *bitchin'* hem of the *bitchin'* robe' *bitchin'* pomegranates were made of *bitchin' ultra*-violet, *infra*-purple and Scarlet *O'Hara bitchin'* yarn and of fine *bitchin'* linen twined. Bells' of pure *bitchin'* gold were also made and put between the *bitchin'* granite pomegranates all around the *bitchin'* hem of the *aforementioned bitchin'* robe'. First a *bitchin'* bell, then a *bitchin' 'granite'* pomegranate *taken for granted*, and thus alternating all around the *bitchin'* hem *as Bezalel kept on bitchin' about his bitchin' labor.* The *bitchin'* hem of the *bitchin'* robe made by *bitchin'* Bezalel was to be worn in performing the *bitchin'* ministry-*all the bitchin' time*, and all this, just as the Lord had commanded *bitchin'* Moses, *who was still unconscious and couldn't at all be bitchin' about being pulverized by bitchin' Bezalel.*

For *bitchin'* Aaron and his *fucked-up punk delinquent* sons there were also *shit-eatin'* woven tunics of fine *mother-humpin'* linen'. There were also the *who' gives a shit* miter of *bitchin'* linen, the ornate *fucked-up* turbans of fine *shit' eatin'* linen and *mother-humpin'* drawers of *who gives a shit* linen *comprised* of fine *bitchin'* linen twined.

Also included were fucked-up sashes of variegated *shit eatin'* work made of fine *mother-humpin'* linen *twisted and* twined and of *who gives a shit ultra*-violet, *infra*-purple and Scarlet *O'Hara bitchin'* yarn, just as the *most excellent* Lord had commanded *fucked-up* Moses.

The *shit eatin'* plate of the sacred *mother humpin'* diadem *(a fuckin' fucked-up crown)* was made of pure *who gives a shit* gold and inscribed, as on a *bitchin'* seal *or walrus* engraving: "Sacred to the Lord." It was tied over the *fucked-up* miter with a *ultra*-violet *shit eatin'* ribbon, as the Lord had commanded *mother humpin' still unconscious* Moses to do.

Thus the entire *who gives a shit* work of the Dwelling of the *bitchin' meeting and greeting* tent was *finally* completed. The *fucked-up* Israelites *by means of Bezalel* did the *shit eatin'* work just as the Lord had commanded the still unconscious *mother humpin'* Moses to do. They *(the crazed who gives a shit Israelites)* then brought to *bitchin' semi-consciou*s Moses the Dwelling, the *fucked-up* tent with all its *shit eatin'* appurtenances, the *mother-humpin'* clasps, the *who gives a shit* boards and the *bitchin'* bars *(where the fucked-up Israelites hung out all the fuckin' time).* They also brought the *shit eatin'* columns, *the mother-humpin'* pedestals and the *notorious who gives a shit* covering of *bitchin*' tahash skins, and also the *fucked-up* curtain veil.

The Ark of the Commandments had its *shit eatin'* poles, the *mother-humpin'* propitiatory *and matching pituitary* lids, the *who gives a shit* table *of contents* with all its *bitchin'* appurtenances, and the *really bitchin' Showtime* Showbread *to be used for the fucked-up* "Really Big Show."

Also included *in the display* were the *shit eatin'* pure gold lamp stand with its *mother-humpin'* lamps set up on it with all its *who gives a shit* appurtenances. *There was also* the *bitchin'* oil for the *fucked-up* light, the golden *shit eatin'* altar, the' *mother-humpin'* anointing oil, the *flagrant* fragrant *who gives a shit* incense, and the *bitchin'* curtain for the *fucked-up entrancing* entrance of the *shit eatin'* tent.

Other important items were the *mother-humpin'* altar of bronze with its *who gives a shit* bronze grating, its *bitchin'* poles and all its *fucked-up* appurtenances. The *fucked-up* appurtenances included the *shit eatin'* laver with its *mother humpin'* base and the *extraordinary who gives a shit* hangings of the *bitchin'* court with their *accompanying fucked-up* columns and *shit eatin'* pedestals.

Other vital accessories were the hand-stitched *mother-humpin'* curtains for the *who gives a shit entrancing* entrance of the *bitchin'* court with its *fucked-up* ropes and *its shit eatin'* tent pegs. *Also provided were all of* the' *mother-humpin'* equipment for the' *who gives a shit* service of the Dwelling of the *really boss bitchin'* meeting *and greeting* tent.

The *fucked-up* service cloths for use in the *shit eatin'* sanctuary *and in the adjacent groovy bird sanctuary,* the *mother-humpin'* vestments for Aaron the *high* priest and for his *repulsive who gives a shit punk delinquent* sons *were also provided for their future fucked-up* ministry.

The *shit eatin' thuggish* Israelites *through the intensive labor of Bezalel (we use the mother humpin' terms affectionately)* had carried out all of the *absurd who gives a shit* work, just as the Lord had commanded *the now semi-conscious fucked-up* Moses to do. *So when bitchin'* Moses *finally became conscious, he* saw that all the *fucked-up* work had been done just as the Lord had commanded, and he blessed the whole *bitchin', shit eatin', mother-humpin', who gives a shit fucked-up* enterprise *that had been singularly completed by Bezalel.*

Bezalel was so infuriated at Moses after he had diligently completed the massive and tedious Ark of the Covenant project that the highly accomplished craftsman marched into the adjacent bird sanctuary tent. Bezalel mercilessly started bashing and battering Moses', whose robe was still partially sewn and tethered to the sanctuary's main center post-frame. Berserk Bezalel was soon joined in his brutal attack by Jethro Reuel', who hated his all-too-cavalier son-in-law Moses as much or maybe even more than the maniac Bezalel did.

Just before Moses was about to expire and leave this world for good, Joshua rambunctiously entered the bird sanctuary and blatantly knocked the very weary Bezalel and the hoary old goat Jethro Reuel to the ground. Then Amalek finally caught up with Joshua. The incensed barbarian scampered into the tent and beat the living feces out of Joshua, Bezalel and out of Jethro Reuel too, thinking that the expert craftsman and Moses' conniving priest father-in-law were both colleagues and accomplices of Joshua.

Next Aaron and his contingent of punk delinquent sons sprinted into the bird sanctuary and started clobbering and thrashing around Amalek, Joshua, Jethro Reuel, Bezalel and Moses, believing that the five had organized a clandestine coalition conspiracy to have them eliminated as the first officially ordained priests of Israel.

Finally, two-dozen fierce Levite warriors hustled into the popular bird sanctuary and beat the living shit out of everybody except the often-abducted Moses', whom' they believed was the only true spiritual medium between the Supernatural and the pathetic Israelites.

Chapter Forty
"Erection of the Dwelling"

The Lord *then* said to Moses, *the only remaining conscious or semi-conscious man in the adjacent bird sanctuary,* "Moses, I never get laryngitis because I'm the Lord, and that's the alpha and the omega *of it*. Now on the first day of the month, *remind Me' later to give both the day and month names,* you shall erect the Dwelling of the meeting *and greeting* tent," the Lord commanded *and demanded.* "On second thought, I suggest that you appoint Bezalel after he wakes up from his deep slumber on the ground over there to construct the Dwelling next to the official meeting and greeting tent."

"Where the hell am I?" *Moses moaned and groaned.* "Why are all of these damned stars and planets swirling around my weak old eyes? Is this Astronomy 101?"

"And Moses," *the martinet and inflexible Lord austerely added,* "put the *sacred* Ark of the Commandments in it *(the portable pre-fab' lift-able Dwelling),* and screen off the Ark with the veil *so that no Israelite will ever see My' face or My' Glory. I tend to be Puritanical at times in terms of My' introverted prudish behavior side,*" the Lord Self-consciously pontificated. "And in addition Moses, bring in the table *of contents* and set it *where it belongs.* Then bring in the *fabulous* lamp stand and set up the *majestic* lamps on it."

"I'm in a fuckin' fog," *Moses confessed to the Voice,* "so I must again be in the blessed mist and midst of the Lord on Mt. Sinai. Yes, that is where I must be right now! I must be standing somewhere on Mt. Sinai!"

"Now Moses, after you perform that perfunctory duty," *the Lord elaborated,* "put the golden altar of incense in front of the Ark of the Commandments, and hang the curtain at the *entrancing* entrance of the *magnificent* dwelling of the *spectacular* meeting *and greeting* tent *that rivals Apollo's splendid temple over in Ethiopia, which as you know is hillbilly country.* Place the laver *without lather* between the meeting *and greeting* tent and the *ornate* altar, *paid for by your poor destitute Israelites by gold and silver coins and objects they had taken and borrowed from civilized and distinguished Egyptians.* Next Moses," *the Lord detailed,* "put water in the laver *without adding any lather.* Then set up the court 'round about *near the roundabout',* and *next* put the curtain at the *entrancing* entrance of the court *in the center of the cul-de-sac."*

"Hey, how come my hands and legs are all bruised up?" Moses asked the all-too-familiar Voice. "I must have run into a couple of mean-spirited big bruisers!"

"Next Moses," said the baritone Voice that sounded a lot like the amateur ventriloquist Jethro Reuel's did, "take the anointing oil and anoint the Dwelling and everything in it, consecrating it and all its furnishing, so that it *(the extravagant White Elephant Dwelling)* will be sacred. *Then Moses,*" the authoritarian Voice further ordered, "anoint the altar of holocausts and all of its appurtenances, consecrating it so that it will be most sacred. Likewise, anoint the laver *without using lather* along with its *debased* base, and thus consecrate it, too."

Moses thought and then finally realized that the mystic Voice sounded much like that of his perverted pedophile father-in-law Jethro Reuel, but he looked toward the ground and saw Jethro lying prone right next to Joshua, Bezalel, Aaron, Amalek, Aaron's depraved punk delinquent sons and four comatose Levites.

"Then Moses," the ethereal Voice continued, "bring Aaron and his *punk juvenile delinquent* sons to the entrance of the meeting *and greeting* tent. *The rogue young men plan to establish a 'semenary' (a type of New Stone Age sex seminary) in the hot arid desert at Succoth (located not far from Fuckoff) in My' honor.* Clothe *that rascally nitwit* Aaron with the sacred vestments and anoint him, thus consecrating him *(the scoundrel nitwit Aaron)* as my *official highest* priest. Bring forward Aaron's *irresponsible punk delinquent* sons also, and clothe them with tunics *so that they can journey and found My' 'semenary' in the hot arid desert at Succoth."*

"*This infernal asshole world is without a doubt bullshit city!"* Moses complained as he held his injured bleeding head and then felt multiple aches and pains all over his aged and decrepit body. *"I don't know what's more fucked-up, the shitty world or me?"*

"And Moses," the haunting Voice beckoned, "as you have anointed their father *Aaron* now *lying before you*, also anoint the *punk juvenile delinquent* offspring *lying before you* as My' *auxiliary* priests. Thus, by being anointed by you *and appointed by Me'*, they shall receive a perpetual *free* 'priesthood' *to wear over their heads during the cold winter months.* They will wear the perpetual 'priest' hood' *in the wintertime* throughout all future generations, *even though each of Aaron's despicable punk juvenile delinquent sons will be dead and buried one generation from now."*

Moses *finally regained his equilibrium, trudged out of the adjacent bird sanctuary and* did exactly what the Lord*'s Voice* had commanded him. On the first *unnamed* day of the first *unknown* month of the second *mystery* year the Dwelling was *satisfactorily* erected *and all the male Israelites celebrated the occasion with nice erections of their own.*

He *(Moses: we're almost at the end now so let's get these puzzling pronouns and antecedents grammatically straight)* placed its *(the Dwelling's) bitchin'* pedestals, set up its *fucked-up* boards, put in its *shit eatin'* bars and *then* set up its *mother-humpin'* columns. He then spread the *who gives a shit* tent over the *portable on-the-go* Dwelling and put the *bitchin'* covering on the *fucked-up* top of the *shit eatin'* tent, as the Lord*'s Voice* had commanded *and demanded* him.

He *(Moses, the patriarch. Look, we respectfully repeat, it's now near the end of the damned story, so please, let's try to get this pronoun-antecedent problem done right at least once)* then took the Commandments and put them in the *sacred* Ark. He placed *mother humpin'* poles alongside the Ark and set the *friggin' who' gives a shit* propitiatory *and pituitary* lids upon it. He *(Moses)* brought the *non-floatable and very sinkable* Ark into the Dwelling and hung the *bitchin'* curtain veil, *so that no Israelite could ever see the Lord's face or His' awesome Glory, whatever the hell that looks like!* The Ark and the Commandments were thus screened off as the *demanding, uncompromising and inflexible* Lord had commanded *His' all-too-gullible dupe* Moses.

He *(Moses. Look guys, for the last time, begin sentences and paragraphs with nouns and not with stupid pronouns)* placed the *fucked-up* lamp stand in the *shit eatin'* meeting *and greeting* tent, opposite the *who gives a shit* table *of contents* on the south side of the *portable on-the-lam hit and run* Dwelling. *It was a rather large undertaking for the bruised and battered patriarch, especially without the assistance of the very versatile Bezalel', who was finally happy at home screwing and sodomizing his four kinky wives and two concubines.*

Moses then set up the *bitchin'* lamps before the *super-fastidious* Lord, as the Lord had *specifically* commanded him. He placed the *fucked-up fools*-gold altar in the *shit eatin'* meeting *and greeting* tent, in front of the *mother-humpin'* veil, and on it he *flagrantly* burned fragrant *who gives a shit* incense, as the *unyielding and only My-way'* Lord had *appropriately* commanded him.

He *(the elderly wimpy Moses)* hung the *bitchin'* curtain at the *entrancing fucked-up* entrance of the *portable on-the-move* Dwelling of the Lord *of future ambushing marauders and blundering area* plunderers. Beware of Israelites offering tokens of friendship, all you peace-loving Canaanites!

He (*the main character in The Wholly Book of Exodus, Moses*) put the *shit eatin'* altar of holocausts in front of the *mother-humpin' entrancing* entrance of the Dwelling of the *who gives a shit* meeting *and greeting* tent, and offered *bitchin' roasted, barbecued* holocausts and *tasteless* cereal, *thus making the first "authentic" human produced frosted flakes* as the Lord had commanded him.

He *(masochistic Moses)* placed the *fucked-up* laver *without lather* between the *shit eatin'* meeting *and greeting* tent and the *mother-humpin'* altar, and *then* the *weary patriarch* put *who gives a shit* water in it for washing *and rinsing the young punk juvenile delinquent priests' personals.*

Moses and Aaron and his *redneck punk juvenile delinquent* sons used the *holy* water to wash their hands, feet, *balls and smelly assholes* there, for they washed themselves whenever they went into the *cunt-lapping* meeting *and greeting* tent or approached the *bitchin'* altar, just as the *stubborn and obdurate* Lord had *tyrannically* commanded.

Finally, he *(the battered, lacerated and badly bruised Moses)* set up the *fucked-up* court around the *on-the-run* Dwelling and the *shit eatin'* altar and hung the *immense pussy-pluggin'* curtain at the *entrancing* entrance of the *mother-humpin'* court. Thus Moses finished all' of the *prescribed cunt lappin'* work' *that* the *obstinate and obdurate* Lord*'s Voice (possibly the perverted pedophile priest Jethro Reuel's ventriloquist voice)* had *deceptively* commanded.

Then the' *ever-present who gives a shit dark funnel* cloud covered the *bitchin'* meeting *and greeting* tent, and the *awesome* Glory of the Lord *that no one was permitted to see* filled the *on-the-move land pirates'* Lord's Dwelling.

Moses *was pessimistic (besides being bludgeoned and maimed) and* could not enter the *fucked-up* meeting *and greeting* tent, because the *shit eatin' dark funnel* cloud *had* settled down upon it, '*mistifying' (mystifying) everyone. The strange, unseen and forbidden awesome* Glory of the Lord filled the tent, *and to this very day, only the Lord knows exactly what His' awesome face and His' awesome Glory really look like.*

Whenever the' *mother-humpin' dark funnel* cloud rose from the *portable on-the-lam'* Dwelling', the' *who gives a shit* Israelites *(using the tornado pattern as their stage cue)* would set out on their *cunt-lappin'* journey *to raid and to pillage innocent Canaanite farmers and their vulnerable settlements.*

But if the *dark pussy-pluggin'* cloud did not lift-off, they *(the cunt lappin' Israelites)* would not go forward *to steal, mutilate, rape, sodomize and plunder prospective Canaanite victims*. Only when it *(the ominous dark bitchin' funnel cloud with the Heavenly steering column)* lifted did they go *forward to 'get the fog' out of there.*

In the *asshole* daytime, the *fucked-up ominous dark funnel* cloud was seen *hovering* over the *moving portable* Dwelling; whereas, at *jerked-off* nighttime, *bitchin' raging* fire was seen inside the *fucked-up* cloud by the whole *shit eatin'* house of Israel in all the *mother-humpin'* stages of the *who' gives a shit lackluster* journey *to Canaan.*

The End

Jay Dubya

About the Author

Jay Dubya is author John Wiessner's initials (J.W.) and also his pen name. John is a retired New Jersey public school English teacher, having taught the subject for thirty-four years. John lives in Hammonton, New Jersey with wife Joanne, and the couple has three grown sons. The book *So Ya' Wanna' Be A Teacher* chronicles Jay Dubya's public school teaching career.

Jay Dubya has written other adult fiction besides *The Wholly Book of Exodus* and its companion book *The Wholly Book of Genesis*. *Black Leather and Blue Denim, A '50s Novel* and its sequel, *The Great Teen Fruit War, A 1960'* Novel are humorous "coming of age" adventure books. *Frat' Brats, A '60s Novel* completes Jay Dubya's action/adventure trilogy. *Pieces of Eight*, *Pieces of Eight, Part II*, *Pieces of Eight, Part III* and *Pieces of Eight, Part IV* are short story/novella collections featuring science fiction, paranormal and humorous plots and themes. *Nine New Novellas*, *Nine New Novellas, Part II*, *Nine New Novellas, Part III* and *Nine New Novellas, Part IV* are also sci-fi/paranormal story collections.

Ron Coyote, Man of La Mangia is adult humor and a satire/parody on Miguel Cervantes' *Don Quixote*, published in 1605. *Mauled Maimed Mangled Mutilated Mythology* is adult satirical literature that retells twenty-one classic myths in parody form. *Fractured Frazzled Folk Fables and Fairy Farces* is adult humor that reorganizes famous children's tales as does its sister book *Fractured Frazzled Folk Fables and Fairy Farces, Part II*. Other satirical humor books authored by Jay Dubya are *Thirteen Sick Tasteless Classics*, *Thirteen Sick Tasteless Classics, Part II*, *Thirteen Sick Tasteless Classics, Part III* and finally *Thirteen Sick Tasteless Classics*, Part *IV*.

John has also authored a trilogy of young adult fantasy novels, *Enchanta*, *Pot of Gold* and *Space Bugs, Earth Invasion*. *The Eighteen Story Gingerbread House* is another children's work written by Jay Dubya.

Jay Dubya likes '50s rock and roll music and he also enjoys pop' songs by the Beach Boys, Beatles, Fleetwood Mac, the Eagles, the Rolling Stones, ELO, John Mellencamp and by John Fogerty. When not writing or listening to music Jay Dubya likes watching *76ers* basketball and *Phillies* and *Yankees* television' baseball games.

www.ingramcontent.com/pod-product-compliance
Lightning Source LLC
Chambersburg PA
CBHW021823090426
42811CB00032B/1992/J